Praise for *Export Marketing Imperative*

In the complex global business environment, obtaining the necessary tools and expertise to compete as a U.S. exporter can be a daunting task. *The Export Imperative* serves as a vital resource for medium sized U.S. exporters seeking to expand markets and provides valuable insight into export finance.

Alan J. Beard
Managing Director
Interlink Capital Strategies

Extraordinary changes in global commerce are rapidly creating large opportunities—and equally large challenges. Dr. Czinkota's latest book, *Export Marketing Imperative*, provides brilliant and original insights that allow the committed international business executive to take much greater—and quicker—advantage of these looming opportunities. Profits, strategic advantage, and superior results await those who apply the superb lessons of this book.

Lew Cramer
Director General (ret.) of the US Commercial Service
Managing Director of Summit Ventures International.

The Export Marketing Imperative imparts to the readers the importance of global trade, the methods of exporting, the pitfalls international businesses can face, the successful paths through which to export and far more. It is clear, concise, readable. It is a great quick reference checklist of all the areas an exporter needs.

Dave Danjczek
Vice President, Administration & Corporate Secretary
Manufacturers Alliance/MAPI
(former Vice President, International Business
Litton Industries, Western Atlas, and Unova)

What to do when the world beats a path to your door—because it will." Not *Whether* but *How* can companies successfully internationalize their business activities will become a decisive question of tomorrow. Anyone who wishes to enter global business firmly in the driver's seat will find an excellent guide here, written by an expert who is intimately familiar with international trade relations. Drawing on years of experience in government, academia, and the private sector, Professor Czinkota and his co-authors furnishes a balanced and succinct analysis of all the aspects crucial to a successful expansion into international markets. From the planning, research, and selection of export markets; marketing strategies; and export channels to issues of securing one's financial investment and the role of governments and organizations in international trade, all the relevant topics are eruditely explained, making the book a value reference for all those looking for a systematic approach to the topic. But *The Export Marketing Imperative* is more than just a comprehensive reference tool—it is also a step-by-step manual for successfully internationalizing business operations. Small and medium-sized businesses in particular will highly profit from this valuable aid.

The Export Marketing Imperative is a valuable package for those interested in planning and managing exports. It covers well all the relevant facets of exports, yet in a very easy-to-read and to-the-point manner. A highly recommendable book.

Hannu Seristö
Professor of International Business
Helsinki School of Economics

This book gives a splendid overview of all the issues relevant to managers, who are confronted with the challenge to internationalize their business through exports. Well-founded scientifically and with equally high practical relevance, the authors show which different export modes exist, which legal and market conditions are to be considered and how marketing and management instruments can be efficiently employed to succeed in the export business. This book is a "must" especially for managers of medium-sized companies, who are responsible for expanding and optimizing the export activities of their firms.

Dr. Bernd Stauss
Chair of Services Management
Catholic University of Eichstaett-Ingolstadt

As one who trains thousands of executives each year about the complex world of trade finance, I find *The Export Marketing Imperative* to be a valuable resource for businesses seeking to compete successfully in today's world marketplace. This book provides a wide range of vital information for both novice exporters and veteran globalists.

**Richard "Chip" Thomas
General Manager
American Export Training Institute**

The *Export Market Imperative* is a "must-read" for any company that intends to survive and compete in today's internet-connected globalized world. With two-thirds of the world's market outside the United States and with fierce and savvy foreign competition, U.S. managers have no choice but to expand their export marketing—and this user-friendly "how-to" book is exactly the guide they need.

**Frank Vargo, Vice President,
International Economic Affairs
NATIONAL ASSOCIATION OF MANUFACTURERS**

THE EXPORT MARKETING IMPERATIVE

Michael R. Czinkota

Ilkka A. Ronkainen

Marta Ortiz-Buonafina

AMERICAN MARKETING ASSOCIATION

THOMSON

Australia • Canada • Mexico • Singapore • Spain • United Kingdom • United States

THOMSON

The Export Marketing Imperative
By Michael R. Czinkota and Ilkka A. Ronkainen

© 2004 by TEXERE, an imprint of Thomson Business and Professional Publishing, a part of the Thomson Corporation. Thomson, the Star logo, TEXERE and Thomson Business and Professional Publishing are trademarks used herein.

ISBN: 0-324-22258-0

Printed and bound in the United States by Phoenix Color
1 2 3 4 5 6 7 07 06 05 04

For more information, contact Thomson Learning, 5191 Natorp Boulevard, Mason, OH 45040. You can also visit our website at www.thomson.com/learning/texere.

Composed by Sans Serif, Inc.

ALL RIGHTS RESERVED No part of this work covered by the copyright hereon may be reproduced or used in any form or by any means—graphic, electronic, or mechanical, including photocopying, recording, taping, Web distribution or information storage and retrieval systems—without the written permission of the author. For permission to use material from this text or product, submit a request online at *http://www.thomsonrights.com.* Any additional questions about permissions can be submitted by email to thomsonrights@thomson.com

This publication is designed to provide accurate and authoritative information in regard to the subject matter covered. It is sold with the understanding that the publisher is not engaged in rendering legal, accounting, or other professional services. If legal advice or other expert assistance is required, the services of a competent professional person should be sought.

The names of all companies or products mentioned herein are used for identification purposes only and may be trademarks or registered trademarks of their respective owners. Texere disclaims any affiliation, association, connection with, sponsorship, or endorsement by such owners.

CONTENTS

Preface xi

1 The Drive to Internationalize 1
  The Process of Internationalizing 1
    International Stages 2
  Motivations to Internationalize 3
    Proactive Motivations 4
    Reactive Motivations 6
  Change Agents 8
    Internal Change Agents 9
    External Change Agents 10
  Summary 11

2 Building the Knowledge Base: Research 13
  The Need for Research 13
  The Tools and Techniques 14
    New Parameters 14
    New Environments 14
    Number of Factors Involved 15
    Broader Definition of Competition 15
  Determining Research Objectives 15
  Determining Information Needs 17
  Sources of Data 17
    Governments 17
    International Organizations 17
    Service Organizations 18
    Trade Associations 18
    Directories and Newsletters 18
    Electronic Information Services 19
    Other Firms 20

Evaluating Data   20
Analyzing and Interpreting Data   20
Export Market Screening: Using Secondary Data   22
    A Step-by-Step Process   22
The Primary Research Process   24
    Research Techniques   25
Export Marketing Information System   26
Environmental Scanning   27
    Delphi Techniques   27
    Scenario Building   28
Summary   28
Appendix A: Information Sources for Marketing Issues   29
Appendix B: The Structure of a Country Commercial Guide   40

3   Export Modes   43

Exports   43
The E-Dimension in Exports   46
Licensing   48
    Assessment of Licensing   48
    Trademark Licensing   50
Franchising   50
Summary   53

4   Export Intermediaries   54

The Role of Intermediaries   54
    Export Management Companies   55
    Webb-Pomerene Associations   58
    Export Trading Companies   59
The Foreign Freight Forwarder   61
Summary   63

5   Financial Management   64

Credit Policy   64
Types of Financial Risk   65
Sources of Financing   66
    Commercial Banks   67

Forfaiting and Factoring   68
Official Trade Finance   69
Managing Foreign Exchange Risk   73
The Foreign Exchange Market   73
Dealing with Financial Crises   75
Summary   77

6 The Role of Government in International Trade   78
Transnational Institutions Affecting World Trade   78
The World Trade Organization (WTO)   78
The International Monetary Fund (IMF)   79
The World Bank   79
Economic Integration   80
Economic Integration and the Export Manager   85
Export Promotion   86
Home Country Political and Legal Environment   88
Export Controls   88
A New Environment for Export Controls   90
Embargoes and Sanctions   91
Regulation of International Business Behavior   91
Host Country Political and Legal Environment   93
Legal Differences and Restraints   95
Influencing Politics and Laws   96
The International Environment   98
Summary   101
Appendix A. The Sales Contract   101
Appendix B. Members of the U.S. Trade Promotion
     Coordination Committee (TPCC)   102

7 Export Market Choice and Development   104
Choosing and Developing a Market   104
Export Market Potential and Market Growth   105
The Strategic Planning Process   105
Internal Analysis   107
Formulating the Export Marketing Strategy   108

Export Country-Market Choice 109

Export Market Growth and Expansion 110
    Concentration versus Diversification 112
    Market Segmentation 113

Summary 115

8 Product Adjustments 116

Product Variables 116

Standardization versus Adaptation 119

Factors Affecting Adaptation 122
    The Market Environment 123
    Climate and Geography 128
    Product Characteristics 128
    Branding 129
    Packaging 131
    Appearance 132
    Method of Operation and Usage 133
    Quality 133
    Service 134

Country–of–Origin Effects 134

Company Considerations 135

Product Counterfeiting 136

Summary 139

9 Pricing 141

Price Dynamics 141

Setting Export Prices 142
    Export Pricing Objectives 142
    Export Pricing Policies 144
    Export Pricing Strategies 145

Export-Related Costs 147

Terms of Sale 150

Terms of Payment 155

Getting Paid for Exports 162

Pricing under Varying Currency Conditions 164

Price Negotiations 167

Leasing 168

Summary 169

10 Export Channel Management 170

Channel Systems 170

Channel Structure 171

Channel Design 172
- Customer Characteristics 173
- Culture 173
- Competition 175
- Character 176
- Capital 177
- Cost 177
- Coverage 178
- Control 179
- Continuity 180
- Communication 180

Selection of Intermediaries 181
- Sources for Finding Intermediaries 182
- Governmental Agencies 183
- Private Sources 187
- Performance 188
- Professionalism 190

The Distributor Agreement 191

Managing Channel Relationships 194
- Factors in Channel Management 195
- Gray Markets 197
- Termination of the Channel Relationship 199

Summary 201

11 International Transportation and Logistics 202

Transportation Infrastructure 202
- Availability of Modes 203
- Ocean Shipping 203
- Air Shipping 204
- Choice of Modes 205
- Transit Time 205
- Predictability 205
- Cost 206
- Noneconomic Factors 207

The International Shipment: Decision Paths 207

The International Shipment: Alternative Modes 209

viii Contents

    Documentation 210
    Assistance with International Shipments 214
  Summary 215

12 **Export Communication and Promotion Strategy** 216
  The Marketing Communications Process 216
  A Promotional Strategy for Exports 218
  Export Promotion Tools 221
    Business/Trade Journals and Directories 221
    Direct Marketing 223
    Internet 224
    Trade Shows and Missions 225
    Certified Trade Fair Program 227
  Personal Selling 228
    Indirect Exports 228
    Direct Exports 229
    Integrated Exports 230
  International Negotiations 232
    Stages of the Negotiation Process 232
    How to Negotiate in Other Countries and Cultures 234
  Summary 237

13 **The Export Marketing Plan** 238
  Selecting the Target Market and Creating Comparative Advantage 238
  Developing and Formulating the Plan 239
  The Financial Flow 243
  The Physical Flow 243
  Document Flow 244
  Implementing the Market Plan 244
  Controlling the Market Plan 245
  Summary 245

About the Authors 246
Index 247

To Ilona
MRC

To Sanna
IAR

To my sister and her children, and to
Astrid, a special thanks to a special friend
M O-B

PREFACE

Welcome to the world of exports in which the old saying "The more things change, the more they stay the same" was never more true than today. Humans have traveled the world in search of new markets since the beginning of recorded history. And occasionally international traders, like Marco Polo, led great revolutionary changes. Today is one of those times, and if you are in business, you can be one of those adventurers.

World trade has taken on an unprecedented the impact on nations, firms and individuals. Consider just two barometers of change during the past thirty years. One concerns the size of export activity: the volume of international trade in goods and services has grown from $ 200 billion to more than $ 9.3 trillion. During virtually all of that time, the growth in the value of trade has greatly exceeded the level of growth of total world output. The second measure is the U.S. trade deficit: Consider that in 1971, President Nixon closed the U.S. gold window and abandoned fixed exchanged rates because of an annual trade deficit of $5 billion. Today, the U.S. trade deficit runs at almost $ 600 billion per year. While that current deficit is considered problematic and undesirable now, thirty years ago it would have been unimaginable, the stuff of science fiction. But most important is the fact that these two measures are indicate of how the world has gone global and created new opportunities for exporters today.

The potential in exporting is so great because the two key changes of this new global economy which have been profound and basic: There have been global shifts in time and space which have resulted in a substantial decrease in the impact of distance. During the late 1960s an individual in Paris who wanted to call New York City would have to check in the morning for the availability of a "trunk" line that afternoon. Today at most locations one can pick up a phone and call anyone virtually anywhere in the world. We can all reach out and be reached ! Distance is no longer an obstacle.

Export channels have been reshaped by the emergence of new production locations, by the unlinkage of production and consumption of services, and by the ability of firms to participate in the global market place through electronic commerce. Multipronged market reach strategies–the privilege of a global few only a decade ago—have become common for many firms today.

The composition of trade has similarly been shifting. During the same 30 years, the trade role of primary commodities has declined precipitously, while the importance of manufactured goods has increased. More recently, however, the growth of trade in services has experienced a sharp upward trend, presaging the diminishing the importance of manufacturing in certain geographic regions. At the same time, new players have emerged who have taken on the role of manufacturing exporters, with activities, prices, and other competitive tools far different from those of "traditional" export players.

The effects of exports have been magnified. Both the opportunities and threats are much greater than ever before. Exports are not unusual anymore. They are what customers, governments and markets expect. But they are still special in that they are a key economic activity that is instrumental to prosperity. Exports bring new growth and expansion to firms, sharpen the competitive edge of managers, and make imports possible. It is only due to exports that consumers get to have the pick among a rich selection of hi quality and low priced imports.

All of which means an increase in freedom for both business and consumers. Of course, that freedom has a price. Businesses can sell their goods and services almost anywhere in the world, but so can competitors in those far-flung locations. Consumers as employees face competition from around the globe. International marketing contains the freedom of unlimited growth potential. Activities which have to constrain themselves to domestic considerations are likely to sooner or later run into limits of expansion. "Everybody has one" becomes a common phrase. When international markets are seen as an opportunity, the limits to growth are reached far less quickly if at all. Different families of products can extend the life of goods or services of a long time. Instead of restrictions, the international marketing paradigm encourages the stripping away of restraints; instead of limitations, there is the pointing out of opportunity. Being passionate about international markets can well open one's eyes to the prospects of freedom.

Freedom also means not being forced to do something one does not want to do. In today's times, many speak about migration pressures that force people to move from their rural homes into urban areas or from their developing countries into industrialized ones. Industrialized nations, in turn, speak about immigration pressure. For both sides, little if any freedom is involved here. The individuals who do the moving would much rather stay home but cannot afford to do so due to economic exigencies. The recipient countries might not want to welcome the migrants but do so in response to political and humanitarian pressures. Both sides are losing or have lost their freedom. Export marketing is instrumental in stemming the tide. It can provide the economic opportunity at home for individuals so that they need not migrate. It also lets individuals become productive contributors to the global economy and, in an organized, proud and above the table fashion, removes sensitive political points of friction.

The chapter of world history which was written in the late part of the 20th century has been most instrumental in showing us how markets, market forces, and the recognition of demand and supply have directly affected human rights and the extent of freedom. That was the time when the longstanding rivalry between socialism and market orientation was resolved. With all humility and gratefulness one can now conclude: Markets were right! The market system has proven its greater efficiency and effectiveness. It has demonstrated its ability to better satisfy the needs of people.

With the U.S. trade deficit at its current size, it seems highly plausible to forecast that change will have to come. One option might be government restrictions of imports. Yet, there is little historic record showing how nations have protected their way to prosperity. That leaves the strengthening of exports a the key option to improve the U.S. trade position, particularly since this activity involves opportunity rather than coercion and, in the words of Willy Sutton that's where the money is and will continue to be.

Currency exchange rates are turning benign—making exports and competition abroad easier. Awareness and cultural sensitivity make the exporter a key protagonist in aligning global values between countries, companies and individuals. With hard work and success, the exporter is a core player for freedom in the world, offering a road leading to growth, peace, and the mergence of values which will let humankind be more human and more kind to each other. The opportunities are there. Now is the time to use them. Exporting is no longer one option, it has become truly imperative. We wish you well in your efforts. Feel free to get in touch with us at either czinkotm@georgetown.edu or ronkaii@georgetown.edu , or ortizm@fia.edu

CHAPTER 1

The Drive to Internationalize

"Why should my firm internationalize?" almost begs the question. It might be better phrased, "What should I do when we get an international order?" Because if your firm has a Web site, it will eventually and inevitably get a nondomestic order. Analogous to the observation of the old-time politician who commented that all politics is local, it can be said that all business is global. The important consideration is what to do when the world beats a path to your door—because it will.

This chapter will describe some of the forces and motivations that lead a company to proactively take its business international and will outline the process that many firms go through as they turn themselves into full-fledged "citizens of the world."

The Process of Internationalizing

The decision to "go global" is dynamic, and it is not susceptible to a "one size fits all" approach. Nevertheless, companies tend to follow certain patterns as they move beyond their own borders, and Exhibit 1.1 presents a reliable model of the typical process of internationalization. It illustrates the interaction between and among components of an organization and shows how a company typically grows into becoming a full participant in the global arena. Using this model as a touchstone, managers can get their bearings when assessing their firm's position and development, and have a tool for planning and plotting future directions and performance.

As a firm expands its activities into the international marketplace, its managers are usually faced with increasing risk and decreasing profits. As with any new venture or initiative, there is a learning curve that every company follows, even with the best planning. Expertise is developed gradually, and during that process there is a high degree of uncertainty. At the same time, the need for upfront investment saps short-term profits. Over the longer term, these factors

EXHIBIT 1.1. A Model of the Internationalization Process

Domestic Expansion	Uninterested Firms	Change Agents and Intermediaries	Concerns
Alternative Strategies	Export Awareness	• External	• Information
	Export Interest	• Internal	• Mechanics
		Stimuli	• Communication
Licensing Franchising	Export Trial	• External	• Sales Effort
	Export Evaluation	• Internal	• Service
		Information Experience Perception	• Delivery
	Export Adaptation		• Regulations
Direct Foreign Investment	Further Activity		

stabilize as the firm becomes more knowledgeable and experienced, but for the short term the ride can become very difficult. Successful performance can be achieved in three ways: effectiveness, efficiency, and competitive strength. Effectiveness is characterized by acquisition of market share abroad and by increased sales. Efficiency is manifest by rising profitability. Competitive strength is reflected by increased market share.

International Stages

In small-market countries, firms may very well be born global, founded for the explicit purpose of marketing abroad because the domestic economy is too small to support their activities. It appears that in some countries more than a third of exporting firms commenced their export activities within two years of establishment. Such *innate*, or start-up, *exporters* may have a distinct role to play in an economy's international trade involvement.

In addition, firms with a strong e-commerce focus may also be gaining rapid global exposure due to the ease of outreach and access. Such rapid exposure, however, should not be confused with internationalization, since it may often take a substantial amount of time to translate exposure into international business activities. In most instances today, firms begin their operations in the domestic market. From their home location, they gradually expand, and, over time, some of them become interested in the international market.

The development of this interest typically appears to proceed in several stages. In each one of these stages, firms are measurably different in their capabilities, problems, and needs. Initially the vast majority of firms are not at all interested in the international marketplace. Frequently, management will not even fill an unsolicited export order if one is received. Should unsolicited orders or other international market stimuli continue over time, however, a firm may gradually become a *partially interested exporter*. Management will then fill unsolicited export orders.

Prime candidates among firms to make this transition from uninterested to partially interested are those companies that have a track record of domestic market expansion. In the next stage, the firm begins to explore international markets gradually, and management is willing to consider the feasibility of exporting. After this *exploratory stage*, the firm becomes an *experimental exporter*, usually to psychologically close countries. However, management is still far from being committed to exporting activities.

At the next stage, the firm evaluates the impact that exporting has had on its general activities. Here, of course, the possibility exists that a firm will be disappointed with its international market performance and will withdraw from these activities. On the other hand, frequently, it will continue to exist as an experienced small exporter. The final stage of this process is that of *export adaptation*. Here a firm is an experienced exporter to a particular country and adjusts its activities to changing exchange rates, tariffs, and other variables. Management is ready to explore the feasibility of exporting to additional countries that are psychologically further away. Frequently, this level of adaptation is reached once export transactions comprise 15 percent or more of sales volume. Just as parking ticket income, originally seen as unexpected revenue, gradually became incorporated into city budgets, the income from export marketing becomes incorporated into the budget and plans of the firm. Already when new product plans are made the question is raised: "How will this play in Osaka, Japan?" In these instances, the firm can be considered a strategic participant in the international market.

Business skills must be developed, relationships cultivated, and resources measured and managed intelligently. But equally important is motivation and the direction and vision that motivation provides.

Motivations to Internationalize

Why does a firm's management decide to go international? The first, maybe obvious, factor in going international is the same as it is for any business decision: determination and commitment to succeed. Management must want to go international and make a serious, determined commitment to identifying

EXHIBIT 1.2. Why Firms Go International

PROACTIVE MOTIVATIONS	REACTIVE MOTIVATIONS
• Profit advantage	• Competitive pressures
• Unique products	• Overproduction
• Technological advantage	• Declining domestic sales
• Exclusive information	• Excess capacity
• Managerial urge	• Saturated domestic markets
• Tax benefit	• Proximity to customers and ports
• Economies of scale	

potential and to making the commitments and preparation necessary to succeed. In short, they must want to do it. This commitment must be more than mere statements in corporate press releases or at stockholders' meetings. It must be able to endure stagnation and sometimes even setbacks and failure that often accompany any new venture or initiative. Obtaining that level of commitment means involving all levels of management early in the export planning process and encouraging their active support and commitment.

A good indication of the degree of corporate commitment is the nature of organizational structure. Someone must have a primary responsibility for exporting. Responsibility means focus. Even if, at the outset, just one person is assigned part time, it is crucial to make that responsibility an important part of a specific person's job description and reward structure.

In addition to wanting to do it, the firm must have the ability—the skill sets and other support—necessary to succeed. At the outset of a program the majority of those resources might not be in-house, but they must be available to the firm in some form.

Of course, motivations are often mixed and usually multiple. One factor alone rarely accounts for any given business activity. Exhibit 1.2 provides an overview of the typical proactive and reactive motivations to go international. Proactive motivations represent stimuli to attempt strategic change. Reactive motivations influence firms that are responsive to environmental changes and adjust to them by changing their activities over time. In other words, proactive firms go international because they want to, while reactive ones go international because they have to.

Proactive Motivations

Profitability is the strongest motivator. Management may perceive international sales as a potential source of higher profit margins or of more added-on profits. Of course, the perception and the reality can differ significantly. High start-up costs often drain initial profitability, especially when the firm has not previously engaged in international market activities. Despite thorough planning, imponderable influences often shift the profit picture substantially. For example, a sudden shift in exchange rates may drastically alter profit forecasts even though they were based on careful market evaluations.

The second major motivator results from distinctiveness of the firm's products or from a unique technological advantage. The firm's offerings might face little competition in international markets or its proprietary technology may be one of a kind in a specialized field. Again, perception and reality should be compared. That means using research as a form of "reality therapy." And if the perception and reality match, it can certainly provide a competitive edge and establish the basis for success. The intensity of marketing's interaction with the research and development function, as well as the level of investment into R&D, has been shown to have a major effect on the success of exported products.

The key question here is how long will such a competitive advantage last. In the past firms could count on dominating international markets for many years. However, the life of such advantages has shrunk dramatically with the rapid increase in the pace of innovation (in both products and technologies) and because of a lack of intellectual property rights protection.

Exclusive market information is another proactive stimulus. This includes knowledge about foreign customers, marketplaces, or market situations that are not widely known by other firms. Such special knowledge may be based on a firm's international research, special contacts, or simply being in the right place at the right time. Although such exclusivity can serve well as an initial stimulus for exporting activities, it will rarely provide prolonged motivation because competitors—at least in the medium run—can be expected to catch up with the information advantage of the firm, particularly in light of the growing ease of global information access.

Tax benefits have historically also played a major motivating role. Many countries offer tax concessions to their firms in order to encourage export activities. In The United States, a tax mechanism called the Exterritorial Income (ETI) Tax Exclusion provides exporting firms with certain tax deferrals, thus making international marketing activities potentially more profitable. However, the rules of the World Trade Organization prohibit the subsidy of exports by all but the poorest countries. For example, the ETI mechanism of the United States was found to be violation of WTO regulations, and the United States was advised to terminate such benefits. It can, therefore, be expected that tax benefits will play a decreasing role in future motivations to export.

A final major proactive motivation is economies of scale. Becoming a participant in exporting activities may enable the firm to increase its output and therefore slide down more rapidly on the learning curve. Ever since the Boston Consulting Group showed that a doubling of output could reduce production costs up to 30 percent, firms have sought this growth. Increased production for the international market can therefore also help in reducing the cost of production for domestic sales and make the firm more competitive domestically as well. Thus, a company's primary motivation with respect to this effect is stated as seeking increased market share. At an initial level of internationalization this may mean an increased search for export markets; later on, it can result in the opening of foreign subsidiaries and foreign production facilities.

Reactive Motivations

Firms act reactively as well as proactively, especially in the face of changes and pressures in the business environment. A prime form of such motivation is the reaction to competitive pressures. A firm may fear losing domestic market share to competing firms that have benefited from the effect of the economies of scale gained by exporting activities. Further, it may fear losing foreign markets permanently to domestic competitors that decide to focus on these markets. Observing that domestic competitors are beginning to internationalize, and knowing that the firm that obtains market share initially most easily retains it, firms frequently enter exporting head over heels. Quick entry may result in similarly quick withdrawal once the firm recognizes that its preparation has been insufficient.

Similarly, overproduction can serve as a major motivation. Historically, during downturns in the domestic business cycle, foreign markets provided an ideal outlet for bloated inventories. Frequently, this kind of *safety-valve activity* was designed for short-term activities only. Instead of developing an exporting perspective by adjusting the marketing mix to needs abroad, firms would simply cut prices, sell their excess inventory, and then leave the market when the domestic market rebounded. In its most egregious form this has been called dumping. Firms that have used such a strategy find it much more difficult to execute it the second time, after they have walked away from business relationships. This reaction from foreign markets and the fact that the major industrial economies appear to be increasingly synchronized may well lead to a decrease in the importance of this motivation over time.

Stable or declining domestic sales of products that are in the declining stage of the product life cycle have a similar motivating effect. Instead of attempting a pushback of the life cycle process at home by adding a cosmetic innovation or, sometimes, in addition to such an effort, the firm may opt to prolong the life of the product by expanding the market. In the past, such efforts often met with success because of the lag times of many product innovations. In particular, markets in many underdeveloped countries did only slowly reach the same level of need and sophistication of markets in more developed nations. Increasingly, however, these lag times, if they still exist at all, are much shorter than they used to be. Nevertheless, this motivation is still particularly valid in less developed countries with respect to high-technology products that have become outdated by the latest innovations in developed markets. Such "just-dated" technology can be highly useful in economic development and offer vast progress in the manufacturing or services sector.

Excess capacity, like overproduction, can also be a powerful motivation. If equipment for production is not fully utilized, firms may see expansion into the international market as an ideal possibility for achieving broader distribution of fixed costs. Alternatively, if all fixed costs are assigned to domestic production, the firm can penetrate international markets with a pricing scheme that focuses mainly on variable costs. Although such a strategy may be useful in the short term, it may result in the offering of products abroad at a cost lower than at home, which in turn may trigger dumping charges. In the long run, fixed costs have to be recovered to ensure replacement of production equipment that growing exporting activities may overtax. Market penetration strategy based on variable cost alone is therefore not feasible over the long term.

The reactive motivation of a saturated domestic market is similar in results to that of declining domestic sales. Again, firms in this situation can use the international market to prolong the life cycle of their product and of their organization.

A final major reactive motivation is proximity to customers and ports. Physical closeness to the international market can often play a major role in the export activities of a firm. For example, Canadian firms established near the U.S. border may not even perceive of their market activities in the United States as exporting. Rather, they are simply an extension of domestic activities, without any particular attention being paid to the fact that some of the products go abroad. Except for some firms close to the Canadian or Mexican border, however, this factor is much less prevalent in North America than in many other parts of the world. Europe, Asia, and South America contain many more countries located much more closely to each other. For example, a European company operating in the heart of Belgium needs to go only fifty miles to be in multiple foreign markets. Companies in such physical circumstances are almost forced to be international.

Then there is the concept of psychic or *psychological proximity*. Geographic closeness to foreign markets may not necessarily translate into real or perceived closeness to the foreign customer. Sometimes cultural variables, legal factors, and other societal norms make a foreign market that is geographically close seem psychologically distant. For example, research has shown that many U.S. firms perceive Canada to be much closer psychologically than Mexico. Even England, mainly because of the similarity in language, is perceived by many U.S. firms to be much closer than Mexico or other Latin American countries, despite the geographic distances. However, in light of the reduction of trade barriers as a result of the North American Free Trade Agreement (NAFTA), and a growing proportion of the U.S. population with Hispanic background, this long-standing perception is changing. Two major issues are at the heart of psychological proximity. First, some of the distance seen by firms is based on perception rather than reality. For example, German firms may view the Austrian market simply as an extension of their home market due to so many superficial similarities, just as many U.S. firms may see the United Kingdom as psychologically very close due to the language similarity. However, the attitudes and values of managers and customers may vary substantially between markets. Too much of a focus on the similarities may let the firm lose sight of the differences. Many Canadian firms have incurred high costs in learning this lesson when entering the United States. Second, closer psychological proximity does make it easier for firms to enter markets. Therefore, for firms new to exporting it may be advantageous to begin this new activity by entering the psychologically closer markets first in order to gather experience before venturing into markets that are farther away.

For the firm that seeks partners for involvement in international markets or managers who search for firms most likely to provide good opportunities, an important consideration should be whether a firm is internationally proactive or reactive. The clearest difference between proactive and reactive firms centers around how they originally entered international markets. Proactive firms are more likely to have solicited their first export order, while reactive firms only began exporting activities after having received an unsolicited order from abroad. And the difference provides an important gauge of the potential for success. The most successful exporters tend to be motivated by proactive factors in their general business operations as well as their international activities. They are more likely to be service-oriented than reactive firms and typically are more marketing and strategy-oriented than reactive firms, which place more emphasis on operational issues. Also, the motivations of firms do not seem to shift dramatically over the short term but are rather stable. Initial motivation for entry into international markets seems to be a good barometer of how the firm's management runs its business otherwise.

Change Agents

For change to take place, someone or something within the firm must initiate it and shepherd it through to implementation. This intervening individual or vari-

EXHIBIT 1.3. Change Agents in the Internationalization Process

FIRM INTERNAL	FIRM EXTERNAL
• Enlightened management • New management • Significant internal event	• Demand • Other firms • Domestic distributors • Banks • Chambers of commerce • Governmental activities • Export intermediaries 　—Export management companies 　—Trading companies

able is here called a **change agent**. Change agents in the internationalization process are shown in Exhibit 1.3.

Internal Change Agents

A primary change agent internal to the firm is enlightened management. The key factor leading to such performance-enhancing enlightenment is the international experience and exposure of management. Examples are when the current management of a firm discovers and understands the value of international markets and decides to pursue exporting opportunities. Such insights are frequently triggered by foreign travel, during which new business opportunities are discovered, or by information that leads management to believe that such opportunities exist. Managers who have lived abroad, have learned foreign languages, or are particularly interested in foreign cultures are likely, sooner rather than later, to investigate whether exporting opportunities would be appropriate for their firm so there is a key business benefit to international travel!

A second set of major internal change agents consists of new management or new employees. Often, managers enter a firm having already had some exporting experience in previous positions and try to use this experience to further the business activities of their new firm. Also, in developing their goals in the new job, managers frequently consider an entirely new set of options for growth and expansion, one of which may be exporting activities.

A significant internal event can be another major change agent. A new employee who firmly believes that the firm should undertake exporting may find ways to motivate management. The development of a new product useful abroad can serve as such an event, as can the receipt of new information about current product uses. As an example, a manufacturer of hospital beds learned that beds it was selling domestically were being resold in a foreign country. Further, the beds it sold for $600 each were resold overseas for approximately $1,300. This new piece of information served to trigger a strong interest on the part of the company's management in entering international markets.

In small and medium-sized firms (firms with fewer than 250 employees), the initial decision to export is usually made by the president, with substantial input provided by the marketing department. The carrying out of the decision—that is, the initiation of actual exporting activities and the implementation of these activities—is then primarily the responsibility of marketing personnel. Only in the final decision stage of evaluating exporting activities does the major emphasis rest again with the president of the firm. In order to influence a firm internally, it therefore appears that the major emphasis should be placed first on convincing the president to enter the international marketplace and then on convincing the marketing department that exporting is an important activity. Conversely, the marketing department is a good place to be if one wants to become active in international business.

External Change Agents

The primary outside influence on a firm's decision to become international is foreign demand. Expressions of such demand through, for example, inquiries from abroad have a powerful effect on initial interest in entering the international marketplace. Unsolicited orders from abroad are a major factor that encourages firms to begin exporting. In the United States, for example, such unsolicited orders have been found to account for more than half of all cases of export initiation by small and medium-sized firms. Due to the growth of corporate Web sites, firms can become unplanned participants in the international market even more often. For example, customers from abroad can visit a Web site and place an international order, even though a firm's plans may have been strictly domestic. Of course, a firm can choose to ignore foreign interest and lose out on new markets. Alternatively, it can find itself unexpectedly an exporter. Such firms can be called accidental exporters. While good fortune may have initiated the export activity, over the longer term the firm must start planning how to systematically increase its international expansion or, at least, how to make more of these accidents happen.

Other major outside influences are the statements and actions of other firms in the same industry. Information that an executive in a competing firm considers international markets to be valuable and worthwhile to develop easily captures the attention of management. Such statements not only have source credibility but also are viewed with a certain amount of fear because a successful competitor may eventually infringe on the firm's business. Formal and informal meetings among managers from different firms at trade association meetings, conventions, or business roundtables therefore often serve as a major change agent.

A third, quite influential, change agent consists of domestic distributors. Often, such distributors are engaged, through some of their other business activities, in exporting. To increase their international distribution volume, they encourage purely domestic firms also to participate in the international market. This is true not only for exports but also for imports. For example, a major customer of a manufacturing firm may find that materials available from abroad, if used in the domestic production process, would make the product available at lower cost. In such instances, the customer may approach the supplier and strongly encourage foreign sourcing.

Banks and other service firms, such as accountants, can serve as major change agents by alerting domestic clients to international opportunities. Although these service providers historically follow their major multinational clients abroad, increasingly they are establishing a foreign presence of their own. They frequently work with domestic clients on expanding their market reach in the hope that their services will be used for any international transactions that result. Chambers of commerce and other business associations that interact with firms locally can frequently heighten exporting interests. In most instances, these organizations function only as secondary intermediaries, because true change is brought about by the presence and encouragement of other managers.

Governmental efforts on the national or local level can also serve as a major change agent. In light of the contributions exports make to growth, employment, and tax revenue, governments increasingly are becoming active in encouraging and supporting exports. In the United States, the Department of Commerce is particularly involved in encouraging exports. Its district offices are charged with increasing the exporting activities of U.S. firms. Frequently, district officers, with the help of voluntary groups such as district export councils, visit firms and attempt to analyze their exporting opportunities.

Increasingly, state and local governments are also actively encouraging firms to participate in the international market. Many states have formed economic development agencies that assist companies by providing information, displaying products abroad, and even helping with financing. Trade missions and similar activities are also being carried out by some of the larger cities. Although it is difficult to measure the effects of these efforts, it appears that due to their closeness to firms, such state and local government authorities can become major factors in influencing firms to go international.

Summary

Firms do not become experienced exporters overnight but rather progress gradually through an international development process. This process is the result of different motivations to internationalize, varying managerial and corporate characteristics of the firm, the influence of change agents, and the capability of the firm to overcome barriers.

The motivations can be either proactive or reactive. Proactive motivations are initiated by the firm's management and can consist of a perceived profit advantage, technological advantage, product advantage, exclusive market information, or managerial urge. Reactive motivations are the responses of management to environmental changes and pressures. Typical are competitive pressures, overproduction, declining domestic sales, or excess capacity. Firms that are primarily stimulated by proactive motivations are more likely to enter international markets aggressively and successfully.

Change agents, both external and internal to the firm, can bring on an international orientation. Typically, these are individuals and institutions that, due to their activities or goals, highlight the benefits of international activities. They can be managers who have traveled abroad or have carried out successful international marketing ventures, banks, or government agencies. Over time, firms will progress through stages of international expertise and activity. In each one of these stages, firms are likely to have a distinct level of interest in the international market and require different types of information and help. Their outlook toward international markets is likely to progress gradually from purely operational concerns to a strategic international orientation. Only at that level will the firm have become a truly committed exporter.

CHAPTER 2

Building the Knowledge Base: Research

It would be trite if it wasn't still so true: A business moves, survives, and grows on information the way an army moves on its ability to get food and fuel. And that certainly holds true for export marketing, where a company is venturing out into new unknown cultures, markets and financial environments. Fortunately, the one thing that we don't lack in today's wired and interconnected world is information. The trick is organizing it, making sense of it, and using it profitably. This chapter will focus on finding and organizing it. Subsequent chapters will show you different ways to use the many different kinds of information available.

The Need for Research

Choosing to export isn't really an issue today. The world will come to your door with the occasional unsolicited Internet order if nothing else. But the problem is that so will your competition. For virtually every business, your marketplace—that means both prospective customers and competitors—is the world. The real issues that you need to ask concern the "where" and the "how."

Here are some questions that every potential export marketer needs to ask:

- What countries offer the best potential for my products?
- What is the nature and size of the country market? The target market?
- What government regulations must the product meet to enter a market?
- What adaptations, if any, are needed for the best product-market fit?
- What channel structure can best serve this market, and what type of channel members are available in the foreign market?
- What factors may affect the pricing strategy and offer?

- How can the product be promoted and what promotional tools can be used successfully?

The answers to these questions will drive your marketing strategy. The quality of information from your research determines how good your marketing strategy is.

The Tools and Techniques

Export and domestic marketing research use the same tools and techniques. The difference is in the environment(s), which is precisely what determines how well those tools and techniques will work and how you will interpret the information they provide. In some instances, entirely new tools and techniques may need to be developed. However, four primary differences are new parameters, new environments, and increase in the number of factors involved, and a broader definition of competition.

New Parameters

In crossing national borders, a firm encounters parameters not found in the home market. Examples include tariff (duties} and no tariff barriers (standards, quotas, etc), foreign currencies and changes in their value, different modes of transportation, port facilities and international documentation. A firm that has done business only domestically will have little or no prior experience with these requirements and conditions. New parameters also emerge because of differing modes of operating internationally. For example, a firm can export, it can license products, it can participate in a joint venture, or it can carry out foreign investment. These parameters must be carefully identified and researched in order to have a complete information base for exporting.

New Environments

When deciding to export, a firm exposes itself to an unfamiliar environment. Many of the assumptions on which the firm was founded and on which its domestic activities are based may not hold true internationally. Export firms need to learn about the culture of the importing country (especially how business is conducted in that country) and understand the political system and its stability and how this might affect the regulation of trade, currency values, and the ability of importers to conduct their business on a regular basis. In addition, exporters need to appreciate the legal system of the importing country in order to understand pertinent legal issues so that they know how to operate within the law. Exporters must also incorporate the technological level of the society into their product, planning, and processes.

In short, all of the assumptions formulated over the year in the domestic market must be reevaluated. This crucial point is often neglected because most managers were born in the environment of their domestic operations and subconsciously learn to understand the domestic constraints and opportunities of their domestic business activities. Export-oriented research helps overcome this deficiency by obtaining information on new environments to help identify the pitfalls, constraints, and opportunities of the export activities.

Number of Factors Involved

Exporters typically enter more than one market at a time. As a result, the number of changing dimensions increases significantly. Even if every dimension is understood, the exporter must be able to understand the similarities and differences of each as well as the interaction between them in each individual country. Each country market must both be evaluated on its own merits, as well as in the context of its interaction with other markets. Because of the sheer number of factors, coordination of the factors becomes increasingly difficult. Export market research can help management in this process.

Broader Definition of Competition

By entering export markets, the firm exposes itself to a much greater variety of competition than existed in the domestic market. In order for the exporter to make realistic assumptions about the export market to enter and serve, it is necessary to understand the competitive environment. The competition faced by an exporter in a target market comes from:

- Other exporters in the domestic market.
- Third-country exporters also exporting to the target market.
- Domestic manufacturers in the importing country.

A thorough analysis of the exporter's main competitors will greatly increase the chances of success in export activities.

Determining Research Objectives

Research objectives will vary from firm to firm for a variety of reasons, but especially because of the marketing situation. After a general review of corporate capabilities, such as personnel resources and the degree of financial exposure and risk that the firm can tolerate, existing diagnostic tools can be used to analyze the target market with a high degree of confidence.

The starting point for market research is market opportunity analysis. The initial aim here is to use a broad-brush approach that quickly and inexpensively narrows down the practical targets for export activities. Such an approach includes a cursory analysis of general market variables, such as total and per capita

GDP, mortality rates, and population figures. These factors make it possible to determine whether the corporation's objectives might be met in those markets. For example, expensive labor-saving consumer products may not be successful in the People's Republic of China because their price may be a significant proportion of the annual income of consumers (per capita GDP) and the perceived benefit to the potential customers may be only minimal. Such cursory evaluation will help reduce the number of markets to be considered to a more manageable number—for example, from 200 to 25.

Next, the researcher will require information about the potential product categories for a preliminary evaluation.

At this stage, the emphasis shifts to focus on market opportunities for a specific product or brand, including existing, latent, and incipient markets. Even though the aggregate industry data may have already been obtained, general information is usually insufficient to make company-specific decisions. For example, the market demand for medical equipment should not be confused with the potential demand for a specific brand. In addition, the research should identify demand-and-supply patterns and evaluate any regulations and standards. Finally, a competitive assessment must match markets with corporate strengths and provides an analysis of the best market potential for specific products. Exhibit 2.1 offers a summary of the various stages in the determination of market potential.

EXHIBIT 2.1. A Sequential Process of Researching Foreign Market Potentials

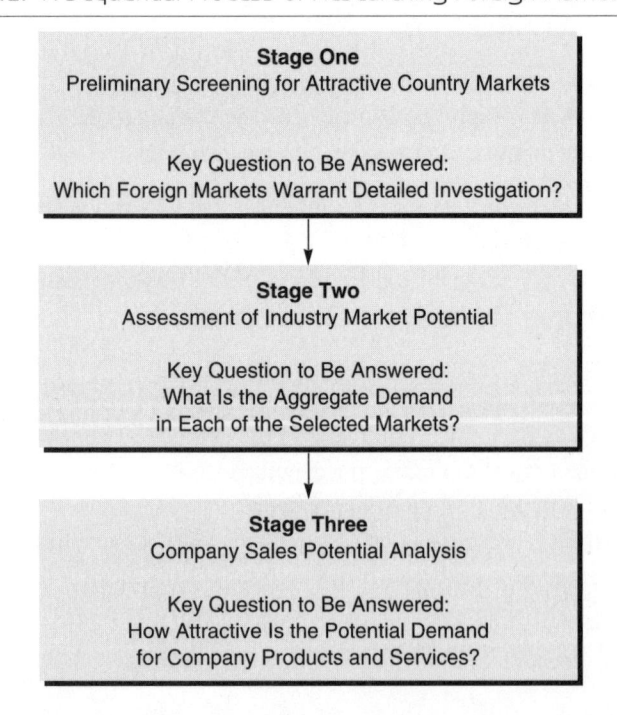

Stage One
Preliminary Screening for Attractive Country Markets

Key Question to Be Answered:
Which Foreign Markets Warrant Detailed Investigation?

↓

Stage Two
Assessment of Industry Market Potential

Key Question to Be Answered:
What Is the Aggregate Demand
in Each of the Selected Markets?

↓

Stage Three
Company Sales Potential Analysis

Key Question to Be Answered:
How Attractive Is the Potential Demand
for Company Products and Services?

Research objectives may include obtaining detailed information on penetrating a market, for designing and fine-tuning the marketing mix, or for monitoring the political climate of a country so that the exporter can expand its operations successfully. The better defined the research objectives are, the better the researcher will be able to determine the information requirements and thus conserve time and the financial resources of the firm.

Determining Information Needs

There are two types of research available for all marketing situations: primary and secondary. Secondary research involves more general, macro issues similar to those that have been discussed thus far, such as industry structure, general market characteristics and structure, and general preferences of the buying public(s) involved. Primary research is used to define or respond to a specific problem that is specific to the company. Primary data is information collected from consumers, competitors, and/or other constituents to obtain input on some specific question or problem the exporter is interested in. This includes information about customer attitudes and product preferences, opinions about the company and competitors' products, and so forth.

Sources of Data

Secondary data is available from a wide variety of sources. The major ones are briefly reviewed here. In addition, Appendix A to this chapter lists a wide variety of publications and organizations that monitor international issues.

Governments

Most countries have a wide array of macro and micro trade data available. Increasingly these data are available on the Internet, which tends to make them much more current than ever before. Closer collaboration between governmental statistical agencies also makes the data more accurate and reliable, since it is now much easier to compare data such as bilateral exports and imports to each other. These information sources are often available at embassies and consulates, whose mission includes the enhancement of trade activities. The commercial counselor or commercial attaché can provide such information.

International Organizations

International organizations often provide useful data for the researcher. The Statistical Yearbook produced by the United Nations (UN) contains international trade data on products and provides information on exports and imports by country. Because of the time needed for worldwide data collection, the information is often dated. Additional information is compiled and made available by specialized sub-structures of the UN. Some of these are the UN Conference on Trade and Development (http://www.unctad.org), which concentrates primarily on international issues surrounding developing nations, such as debt and market access, the UN Center on Transnational Corporations, and the International Trade Center (http://www.intracen.org). The *World Bank Atlas*, published by the World Bank (http://www.worldbank.org) provides useful general data on population, growth trends, and GNP figures. The World Trade Organization (http://www.wto.org) and the Organization for Economic Cooperation and Development (http://www. oecd.org) also publish quarterly and annual data on their member countries. Organizations such as the International Monetary Fund (http://www.imf.org) and the World Bank publish summary economic data and occasional staff papers that evaluate region-or country-specific issues in depth.

Service Organizations

Banks, accounting firms, freight forwarders, airlines, and international trade consultants can be invaluable sources of trade-related information. Frequently, they are able to provide data on business practices, legislative, or regulatory requirements, and political stability as well as basic trade data. Although some of this information is available without charge, its basic intent is to serve as an "appetizer." Much of the initial information is quite general in nature; more detailed answers often require an appropriate fee.

Trade Associations

Associations such as world trade clubs and domestic and international chambers of commerce (for example, the American Chamber of Commerce abroad) can provide valuable information about local markets. Often, files are maintained on international trade issues and trends affecting exporters. Useful information can also be obtained from industry associations. These groups, formed to represent entire industry segments, often collect from their members a wide variety of data that are then published in an aggregate form. The information provided is often quite general in nature because of the wide variety of clientele served. It can provide valuable initial insights into international markets, since it permits a benchmarking effort through which the exporter can establish how it is faring when compared to the competition.

Directories and Newsletters

Many industry directories are available on local, national, and international levels. These directories primarily serve to identify firms and to provide general background information, such as the name of the chief executive officer, the address and telephone number, and some information about a firm's products. The quality of a directory depends, of course, on the quality of input and the frequency of updates. Some of the directories are becoming increasingly sophisticated and can provide quite detailed information to the researcher.

Many newsletters are devoted to specific international issues such as international trade finance, international contracting, bartering, countertrade, international payment flows, and customs news. Published by banks or accounting firms in order to keep their clientele current on international developments, newsletters usually cater to narrow audiences but can provide important information to the firm interested in a specific area.

Electronic Information Services

When information is needed, managers often cannot spend a lot of time, energy, or money finding, sifting through, and categorizing existing materials. Consider laboring through every copy of every trade publication to find out the latest news on how environmental concerns are affecting marketing decisions in Mexico. With electronic information services, search results can be obtained almost immediately. International online computer database services, numbering in the thousands, can be purchased to supply information external to the firm, such as exchange rates, international news, and import restrictions. Most database hosts do not charge any sign-up fee and request payment only for actual use. The selection of initial database hosts depends on the choice of relevant databases, taking into account their product and market limitations, language used, and geographical location.

A large number of databases and search engines provide information about products and markets. Many of the main news agencies through online databases provide information about events that affect certain markets. Some databases cover extensive lists of companies in given countries and the products they buy and sell. A large number of databases exist that cover various categories of trade statistics. The main economic indicators of the UN, IMF, OECD, and EU are available online. Standards institutes in most of the G7 nations provide online access to their databases of technical standards and trade regulations on specific products.

There is a significant amount of international trade and economic data available from domestic and international organizations. A significant number of databases can be found online and accessed either free or for a fee. For the U.S. exporter, a primary database is the National Trade Data Bank (NTDB). This database is a service of the U.S. Department of Commerce for the export community. The NTDB provides access to Exporting Insights reports, Country Commercial Guides, Industry Sector Analysis reports, Market Research reports, Best Market reports and other programs prepared by the Economics and Statistical Administration. It includes an International Trade Library with a comprehensive collection of over 40,000 documents related to international trade. All are full text searchable, as well as keyword searchable by country or product. This database is second to none as it provides *relevant* and *timely* information for export market assessment (www.stat-usa.gov).

However, there are also drawbacks. In spite of the ease of access to data on the Internet, search engines cover only a portion of international publications. Also, they are heavily biased toward English-language publications. As a result, sole reliance on electronic information may cause the researcher to lose out on valuable input. Electronic databases should therefore be seen as only one important dimension of research scrutiny.

Other Firms

Often other firms can provide useful information for exporting purposes. Firms appear to be more open about their international than about their domestic marketing activities. On some occasions, valuable information can also be obtained from foreign firms and distributors.

Evaluating Data

Before obtaining secondary data, the researcher needs to evaluate their appropriateness for the task at hand. As the first step of such an evaluation, the quality of the data source needs to be considered with a primary focus on the purpose and method of the original data collection. Next, the quality of the actual data needs to be assessed, which should include a determination of data accuracy, reliability, and recency. Obviously, outdated data may mislead rather than improve the decision-making process. In addition, the compatibility and comparability of the data need to be considered. Since they were collected with another purpose in mind, we need to determine whether the data can help with the issue of concern to the firm. In international research it is also important to ensure that data categories are comparable to each other, in order to avoid misleading conclusions.

Analyzing and Interpreting Data

Once the data have been obtained, the researcher must use research creativity to make good use of them. This often requires the combination and cross-tabulation of various sets of data or the use of proxy information in order to arrive at conclusions that address the research objectives. A *proxy variable* is a substitute for a variable that one cannot directly measure. For example, the market penetration of television sets may be used as a proxy variable for the potential market demand for DVD players. Similarly, in an industrial setting, information about plans for new port facilities may be useful in determining future containerization requirements. Also, the level of computerization of a society may indicate the future need for software.

The researcher must go beyond the scope of the data and use creative inferences to arrive at knowledge useful to the firm. However, such creativity brings risks. Once the interpretation and analysis have taken place, a consistency check must be conducted. The researcher should always cross-check the results with other possible sources of information or with experts.In addition, the researcher should take another look at the research methods employed and, based on their usefulness, determine any necessary modifications for future projects. This will make possible the continuous improvement of international market research activities and enables the corporation to learn from experience.

As mentioned previously, it is important to be aware of different laws and attitudes in different countries. For example, in 2002, the European Union passed a directive on privacy and electronic communications. Extending earlier legislation, it maintains high standards of data privacy to ensure the free flow of data throughout the 15 member states. The new directive requires member states to block transmission of data to non-EU countries if these countries do not have domestic legislation that provides for a level of protection judged as adequate by the European Union. The EU has a strict interpretation of its citizens' rights to privacy. There is an opt-in approach for unsolicited e-mails: Online marketing firms and other Internet operators can send commercial e-mails only after the customer has specifically asked them to do so. The placement of invisible data-tracking devices such as "cookies" on a computer is prohibited until after a user has been provided with adequate information about their purpose.

The directive also reflects a EU compromise in light of the September 11 attacks and the growing frequency of cybercrime. Due to requests by key e-commerce partners, such as the United States, revisions were made to EU policy to accommodate criminal investigation. Under the new directive, companies in the EU will still have to erase information immediately after the one- to-two month period needed for billing purposes. However, governments can now require operators to store data for longer periods of time, if deemed necessary for security reasons. In order to settle conflicts between divergent government policies, companies are increasingly likely to adapt global privacy rules for managing information online and to get certified by watchdog groups, which tell users when a site adheres to specific privacy guidelines. Overall, the exporter must pay careful attention to the privacy laws and expectations in different nations and to possible consumer reactions to the use of data in the marketing effort.

Export Market Screening: Using Secondary Data

The exporter can rely primarily on secondary data for the basis of export market analysis. However, the researcher must exercise caution in evaluating the information reliability and accuracy.

Most U. S. government publications and foreign trade data, such as the International Trade Administration (www.web.ita.doc.gov/), can be accessed via the Internet. Other types of international organizations such The World Trade Organization (www.wto.org) and International Monetary Fund (www.imf.org) provide updated economic and trade information. Most foreign governments and other international organizations have Web sites providing useful information.

A Step-by-Step Process

- **Step 1: Export Marketing Screening**

  The first step in export market research is the screening of potential markets for a particular product to be exported. The goal is to evaluate a market for a specific product or product category in order to identify the opportunities that may be available for exporting.

  For example, a U.S. exporter of road tractors for agricultural use would find that key information is available from *The World Bank Atlas*, a CD-ROM-based database available for commercial users. This database provides detailed information about U.S. exports to the world and is searchable by product category, specific product, and ranked country markets. It also provides information about total value and volume of exports and average price in export markets.

  In order to use this database, the researcher needs to obtain the Schedule B number under which the product is classified. The system, called The International Harmonized Commodity Classification System (HS-based Schedule B) is used by the U.S. Department of Commerce, Bureau of the Census, to classify all products leaving the United States.

  Millions of trade transactions occur each year. These transactions are classified under approximately 8,000 product categories leaving the United States (http://www.census.gov). The Schedule B Commodity Classification assigns a unique 10-digit number to each specific product. Then the classification system aggregates products into 6, 4, and 2-digit broader product categories. For example, to obtain the product 10-digit number for tractors for agricultural use, you would go to:

Chapter 87	Vehicles, except railway or tramway, and parts, etc.
8701	Tractors (other than tractors of heading 8709)
870190	Tractors suitable for agricultural use
8701901030	Tractors (40 hp or more but less than 60 hp)

There are 8 tractor classifications according to horsepower or hp. With this 10-digit number, one can look at all the countries that the United States exports to, ranked in terms of value and volume of exports. The table obtained from the *World Bank Atlas* details Total Value of U.S. exports to the world ranked starting with largest country exported to. It also includes the percentage change in exports in the last two years shown. A sample of the table obtained from the *World Bank Atlas* is shown in Exhibit 2.2. With this data on hand and setting selection criteria, the exporter can single out one or two countries for further research.

- **Step 2: Target Market Assessment**
  The exporter now needs to collect specific data to evaluate the quality of the market he or she wants to export to. This requires information related to the issues that must be decided on to formulate a marketing strategy. The type of information needed is listed below.

Economic Environment and Sector Analysis. The target market assessment must start with an evaluation of trends in the economy and the particular sector under analysis. For example, GDP growth rate is particularly important as a country's imports income elastic. In other words, a growing economy and/or sector affects imports positively. Similarly, it is necessary to identify customer characteristics and develop estimates of market size (overall consumption of the product) to have a reasonable understanding of the market.

Foreign Government Import Trade Regulations. It is necessary to identify any trade restrictions, which may affect the importation of one's product into the target country. This includes any type of tariff and non-tariff barriers that may influence demand. Similarly, any domestic barriers such as export controls that affect the exportation of the product from the home market must be identified.

Marketing Infrastructure. Identification of factors affecting the marketing of a product is the key to a successful and viable marketing strategy. The exporter needs to know about the availability of channels of distribution, the distribution alternatives and types of channel intermediaries available in the foreign market, the communication infrastructure, the physical infrastructure, particularly ocean and air transportation, and carrier availability. An insight into business practices and cultural idiosyncrasies is a necessary and important complement of the marketing information as it provides a framework for formulating the marketing strategy.

Competitive Analysis. A target market assessment is incomplete without a thorough analysis of the competition and competitive offerings. The type of information that is generally required to evaluate competitors include:

- General information about firms offering similar products in the target market, their financial strength, sales in export markets and market share.
- Information about the competitor's marketing strategy, such as product line, prices, credit and service policies, and distribution strategy.
- Evaluation of competitors' products through actual product comparisons and visits to the target market and/or trade fairs where products are exhibited. An evaluation of the firms' sales materials such as catalogues and sales conditions are also merited.

After collecting and evaluating the data, the exporter is ready to prepare the export marketing strategy that is based on factual data. Experience will help the exporter fill in the gaps that may exist in the information collected. The output is a well-informed outline for a sound marketing strategy and can help the exporter tap the target market potential.

The Primary Research Process

Primary research addresses those questions to which secondary data cannot supply answers, such as product-specific or company-specific questions. Conducting primary research internationally can be complex due to different environments, attitudes, and market conditions. Yet, it is precisely because of these differences that such research is necessary. Nonetheless, at this time, marketing research is still mainly concentrated in the industrialized nations of the world. Global marketing research expenditures were estimated to be $15.9 billion in 2002. Of that amount, about three-quarters were spent in the United States and the European Union.

Primary research is essential for the formulation of international strategic marketing plans. One particular area of research interest is market segmentation. Historically, firms segmented international markets based on macro variables such as income per capita or consumer spending on certain product categories. Increasingly, however, firms recognize that psychographically based segmentation variables, such as lifestyles, attitudes, or personality, play a major role in identifying similar consumer groups in different countries, which can then be targeted across borders.

The exporter should turn to primary data only if some pressing research problem is still present after the secondary research process has been finalized. Primary data collection involves collecting data through communication and observation, and it involves some kind of contact with a respondent or respondents who answer questions, as well as some kind of interview or questionnaire administration. In all cases, it requires careful identification of respondents in order to get reliable and valid information. In the past, this type of research has been more expensive than secondary data collection; however, online research has been growing in popularity and has begun to be a reliable and less costly alternative.

Business-to-business (B-2-B) research tends to be easier and less expensive than consumer research. In B-2-B research, questions are addressed to a smaller, better defined group of respondents than possible participants in consumer research, where respondents are likely to be considerably less homogeneous. Consumer research often involves more sophisticated analytic and evaluation processes such as sampling and various kinds of statistical evaluation. Finding and then affording relevant samples of potential market segments can become very expensive. Thus, export-driven consumer research can be difficult to implement and use due to cost and other technical problems, such as questionnaire formulation, translation, implementation, etc.

Research Techniques

Face-to-face interviews and online questionnaires are generally regarded as the most effective B-2-B research techniques. Face-to-face interviews with customers, distributors, and government officials can be useful in obtaining information about import regulations, product preferences, and adaptation requirements. In particular, distributors can be an important source of customer preferences and distribution problems. A typical problem with B-2-B research is getting a sufficiently large sample of respondents. Online questionnaires can be especially helpful in expanding the reach of a survey and obtaining market information, product preferences, and changing demand patterns from a larger pool of respondents. Of course, the quality of responses is always directly related to the quality of the respondents in the pool.

Finally, for B-2-B research to be useful, the exporter must be able to ascertain the quality of the data collected in terms of the three factors that influence the quality of research:

- Validity or the extent to which the research measures what is intended to measure.
- Reliability, or the extent to which the research measures are free of error; that is, that the questions are understood to mean the same thing to all respondents.

- Representativeness, or the extent to which the respondent pool can answer the questions with knowledge and understanding of the problem.

Export Marketing Information System

Export marketing research projects represent only a part of an organization's ongoing market information needs. In most companies an information system is already in place to provide decision-makers with basic data for ongoing decisions. For example, an export marketer needs periodic updates on foreign government regulations and tariff restrictions. However, this is just part of a larger system that includes similar domestic information. Of course, such international information is more complex than it is for the domestic market, but the process is similar. This type of information can be stored in an information system to support daily management decisions. Defined as "an integrated system of data, statistical analysis, modeling, and display formats using computer hardware and software technology," such a system serves as a mechanism to coordinate the flow of information to export managers for decision-making purposes.

To be useful to a decision-maker, the information system needs various attributes:

1. Relevance: The data gathered must have meaning for the decision-making process.
2. Timeliness: It must be available when needed (usually *now*). It is of little benefit to the exporter if the decision information that is needed today does not become available until a month from now.
3. Flexibility: It must be available in the format needed by management. A great effort must be made to make international data comparable to each other.
4. Accuracy: This should go without saying. A system that provides incorrect information leads to poor decisions of no value.
5. Thoroughness: It must be reasonably comprehensive. Because of interrelationship between variables, factors that may influence a particular decision must be appropriately represented in the information system.
6. Convenient: The system must be easy to use and to access.

More international information systems are being developed successfully due to the progress of computer technology. Similarly, a significant amount of trade data is now available online. Companies can also use internal data, such as accounting and financial, and data from their subsidiaries and channels of distribution to complete the information base. In addition, many organizations put mechanisms into place to enrich the data flow. Such tools are environmental scanning, Delphi studies, and scenario building.

Environmental Scanning

Any changes in the business environment, whether domestic or foreign, may have serious repercussions on the export marketing activities of the firm. Managers need to track new developments and obtain continuous updates of the export environment. To carry out this task, some large corporations have formed environment scanning groups. These groups conduct a range of activities that enable them to continuously receive information on political, social, and economic affairs internationally and on changes in the attitudes of leaders of public institutions, particularly as they relate to the country's imports; and possibly upcoming changes in export markets. The complexity of the environmental scanning process may vary with the size of the firm and market coverage; however, in today's competitive environment, doing little to keep up with environmental changes can seriously hamper export activities.

There are several methods of environmental scanning One method focuses on collecting quantitative information. For example, the U.S. Census Bureau collects, evaluates, and adjusts a wide variety of demographic, social, and economic characteristics of foreign countries. Specific country analysis, sector analysis, and marketing reports are available to the export community through the *National Trade Data Bank – NTDB*. Similar factual information can be obtained from international organizations such as Euromonitor Publications, the World Bank, or the United Nations.

There is, of course, a trade-off between the breadth and depth of the information obtained, and the cost of obtaining it. The continuous evolution of data-processing capabilities has reduced the problems of breadth, depth, and timeliness as more and more governments and international organizations make data available online. Yet the cost of the better databases can affect the cost of acquiring data and can be a major impediment to the the development of environmental scanning systems.

Delphi Techniques

To complement the information obtained from factual data, managers resort to the use of qualitative data-gathering methods. Delphi studies are one such method. These studies can be particularly useful in export marketing because they provide input on the judgment and experience of experts or practitioners on the field. They seek to obtain answers from those who know instead of seeking average answers from persons with limited knowledge.

Typically, Delphi studies are carried out with groups of about thirty well-chosen participants who possess particular in-depth expertise in an area of concern. The participants are asked via e-mail or fax to identify the major issues under discussion. They are asked to rank their statements in order of importance and explain the rationale for the rank given. Next, the aggregate information is returned to the participants. They are asked to review the statements and are encouraged to agree or disagree with various rank orders and statements. After several rounds of this process, a reasonably coherent consensus can be developed.

The Delphi technique is very useful and feasible as it uses e-mail and facsimile as a form of communication to bridge large distances at a reasonable cost. One drawback of the technique is that it requires several steps and therefore, time before needed information is obtained. A small exporting firm may view this process as somewhat cumbersome. However, the Delphi information can provide crucial insights into factual data available for the marketing information system.

Scenario Building

Some companies use scenario analysis to look at different configurations of key variables in the international market. For example, economic growth rates, import penetration, trade growth, population growth, trade regulation, etc., can vary over time By projecting such variations for medium-to long-term periods, companies can envision completely new environmental conditions. These conditions are analyzed for their potential domestic and international impact on company strategy.

Of major importance in scenario building is the identification of crucial trend variables and the degree of variation. For scenarios to be useful, the exporter must analyze and respond to any observed variation by formulating contingency plans. Such planning will broaden horizons and prepare the manager for unexpected situations. It also may result in shorter response times to actual occurrences by honing response capabilities. The difficulty, of course, is to devise scenarios that are unusual enough to trigger new thinking yet sufficiently realistic to be taken seriously by management.

Summary

Constraints of time, resources, and expertise are the major inhibitors of international marketing research. Nevertheless, firms need to carry out planned and organized research in order to explore global market alternatives successfully. Such research needs to be closely linked to the decision-making process.

Export market research differs from domestic research in that the environment, which determines how well tools, techniques, and concepts apply, is different abroad. In addition, the manager needs to deal with new parameters, such as duties, exchange rates and international documentation, a greater number of interacting factors, and a much broader definition of the concept of competition.

Given the scarcity of resources, companies beginning their international effort often need to use data that have already been collected, that is, secondary data. Such data are available from governments, international organizations, directories, trade associations, or online databases.

To respond to specific information requirements firms frequently need primary research. The researcher needs to select an appropriate research technique to collect the information needed. Sensitivity to different international environments and cultures will guide the researcher in deciding whether to use interviews, focus groups, observation, surveys, or experimentation as data collection techniques. The same sensitivity applies to the design of the research instrument, where issues such as question format, content, and wording are decided. Also, the sampling plan needs to be appropriate for the local environment in order to ensure representative and useful responses.

Once the data have been collected, care must be taken to use analytical tools appropriate for the quality of data collected so that management is not misled about the sophistication of the research. Finally, the research results must be presented in a concise and useful form so that management can benefit in its decision-making, and implementation of the research needs to be tracked. To provide ongoing information to management, an international information support system is useful. Such a system will provide for the systematic and continuous gathering, analysis, and reporting of data for decision-making purposes. It uses a firm's internal information and gathers data via environmental scanning, Delphi studies, or scenario building, thus enabling management to prepare for the future and hone its decision-making skills.

Appendix A
Information Sources for Marketing Issues

European Union

EUROPA
The umbrella server for all institutions
http://www.europa.eu.int

CORDIS
Information on EU research programs
http://www.cordis.lu

Council of the European Union
Information and news from the Council with sections covering Common Foreign and Security Policy (CFSP) and Justice and Home Affairs
http://ue.eu.int

Court of Auditors
Information notes, annual reports, and other publications
http://www.eca.eu.int

Court of Justice
Overview, press releases, publications, and full-text proceedings of the court
http://europa.eu.int/cj/en/index.htm

Citizens Europe
Covers rights of citizens of EU member states
http://citizens.eu.int

Delegation of the European Commission to the United States
Press releases, EURECOM: Economic and Financial News, EU-U.S. relations, information on EU policies and Delegation programs
http://www.eurunion.org

Euro
The Single Currency
http://euro.eu.int

EUDOR (European Union Document Repository)
Bibliographic database
http://www.europa.eu.int/eur-lex

EUROPARL
Information on the European Parliament's activities
http://www.europarl.eu.int

European Agency for the Evaluation of Medicinal Products
Information on drug approval procedures and documents of the Committee for Proprietary Medicinal Products and the Committee for Veterinary Medicinal Products
http://www.emea.eu.int

European Bank for Reconstruction and Development
One Exchange Square
London EC2A 2EH
United Kingdom
http://www.ebrd.com

European Centre for the Development of Vocational Training
Information on the Centre and contact information
http://www.cedefop.gr

European Community Information Service
200 Rue de la Loi
1049 Brussels, Belgium
and
2100 M Street NW, 7th Floor
Washington, DC 20037

European Environment Agency
Information on the mission, products and services, and organizations and staff of the EEA
http://www.eea.eu.int

European Investment Bank
Press releases and information on borrowing and loan operations, staff, and publications
http://www.eib.org

European Monetary Institute
Name: European Central Bank
http://www.ecb.int

EuroStat
http://europa.eu.int/comm/eurostat

European Training Foundation
Information on vocational education and training programs in Central and Eastern Europe and Central Asia
http://www.etf.eu.int

European Union
200 Rue de la Loi
1049 Brussels, Belgium
and 2100 M Street NW 7th Floor
Washington, DC 20037
http://www.eurunion.org

Office for Harmonization in the Internal Market
Guidelines, application forms, and other information to registering an EU trademark
http://www.oami.eu.int/en/default.htm

United Nations

http://www.un.org

Conference of Trade and Development
Palais des Nations
1211 Geneva 10
Switzerland
http://unctad.org

Department of Economic and Social
    Development
1 United Nations Plaza
New York, NY 10017
http://www.un.org/ecosocdev/

Industrial Development Organization
1660 L Street NW
Washington, DC 20036
and
Post Office Box 300
Vienna International Center
A-1400 Vienna, Austria
http://www.unido.org

International Trade Centre
UNCTAD/WTO
54–56 Rue de Mountbrillant
CH-1202 Geneva
Switzerland
http://www.intracen.org

United Nations Educational, Scientific and
    Cultural Organization
2 United Nations Plaza, Suite 900
New York, NY 10017
http://www.unesco.org

UN Publications
Room 1194
1 United Nations Plaza
New York, NY 10017
http://www.un.org/pubs/sales.htm

U.S. Government

Agency for International Development
Office of Business Relations
Washington, DC 20523
http://www.usaid.gov

Customs Service
1301 Constitution Avenue NW
Washington, DC 20229
http://www.customs.ustreas.gov

Department of Agriculture
12th Street and Jefferson Drive SW
Washington, DC 20250
http://www.usda.gov

Department of Commerce
Herbert C. Hoover Building
14th Street and Constitution Avenue NW
Washington, DC 20230
http://www.commerce.gov

Department of State
2201 C Street NW
Washington, DC 20520
http://www.state.gov

Department of the Treasury
15th Street and Pennsylvania Avenue NW
Washington, DC 20220
http://www.ustreas.gov

Federal Trade Commission
6th Street and Pennsylvania Avenue NW
Washington, DC 20580
http://www.ftc.gov

FedStats
http://www.fedstats.gov

Global Trends 2015
http://www.cia.gov/cia/
    publications/globaltrends2015

International Trade Commission
500 E Street NW
Washington, DC 20436
http://www.usitc.gov

Small Business Administration
409 Third Street SW
Washington, DC 20416
http://www.sbaonline.sba.gov

U.S. Census Bureau
http://www.census.gov

U.S. House of Representatives Law Library
http://lectlaw.com/in11/1.htm

U.S. Trade and Development Agency
1621 North Kent Street
Rosslyn, VA 22209
http://www.tda.gov

World Fact Book
http://www.odci.gov/cia/
   publications/factbook/index.html

World Trade Centers Association
60 East 42nd Street
Suite 1901
New York, NY 10165
http://www.wtca.org

Council of Economic Advisers—
http://www.whitehouse.gov/cea

Department of Defense—
http://www.dod.gov

Department of Energy—
http://www.energy.gov

Department of Interior—
http://www.doi.gov

Department of Labor—
http://www.dol.gov

Department of Transportation—
http://www.dot.gov

Environmental Protection Agency—
http://www.epa.gov

National Trade Data Bank—
http://www.stat.usa.gov

National Economic Council—
http://www.whitehouse.gov/nec

Office of Management and Budget—
http://www.whitehouse.gov/omb

Office of the U.S. Trade Representative—
http://www.ustr.gov

Overseas Private Investment Corporation—
http://www.opic.gov

Selected Organizations

Academy for Educational Development
1401 New York Avenue NW
Suite 1100
Washington, DC 20005
http://www.aed.org

American Bankers Association
1120 Connecticut Avenue NW
Washington, DC 20036
http://www.aba.com

American Bar Association
Section of International Law and Practice
750 N. Lake Shore Drive
Chicago, IL 60611
and
1800 M Street NW
Washington, DC 20036
http://www.abanet.org/intlaw/
   home.html

American Management Association
440 First Street NW
Washington, DC 20001
http://www.amanet.org

American Marketing Association
311 S. Wacker Drive, Suite 5800
Chicago, IL 60606
http://www.marketingpower.com

American Petroleum Institute
1220 L Street NW
Washington, DC 20005
http://www.api.org

Asia-Pacific Economic Cooperation Secretariat
438 Alexandra Road
#41–00, Alexandra Road
Singapore 119958
http://www.apecsec.org.sg

Asian Development Bank
2330 Roxas Boulevard
Pasay City, Philippines
http://www.adb.org

Association of South East Asian Nations (ASEAN)
Publication Office
c/o The ASEAN Secretariat
70A, Jalan Sisingamangaraja
Jakarta 11210
Indonesia
http://www.asean.or.id

Better Business Bureau
http://www.bbb.org

Canadian Market Data
http://www.strategis.ic.gc.ca

Chamber of Commerce of the United States
1615 H Street NW
Washington, DC 20062
http://www.uschamber.org

Commission of the European Communities to the United States
2100 M Street NW
Suite 707
Washington, DC 20037
http://www.eurunion.org

Conference Board
845 Third Avenue
New York, NY 10022
and
1755 Massachusetts Avenue
NW Suite 312
Washington, DC 20036
http://www.conference-board.org

Deutsche Bundesbank
Wilhelm-Epstein-Str. 14
P.O.B. 10 06 02
D-60006 Frankfurt am Main
http://www.bundesbank.de

Electronic Industries Alliance
2001 Pennsylvania Avenue NW
Washington, DC 20004
http://www.eia.org

Export-Import Bank of the United States
811 Vermont Avenue NW
Washington, DC 20571
http://www.exim.gov

Federal Reserve Bank of New York
33 Liberty Street
New York, NY 10045
http://www.ny.frb.org

Gallup Organization
http://www.gallup.com

Greenpeace
http://www.greenpeace.org

Iconoculture
http://iconoculture.com

Inter-American Development Bank
1300 New York Avenue NW
Washington, DC 20577
http://www.iadb.org

International Bank for Reconstruction and Development (World Bank)
1818 H Street NW
Washington, DC 20433
http://www.worldbank.org

International Monetary Fund
700 19th Street NW
Washington, DC 20431
http://www.imf.org

International Telecommunication Union
Place des Nations
Ch-1211 Geneva 20
Switzerland
http://www.itu.int

IRSS (Institute for Research in Social Science)
http://www.irss.unc.edu/data_archive/home.asp

LANIC (Latin American Network Information Center)
http://www.lanic.utexas.edu

Marketing Research Society
111 E. Wacker Drive, Suite 600
Chicago, IL 60601

Michigan State University Global EDGE
http://globaledge.msu.edu/ibrd/ibrd.asp

National Association of Manufacturers
1331 Pennsylvania Avenue
Suite 1500
Washington, DC 20004
http://www.nam.org

National Federation of Independent
  Business
600 Maryland Avenue SW
Suite 700
Washington, DC 20024
http://www.nfib.org

Organization for Economic Cooperation
  and Development (OECD)
2 rue Andre Pascal
75775 Paris Cedex Ko, France
and
2001 L Street NW, Suite 700
Washington, DC 20036
http://www.oecd.org

Organization of American States
17th and Constitution Avenue NW
Washington, DC 20006
http://www.oas.org

The Roper Center for Public Opinion
  Research
http://www.ropercenter.uconn.edu

Roper Starch Worldwide
http://www.roper.com

Transparency International
Otto-Suhr-Allee 97–99
D-10585 Berlin
Germany
http://www.transparency.org

Indexes to Literature

Business Periodical Index
H.W. Wilson Co.
950 University Avenue
Bronx, NY 10452

New York Times Index
University Microfilms International
300 N. Zeeb Road
Ann Arbor, MI 48106
http://www.nytimes.com

Public Affairs Information Service Bulletin
11 W. 40th Street
New York, NY 10018

Wall Street Journal Index
University Microfilms International
300 N. Zeeb Road
Ann Arbor, MI 48106
http://www.wsj.com

Directories

American Register of Exporters and
  Importers
38 Park Row
New York, NY 10038

Arabian Year Book
Dar Al-Seuassam Est. Box 42480
Shuwahk, Kuwait

Directories of American Firms Operating
  in Foreign Countries
World Trade Academy Press
Uniworld Business Publications Inc.
50 E. 42nd Street
New York, NY 10017

The Directory of International Sources of
  Business Information
Pitman
128 Long Acre
London WC2E 9AN, England

Encyclopedia of Associations
Gale Research Co.
Book Tower
Detroit, MI 48226

Polk's World Bank Directory
R.C. Polk & Co.
2001 Elm Hill Pike
P.O. Box 1340
Nashville, TN 37202

Verified Directory of Manufacturers'
   Representatives
MacRae's Blue Book Inc.
817 Broadway
New York, NY 10003

World Guide to Trade Associations
K.G. Saur & Co.
175 Fifth Avenue
New York, NY 10010

Encyclopedias, Handbooks, and Miscellaneous

A Basic Guide to Exporting
U.S. Government Printing Office
Superintendent of Documents
Washington, DC 20402

Doing Business In . . . Series
Pricewaterhouse Coopers
1251 Avenue of the Americas
New York, NY 10020

Economic Survey of Europe
United Nations Publishing Division
1 United Nations Plaza
Room DC2–0853
New York, NY 10017

Economic Survey of Latin America
United Nations Publishing Division
1 United Nations Plaza
Room DC2–0853
New York, NY 10017

Encyclopedia Americana, International
   Edition
Grolier Inc.
Danbury, CT 06816

Encyclopedia of Business Information
   Sources
Gale Research Co.
Book Tower
Detroit, MI 48226

Europa Year Book
Europa Publications Ltd.
18 Bedford Square
London WCIB 3JN, England

Export Administration Regulations
U.S. Government Printing Office
Superintendent of Documents
Washington, DC 20402

Exporters' Encyclopedia—World
   Marketing Guide
Dun's Marketing Services
49 Old Bloomfield Rd.
Mountain Lake, NJ 07046

Export-Import Bank of the United States
   Annual Report
U.S. Government Printing Office
Superintendent of Documents
Washington, DC 20402

Exporting for the Small Business
U.S. Government Printing Office
Superintendent of Documents
Washington, DC 20402

Exporting to the United States
U.S. Government Printing Office
Superintendent of Documents
Washington, DC 20402

Export Shipping Manual
U.S. Government Printing Office
Superintendent of Documents
Washington, DC 20402

Foreign Business Practices: Materials on
   Practical Aspects of Exporting,
   International Licensing, and Investing
U.S. Government Printing Office
Superintendent of Documents
Washington, DC 20402

A Guide to Financing Exports
U.S. Government Printing Office
Superintendent of Documents
Washington, DC 20402

Handbook of Marketing Research
McGraw-Hill Book Co.
1221 Avenue of the Americas
New York, NY 10020

Periodic Reports, Newspapers, Magazines

Advertising Age
Crain Communications Inc.
740 N. Rush Street
Chicago, IL 60611
http://www.adage.com

Advertising World
Directories International Inc.
150 Fifth Avenue, Suite 610
New York, NY 10011

American Demographics
http://www.americandemo
   graphics.com

Arab Report and Record
84 Chancery Lane
London WC2A 1DL, England

Asian Demographics
http://www.asiandemographics.com

Barron's
University Microfilms International
300 N. Zeeb Road
Ann Arbor, MI 48106
http://www.barrons.com

Business America
U.S. Department of Commerce
14th Street and Constitution Avenue NW
Washington, DC 20230
http://www.doc.gov

Business International
Business International Corp.
One Dag Hammarskjold Plaza
New York, NY 10017

Business Week
McGraw-Hill Publications Co.
1221 Avenue of the Americas
New York, NY 10020
http://www.businessweek.com

Commodity Trade Statistics
United Nations Publications
1 United Nations Plaza
Room DC2–0853
New York, NY 10017

Conference Board Record
Conference Board Inc.
845 Third Avenue
New York, NY 10022

Customs Bulletin
U.S. Customs Service
1301 Constitution Avenue NW
Washington, DC 20229

The Dismal Scientist
http://www.economy.com/dismal

Dun's Business Month
Goldhirsh Group
38 Commercial Wharf
Boston, MA 02109

The Economist
Economist Newspaper Ltd.
25 St. James Street
London SWIA 1HG, England
http://www.economist.com

Europe Magazine
2100 M Street NW Suite 707
Washington, DC 20037

The Financial Times
Bracken House
10 Cannon Street
London EC4P 4BY, England
http://www.ft.com

Forbes
Forbes, Inc.
60 Fifth Avenue
New York, NY 10011
http://www.forbes.com

Fortune
Time, Inc.
Time & Life Building
1271 Avenue of the Americas
New York, NY 10020
http://www.fortune.com

Global Trade
North American Publishing Co.
401 N. Broad Street
Philadelphia, PA 19108

Industrial Marketing
Crain Communications, Inc.
740 N. Rush Street
Chicago, IL 60611

International Encyclopedia of the Social Sciences
Macmillan and the Free Press
866 Third Avenue
New York, NY 10022

International Financial Statistics
International Monetary Fund
Publications Unit
700 19th Street NW
Washington, DC 20431
http://www.imf.org

Investor's Daily
Box 25970
Los Angeles, CA 90025

Journal of Commerce
100 Wall Street
New York, NY 10005
http://www.joc.com

Lexis-Nexis Legal Express Info Service
http://www.michie.com

Sales and Marketing Management
Bill Communications Inc.
633 Third Avenue
New York, NY 10017

Tomorrow
Global Environment Business
http://www.tomorrow-Web.com

Wall Street Journal
Dow Jones & Company
200 Liberty Street
New York, NY 10281
http://www.wsj.com

World Agriculture Situation
U.S. Department of Agriculture
Economics Management Staff
http://www.econ.ag.gov

Pergamon Press Inc.
Journals Division
Maxwell House
Fairview Park
Elmsford, NY 10523

Trade Finance
U.S. Department of Commerce
International Trade Administration
Washington, DC 20230
http://www.doc.gov

World Trade Center Association (WTCA) Directory
60 East 42nd Street
Suite 1901
New York, NY 10048
http://www.wtca.com

Media Guide International: Business/ Professional Publications
Directories International Inc.
150 Fifth Avenue, Suite 610
New York, NY 10011

World Wide Web Virtual Law Library
http://www.law.indiana.edu/v-lib

Selected Trade Databases

News agencies
Comline-Japan Newswire
Database Omninews
Dow Jones News
Lexis-Nexis
Nikkei Shimbun News
Reuters Monitor
UPI

Trade Publication References with Bibliographic Keywords
Agris
Biocommerce Abstracts & Directory
Findex
Frost (short) Sullivan Market Research Reports
Marketing Surveys Index
McCarthy Press Cuttings Service
Paperchem
PTS F & S Indexes
Trade and Industry Index

Trade Publication References with Summaries
ABI/Inform
Arab Information Bank
Asia-Pacific
BFAI
Biobusiness
CAB Abstracts
Chemical Business Newsbase
Chemical Industry Notes
Caffeeline
Delphes
InfoSouth Latin American Information System
Management Contents
NTIS Bibliographic Data Base
Paperchem
PIRA Abstract
PSTA
PTS Marketing & Advertising Reference Service
PTS PromtRapra Abstracts
Textline
Trade & Industry ASAP
World Textiles

Full Text of Trade Publications
Datamonitor Market Reports
Dow Jones News
Euromonitor Market Direction
Federal News Service
Financial Times Business Report File
Financial Times Fulltext
Globefish
ICC Key Notes Market Research
Investext
McCarthy Press Cuttings Service
PTS Promt
Textline
Trade & Industry ASAP

Statistics
Agrostat (diskette only)
Arab Information Bank
ARI Network/CNS
Comext/Eurostat
Comtrade
FAKT-German Statistics
Globefish
IMF Data
OECD Data
Piers Imports
PTS Forecasts
PTS Time Series
Reuters Monitor
Trade Statistics
Tradstat World Trade Statistics
TRAINS (CD-ROM being developed)
U.S. I/E Maritime Bills of Lading
U.S. Imports for Consumption
World Bank Statistics

Price Information
ARI Network/CNS
Chemical Business Newsbase
COLEACP
Commodity Options
Commodities 2000
Market News Service of ITC
Nikkei Shimbun News Database
Reuters Monitor
UPI
U.S. Wholesale Prices

Company Registers
ABC Europe Production Europe
Biocommerce Abstracts & Directory
CD-Export (CD-ROM only)
Company Intelligence
D&B Duns Market Identifiers
 (U.S.A.)
D&B European Marketing File
D&B Eastern Europe
Dun's Electronic Business Directory
Firmexport/Firmimport
Hoppenstedt Austria
Hoppenstedt Benelux
Hoppenstedt Germany
Huco-Hungarian Companies
ICC Directory of Companies
Kompass Asia/Pacific
Kompass Europe (EKOD)
Mexican Exporters/Importers
Piers Imports
Polu-Polish Companies
SDOE
Thomas Register
TRAINS (CD-ROM being developed)
UK Importers
UK Importers (DECTA)
U.S. Directory of Importers
U.S. I/E Maritime Bills of Lading
World Trade Center Network

Trade Opportunities, Tenders
Business
Federal News Service
Huntech-Hungarian Technique
Scan-a-Bid
Tenders Electronic Daily
World Trade Center Network

Tariffs and Trade Regulations
Celex
ECLAS
Justis Eastern Europe (CD-ROM only)
Scad
Spearhead
Spicer's Centre for Europe
TRAINS (CD-ROM being developed)
U.S. Code of Federal Regulations
U.S. Federal Register
U.S. Harmonized Tariff Schedule

Standards
BSI Standardline
Noriane/Perinorm
NTIS Bibliographic Data Base
Standards Infodisk ILI (CD-ROM only)

Shipping Information
Piers Imports
Tradstat World Trade Statistics
U.S. I/E Maritime Bills of Lading

Others
Fairbase
Ibiscus

Appendix B

The Structure of a Country Commercial Guide

The U.S. Commercial Service

The following is an example of governmental research made available to firms. Country commercial guides provide a condensed and business-focused overview of business customs, conditions, contacts, and opportunities. Using such guides can be of major help in getting started in unfamiliar territory.

Guide for Austria

Table of Contents
Chapter 1 Executive Summary
Chapter 2 Economic Trends and Outlook
    A. Major Trends and Outlook
    B. Government Role in the Economy
    C. Balance of Payments Situation
    D. Infrastructure Situation
Chapter 3 Political Environment
    A. Nature of Political Relationship with the United States
    B. Major Political Issues Affecting the Business Climate
    C. The Civil Society
    D. Synopsis of the Political System.
Chapter 4 Marketing U.S. Products and Services
    A. Distribution and Sales Channels
    B. Product Pricing Structures
    C. Retail Trends
    D. Use of Agents/Distributors; Finding a Partner
    E. Franchising
    F. Joint Ventures and Licensing
    G. Steps to Establishing an Office
    H. Selling Factors and Techniques
    I. Advertising and Trade Promotion
    J. Pricing Products
    K. Sales Services and Customer Support
    L. Selling to the Government
    M. Protecting Your Product from IPR Infringement
    N. Need for a Local Attorney

Chapter 5   Leading Sectors for U.S. Exports
  A. Best Prospects for Non-Agricultural Products
  B. Best Prospects for Agricultural Products

Chapter 6   Trade Regulations, Customs, and Standards
  A. Customs Regulations and Tariff Rates
  B. Non-Tariff Trade Barriers
  C. Import Taxes Including Value Added Taxes
  D. Import License Requirements
  E. Temporary Goods Entry Requirements
  F. Special Import/Export Requirements
  G. Labeling Requirements
  H. Prohibited Imports
  I. Warranty and Non-Warranty Repairs
  J. Export Controls
  K. Standards
  L. Free Trade Zones/Warehouses
  M. Membership in Free Trade Agreements
  N. Customs Contact Information

Chapter 7   Investment Climate
  A. Openness to Foreign Investment
  B. Conversion and Transfer Policies
  C. Expropriation and Compensation
  D. Dispute Settlement
  E. Performance Requirements/Incentives
  F. Right to Private Ownership and Establishment
  G. Protection of Property Rights
  H. Transparency of the Regulatory System
  I. Efficient Capital Markets and Portfolio Investment
  J. Political Violence
  K. Corruption
  L. Bilateral Investment Agreements
  M. OPIC and Other Investment Insurance Programs
  N. Labor
  O. Foreign Trade Zones/Free Ports
  P. List of Major Foreign Investors

Chapter 8   Trade and Project Financing
  A. Synopsis of Banking System
  B. Foreign Exchange Controls Affecting Trading
  C. General Financing Ability
  D. How to Finance Exports/Methods of Payment
  E. Types of Available Export Financing and Insurance
  F. Project Financing Available
  G. List of Banks with Correspondent U.S. Banking Arrangements

Chapter 9   Business Travel
- A. Business Customs
- B. Travel Advisory and Visas
- C. Holidays
- D. Business Infrastructure

Chapter 10   Economic and Trade Statistics
- **Appendix A.** Country Data
- **Appendix B.** Domestic Economy
- **Appendix C.** Trade
- **Appendix D.** Foreign Direct Investment

Chapter 11   U.S. & Austrian Contacts
- A. Austrian Government Agencies
- B. Austrian Trade Associations/Chambers of Commerce
- C. Austrian Market Research Firms
- D. Austrian Commercial Banks
- E. U.S. Commercial Service
- F. U.S.–Based Multipliers
- G. Washington-Based U.S. Government Contacts

Chapter 12   Market Research
- A. Foreign Agriculture Service Commodity Reports/Market Briefs
- B. Department of Commerce Industry Subsector Analyses

Chapter 13   Trade Event Schedule
- A. Scheduled Agricultural/Food Trade Events
- B. Scheduled Trade Events—U.S. Commercial Service Vienna

CHAPTER 3

Export Modes

Exporting is the great learning experience of international operations. In its different formats, it is the most common way of conducting business across borders. Originators' involvement can range from minimal to extensive, conducted jointly with partners to completely independently, and involve products, services, or intellectual property. This chapter will focus on the different modes of exports, including licensing.

Exports

The major approaches to exports are usually distinguished by the number, location, and nature of intermediaries between the originator and the customer as well as the level of involvement the originator has in the process. Exhibit 3.1 provides a summary of these modes.

The level of involvement refers to the degree to which the exporter knows that its products are being exported and its interest in the process. For example, goods can be bought by a domestic firm that in turn sells it abroad. Active exporting means that the originator is integrally involved in the planning for and execution of the exports.

EXHIBIT 3.1. Export Modes

		LEVEL OF INVOLVEMENT	
		PASSIVE	ACTIVE
CONTACT WITH TARGET MARKET	INDIRECT	"Exporting in your own backyard"	EMCs, ETCs
	DIRECT	Sales through the Web without knowledge of originator	Importers Sales office

EXHIBIT 3.2. Types of Export Operations

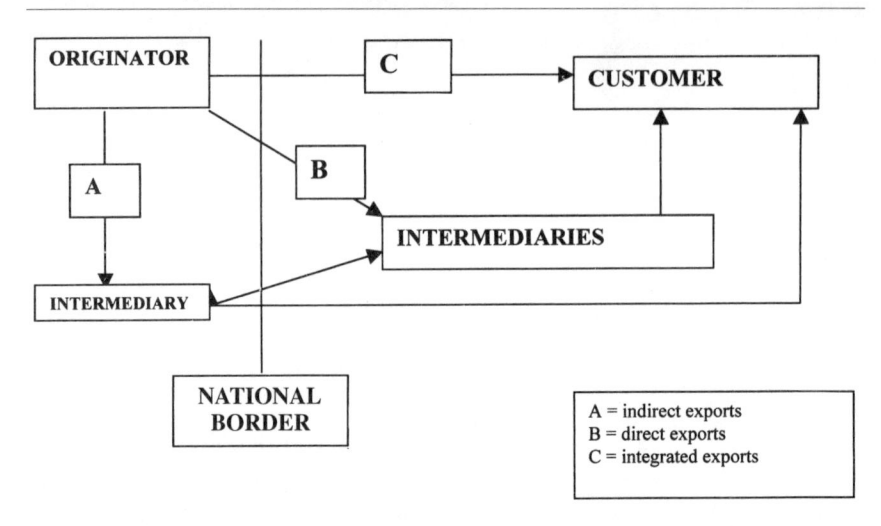

```
ORIGINATOR ────────┬──── C ────────────► CUSTOMER
    │              │                         ▲   ▲
    │   ┌───┐      │                         │   │
    │   │ A │   ┌─────┐                      │   │
    │   └───┘   │  B  │                      │   │
    │           └─────┘                      │   │
    │              │                         │   │
    ▼              ▼                         │   │
┌────────────┐   ┌─────────────────────┐     │   │
│INTERMEDIARY│──►│   INTERMEDIARIES    │─────┘   │
└────────────┘   └─────────────────────┘─────────┘
    │
    │       ┌──────────┐
    │       │ NATIONAL │     A = indirect exports
    │       │  BORDER  │     B = direct exports
    │       └──────────┘     C = integrated exports
```

The contact with the target market can take place in multiple ways as shown in Exhibit 3.2. Indirect exports (A) occur through a domestically based entity that acts either on its own behalf or on the behalf of the originator. In direct exports (B), the originator has a contact with the targeted market, typically through an importer. In integrated exports (C), the originator deals with the customer without intermediaries either from its home base or through its own sales office in the customer's market.

With passive indirect exports, or when exporting at home, the originator may be selling to large domestic companies (such as Boeing, which has hundreds of domestic suppliers) or trading companies purchasing for their own foreign affiliates or for projects awarded to them, export merchants buying for their own account, other exporters interested in rounding out their product lines, or government financed transactions (including aid) that require local goods. While indirect exports may be a result of unwitting participation, some firms may also choose this method of market entry as a strategic alternative that conserves effort and resources while still taking advantage of the demand abroad. Many companies may turn into active exporters once they realize the profit opportunity they miss (i.e., the so-called demonstration effect).

With more companies engaging in e-business operations, it is possible that sales are made abroad to customers without the knowledge or interest of the e-commerce site owner (i.e., passive direct exports). Naturally, there is a tremendous loss of opportunity in not knowing who or where potential customers are. Many companies outsource their services to facilitators such as air express carriers and may thus be oblivious as to their customer base. In addition to lost opportunities due to lack of interest, some originators may have to worry about legal repercussions. A U.S. computer maker, for example, was fined $50,000 by the U.S. Department of Commerce for having (unknowingly) shipped its products to Iran, a country on the sanctions list due to its sponsorship of terrorism.

In typical active indirect exports, a domestic intermediary specializing in foreign markets, an agent (such as an export management company) or an export corporation established under specific legislation for exports (such as an export trading company) will take over the originator's export function. The tasks that EMCs and ETCs perform are discussed in Chapter 4. They provide their market- and firm-specific assets to the use of the originator in exchange for a fee. In some cases, the originator may well be a part of an export trading company joining other similar companies and other export facilitators in the export effort to minimize individual risk of market development.

Indirect exports are a cost-effective method to be used in the early stages of the internationalization process. However, this mode may not lead to the level of necessary learning for the originator to take more control at a later stage. Intermediaries, especially domestic ones, may try to keep the originator dependent on them by keeping vital information close to heart and final customers loyal to their services rather than to the products of the originator.

Active direct exports occur when the originator has contact with entities in the targeted market. These entities include import agents or importers (whether wholesalers or retailers), buying organizations for independent retailers, or foreign trading companies (either privately or publicly owned). The level of involvement by the originator is substantial in taking care of the marketing and sales tasks as well as in participating in the exporting routines. In controlling these dimensions of exporting, the originator accumulates experience and expertise. In choosing to use direct exports, it is assumed that the company has the necessary readiness both organizationally and in terms of product to do so. Sufficient investment has to be made in capabilities to control intermediaries abroad and in the firm's abilities to support them, and, therefore, do a better job for the originator.

At some stage of the firm's internationalization process, the decision may be made to deal directly with customers. The result is integrated exports, where the originator may establish a sales office in the target market. The investment could be the opening, for example, of a German or EU sales office. Although this type of move indicates a long-term commitment to a market, it is far riskier than indirect or direct exports because the firm is making a major financial investment. If the exporter moves from an agency agreement with an importer to a sales office, its costs for that market are now fixed costs (i.e., will be incurred even if no sales are made) instead of previous variable costs. The firm has to be careful in the transition stage from using an intermediary to a sales office in that customers may show more loyalty to a discarded intermediary than to the firm's products, thereby resulting in sales losses. This is at least partly why one of the most popular methods of establishing a sales office is to acquire an existing intermediary to form the base of a firm-owned entity. Setting up and operating even a modest sales office may be expensive. The cost of an office manager and a secretary can easily reach the equivalent of $100,000, while a full-scale sales office will cost $500,000 on an annual basis. Real estate costs are a major ingredient the closer the office is to a major business district.

The E-Dimension in Exports

E-commerce, the ability to offer goods and services over the Web (both B2C and B2B) is expected to reach a compound growth rate of 100 percent in the next few years around the world. Marketing through the Internet can help exporters obtain ongoing information about their target market, thus enhancing responsiveness and competitiveness, allowing them to explore more markets and increase their global reach. E-exporting can provide a bridge for time differences in international markets in being available 24 hours a day.

In a B2B setting, use of the Internet can be extremely helpful to contact small and medium-sized importers such as manufacturers, retailers, and wholesalers. In addition, large national chains can be more effectively reached with online marketing. Direct export channels can help the exporter build relationships with their market, as well as sell, promote, and distribute their product offering more efficiently.

Personal selling can be used more efficiently to perform the sales contact, supported by other traditional direct marketing tools, such as post-sales services, technical support, and follow-up in order to build a strong relationship with the customer.

Internet marketing is now feasible for the B2C markets as computer use continues to grow among individual users. The strategy to reach consumer markets traditionally has been conducted through indirect marketing, relying on contact with the foreign distributor for the implementation of the export marketing activities and to reach the largest number of consumers. This direct marketing strategy may include, for example, such tools as e-mail, e-retailing, and telemarketing. This allows the exporter, through computer-based contacts, to present, promote, and sell products in foreign markets as well as improve availability by tailoring product assortment to the particular foreign market and facilitate transactional services in the target market.

The challenges faced in terms of response and delivery capabilities can be overcome by outsourcing services or by building international distribution networks. Air express carriers such as DHL, FedEx, and UPS offer full-service packages that leverage their own Internet infrastructure with customs clearance and e-mail shipment notification. If a company needs help in order fulfillment and customer support (including the handling of returns), logistics centers offer warehousing and inventory management services as well as same-day delivery from in-country stocks. DHL, for example, has seven express logistics centers and 45 strategic parts centers worldwide, with key centers in Bahrain for the Middle East, Brussels for Europe, and Singapore for Asia-Pacific. Some companies elect to build their own international distribution networks. Both QVC, a televised shopping service, and amazon.com, an online retailer of books and consumer goods, have distribution centers in Britain and Germany to take advantage of the European Internet audience and to fulfill more quickly and cheaply the orders generated by their Web sites.

Although English has long been perceived as the lingua franca of the Web, the share of non-English speakers worldwide has increased to 65 percent. It has also been shown that Web users are three times more likely to buy when the offer is made in their own language. However, not even the largest of firms can serve all markets with a full line of their products. Getting a Web site translated and running is an expensive proposition and, if done correctly, time-consuming as well. If the site is well developed, it will naturally lead to expectations that order fulfillment will be of equal caliber. Therefore, any worldwide Web strategy has to be tied closely with the company's overall growth strategy in world markets.

A number of hurdles and uncertainties are keeping some companies out of global markets or preventing them from exploiting these markets to their full potential. Some argue that the World Wide Web does not live up to its name, since it is mostly a tool for the United States and Europe. Yet, as Internet penetration levels increase in the near future, due to technological advances, improvements in many countries' Web infrastructures, and customer acceptance, e-business will become truly global.

The exporter has to be sensitive to the governmental role in e-commerce. No real consensus exists on the taxation of e-commerce, especially in the case of cross-border transactions. While the United States and the EU have agreed not to impose new taxes on sales through the Internet, there is no uniformity in the inter-national taxation of transactions. Other governments believe, however, that they have something to gain by levying new e-taxes. Until more firm legal precedents are established, international exporters should be aware of their potential tax liabilities and prepare for them, especially if they are considering substantial e-commerce investments. One likely scenario is an e-commerce tax system that closely resembles sales taxes at physical retail outlets. Vendors will be made responsible for collecting sales taxes and forwarding them to the governments concerned, most likely digitally. Another proposal involves the bit-tax, a variation of the Internet access tax.

Government will also come to terms with issues related to pricing and access to the Internet. The private sector argues for the highest possible ability to safeguard its databases, to protect cross-border transmission of confidential information, and to conduct secure financial transactions using global networks. This requires an unrestricted market for encryption products that operate globally. However, some governments, especially the United States, fear that encryption will enable criminals and terrorist organizations to avoid detection and tracking. Therefore, a strong argument is made in favor of limiting the extent of encryption.

Licensing

Licensing constitutes the export of intangibles, typically intellectual property.

Under a licensing agreement, one firm, the licensor, permits another to use its intellectual property in exchange for compensation in the form of a royalty. The recipient firm is the licensee. The property might include patents, trademark, copyrights, technology, technical know-how, or specific marketing skills. For example, a firm that has developed new packaging for liquids can permit other firms abroad to use the same process. Licensing therefore amounts to exporting and importing tangibles and intangibles. Licensing can be an excellent way to expand one's markets.

Assessment of Licensing

Licensing has intuitive appeal to many potential exporters. As an entry strategy, it may require neither capital investment, nor knowledge, nor marketing strength in foreign markets. A licensing agreement may include the use of intellectual property as well as purchase of intermediate goods. The license may bring not only royalty income but also profits from the import of materials and components needed to develop the product or concept in the foreign market. It provides an opportunity to obtain additional return on research and development investments already incurred. After initial costs, the licensor can reap benefits from royalties and the sale of goods until the end of the license.

Licensing reduces the risk of exposure to government intervention in that the licensee is typically a local company that can provide leverage against government action. Licensing will help to avoid host-country regulations that are focused in equity ventures. Similarly, import tariffs can be reduced and, in instances, eliminated when licensing involves the production of goods and services for the local economy. Licensing may also serve as a stage in the internationalization of the firm by providing a means by which foreign markets can be tested without major involvement of capital or management time. Similarly, licensing can be used as a strategy to preempt a market before the entry of competition, especially if the licensor's resources permit full-scale involvement only in selected markets.

A final reason for the growth in licensing is the gradual implementation of intellectual property rights protection. In many countries pirated technology, processes, and products are still abundant. Progress by the World Trade Organization (WTO), however, has improved the protection of intellectual property and the enforcement of such protection by governments. With greater protection of their proprietary knowledge, companies are more willing to transfer such knowledge internationally. In instances of high levels of piracy, a licensing agreement with a strong foreign partner may also add value because now the partner becomes a local force with a distinct interest in rooting out unlicensed activities.

Licensing also offers a foreign entry opportunity for immediate market entry with a proven concept. The risk of R&D failures is reduced, as is the cost of designing around the licensor's patents, or the fear of patent infringement litigation. Furthermore, most licensing agreements provide for ongoing cooperation and support, thus enabling a licensee to benefit from new developments.

In addition, licensing may enable an exporter to enter a foreign market that is closed to either imports or direct foreign investment. Licensing arrangements may also enable the licensor to negotiate parallel contracts that are not related directly to the agreement but provide foreign purchases of materials and components of unrelated activities. The licensor can thereby expand participation in the particular market as an exporter.

Licensing is not without disadvantages. It has come under criticism from supranational organizations such as the United Nations Conference of Trade and Development (UNCTAD). It has been alleged that licensing provides a mechanism by which older technology is capitalized on by industrialized-country multinational corporations (MNCs). Licensees may often want labor-intensive techniques or machinery, however. For example, in order to produce Guinness Stout in Nigeria, Guinness Brewery imported licensed equipment that had been used in Ireland in the early 1900s. Even though this equipment was obsolete by Western standards, it had additional economic life in Nigeria due to lack of competition.

Licensing often leaves the foreign marketing functions to the licensee. As a result, the licensor may not gain sufficient exporting expertise to ready itself for subsequent global market penetration. Moreover, the initial toehold in the foreign market may not be a foot in the door. Depending on the licensing arrangement, quite the opposite may take place. In exchange for a royalty, the licensor may create its own competitor not only in the markets for which the agreement was made, but also in third markets. As a result, many companies are hesitant to enter into many licensing agreements. For example, Japanese firms are delighted to sell goods to China but are unwilling to license the Chinese to produce the goods themselves. They fear that because of the low wage structure in China, such licenses could create a powerful future competitor in markets presently held by Japan.

Licensing agreements typically have limits. Although terms may be extended one time after the startup period, additional extensions are not readily permitted by a number of foreign governments. If the licensing ties in with the licensor's global marketing network, quality control in terms of production and marketing effort can become a concern. For the exporting firm, the value of present and future export sales can be a significant determinant in using licensing with export operations.

Trademark Licensing

For companies that can trade on their names and characters, *trademark licensing* has become a substantial source of worldwide revenue. The names and logos of designers, literary characters, sports teams, and movie stars appear on merchandise such as clothing, games, food and beverages, gifts and novelties, toys, and home furnishings. The licensors are likely to make millions of dollars with little effort, whereas the licensees can produce a branded product that consumers will recognize immediately. Fees can range between 7 and 12 percent of net sales for merchandising license agreements.

Both licensor and licensee may run into difficulty if the trademark is used for a product far removed from the original success or if the licensed product casts a shadow on the reputation of the licensor. In licensing a trademark, consumer perceptions have to be researched to make sure the brand's positioning will not change. As an example, when Lowenbrau was exported to the United States, it was the number-one imported beer sold in the market. However, when the product name was licensed to Miller Brewing Company for domestic production, the beer's positioning (and subsequently its target audience) changed drastically in the minds of the consumers, resulting in a major decline in sales.

Franchising

Franchising is a form of licensing in which a parent company (the franchiser) grants another, independent entity (the franchisee) the right to do business in a prescribed manner. The right can take the form of selling a franchiser's products or using the name, production and marketing techniques, or general business approach. Usually, franchising involves a combination of all these elements. The major forms of franchising are manufacturer-retailer systems (such as car dealerships), manufacturer-wholesaler systems (such as soft drink companies), and service firm-retailer systems (such as lodging services and fast food outlets).

Franchising originated in Bavaria, but various types of businesses in many countries have adopted it. In 2002, global franchise sales by 16,000 franchisers and one million franchisees were estimated to be more than $1.5 trillion.

One can differentiate between product/trade franchising, where the major emphasis rests on the product and commodity to be sold, and business format franchising, where focus is on the ways of doing business. Even though many franchising firms are large, franchising can be a useful exporting expansion for the exporter, particularly product/trade franchising.

The typical reasons for the international expansion of franchise systems are market potential, financial gain, and saturated domestic markets. U.S. franchisers expanded dramatically in Europe in the mid-1980s, taking advantage of the strong dollar. The initial impetus for Computer Land's expansion into the Asia/Pacific region was "Asian entrepreneurs coming knocking on our door asking for franchises."

From a franchisee's perspective, the franchise is beneficial because it reduces risk by implementing a proven concept. In Malaysia, for example, the success rate in the franchise business is 90 percent, compared to 80 percent failure of all new businesses.

Franchising agreements are also beneficial from the governmental perspective. From a source-country view, franchising does not replace exports and export jobs. From a recipient-country view, franchising requires little outflow of foreign exchange, and the bulk of the profits generated remain within the country.

With all its benefits, franchising encounters some problems. One key issue is that companies first need to find out what their special capabilities are. This requires an identification and codification of knowledge assets in the firm. After such an investigation, companies can launch an aggressive program to share knowledge. For example, Dow Chemical, after a knowledge audit, was able to sign licensing agreements that are said to yield an estimated $100 million.

A second concern is the need for a great degree of standardization. Without such standardization, many of the benefits of transferred know-how are lost. Typically, such standardization includes the use of a common business name, similar layout, and similar production or service processes. Apart from leading to efficient operations, all these factors will also contribute to a high degree of international recognition. However, standardization does not mean 100 percent uniformity. Adjustment may be necessary in the final end product so that local market conditions can be taken into account. For example, fast-food outlets in

Europe often need to serve beer and wine to be attractive to the local clientele. In order to enter the Indian market, McDonald's has developed beefless burgers; Domino's Pizza in Japan serves seafood and eggplant pizza. The key to success in the development of a successful franchising program is to maintain a high degree of recognizability and efficient benefits while being responsive to local cultural preferences.

Another key issue is the protection of the total business system that a franchise offers. Whereas it is possible to protect a name, the type of product or service and the general style of operation can be readily copied abroad. As a result, franchise operations may meet competition head-on shortly after their introduction.

Government intervention can also represent major problems. For example, government restrictions on the type of services to be offered or on royalty remission can prevent franchising arrangements or lead to a separation between company and its franchises. Similarly, selection and training of franchisees presents another key concern. Many franchise systems have run into difficulty by expanding too quickly and granting franchises to unqualified entities. Although the local franchisee knows the market best, the franchiser still needs to understand the market for product adaptation purposes and operational details.

The franchiser should be the conductor of a coordinated effort by the individual franchisees—for example, in terms of sharing ideas and engaging in joint marketing efforts, such as cooperative advertising. However, even here difficulties can emerge consisting mostly of complications in selecting appropriate advertising media, effective copy testing, effective translation of franchiser's message, and the use of appropriate sales promotion tools. Exhibit 3.3 summarizes research findings regarding the challenges faced in international franchising.

To encourage better-organized and more successful growth, many companies turn to a master franchising system, wherein foreign partners are selected and awarded the rights to large territories in which in turn they subfranchise. As a result, the franchiser gains market expertise and an effective mechanism for new franchises without incurring costly mistakes. However, in order to preserve control, many companies also prefer to own their outlets abroad.

Franchising represents an additional opportunity for the firm that is already engaged in exporting. While franchising is often thought of as a foreign market entry strategy for large firms, it is also a viable alternative for the small business firm. However, the exporter needs to recognize the additional risks and financial involvement that such a strategy entails. The exporting firm may be a step ahead of a firm with no international experience. By considering franchise operations, the exporting firm can expand its opportunities if the right concept is found.

EXHIBIT 3.3. Key Impediments to International Franchising

- Meeting and training qualified and reliable franchisees overseas
- Security and protection of industrial property and trademarks in foreign countries
- Keeping current with market prospects overseas
- Familiarity with business practices overseas
- Foreign government regulations on business operations
- Foreign regulations or limitations on entry of franchise business
- Negotiation with foreign franchises
- Collection and transfer of franchise fee
- Control of quality or quantity of product or service
- Providing technical support overseas
- Pricing franchise for a foreign market
- Promotion and advertising opportunities for franchise overseas
- Sourcing and availability of raw materials, equipment, and other products
- Shipping and distribution of raw materials required to operate a foreign franchise
- Financing franchise operations overseas
- Shipping and handling of equipment needed to operate a foreign franchise

SOURCE: Adapted from Ben L. Kedia, David J. Ackerman, and Robert J. Justis, "Changing Barriers to the Internationalization of Franchising Operations: Perceptions of Domestic and International Franchisors," *The International Executive* 37 (July/August 1995): 329–348.

Summary

Exporting can be conducted in a a variety of modes reflecting varying degrees of contact with the marketplace (ranging from indirect to direct). This is an evolutionary process in which the firm gradually takes more control of the internationalization process. At the final stage, the firm may start dealing with customers without any intermediary involvement. One of the direct modes of exporting is e-commerce, both B2B or B2C. Firms with significant intellectual property may choose to enter markets through licensing or franchising. If the firm's competitive advantage ids in the development of new ideas and technologies rather than market development itself, licensing is often an efficient way to internationalize.

CHAPTER 4

Export Intermediaries

Companies and their managers often recognize the value of exporting but lack sufficient capital or human resources to capitalize on the potential. This chapter focuses on export intermediaries, such as Export Management Companies, Export Trading Companies, Webb-Pomerene associations, and foreign freight forwarders, as ways of participating in international markets.

The Role of Intermediaries

When a company first considers exporting, the first reality it encounters is lack of knowledge concerning the foreign market environment, namely information concerning market size, market access, and marketing and economic data for decision-making. Without this type of information, it is very difficult if not impossible to make key decisions about matters such as product specialization, market penetration, and distribution (including achieving economies of scale in procurement, marketing, and shipping).

Because of these problems, many export-capable firms may not care to export directly: however, they can accomplish the same objective by using international marketing intermediaries. One of the possibilities is the selling of merchandise to a domestic firm that in turn sells it abroad. For example, many products are sold to multinational corporations that use them as inputs for their foreign sales. Similarly, products sold to the U.S. Department of Defense may ultimately be shipped to military outposts abroad. Alternatively, an exporter may buy products domestically or internationally to round out an international product line that a foreign buyer may purchase during a visit to the United States.

Exporting, however, can best be accomplished by selling products or services directly to an importer abroad. A company seeking to get started in exporting can turn to specialized marketing organizations to help them start and build their export activities. These export intermediaries can be particularly useful to small manufacturers and export middlemen who wish to enter and/or develop a larger scale export activity but lack the expertise and personnel to do so. In such cases, specialized marketing intermediaries are crucial to the success of potential exporters because their special expertise can help overcome knowledge and performance gaps of firms. Often, they have detailed information about the competitive conditions in certain markets or they have personal contacts with potential buyers abroad. They can also assist by evaluating credit risks, calling on customers abroad in person, and handling the physical delivery of the product to the buyer.

Export Management Companies

Export management companies, also known as EMCs, are a unique type of international marketing intermediary that exclusively represents U.S. manufacturers in export markets. EMCs serve many or select export markets and may represent specific products or product categories. According to the Federation of International Trade Associations(FITA), all manufacturers without export experience should explore the use of an EMC. Even more experienced exporters should consider using an EMC for select products and/or select markets.[1] See Exhibit 4.1.

EMCs are independent firms that act as an export department for noncompeting manufacturers. An EMC has two primary functions: first, it acts as a merchant wholesaler for domestic U.S. manufacturers; i.e., it takes title to goods for resale and operates internationally on its own account. Second, it acts as a sales representative abroad; i.e., it serves as an exclusive agent to the manufacturer in foreign countries.

The EMC as merchant wholesaler. When operating as a merchant wholesaler, the EMC becomes a distributor, offering the manufacturer a conventional channel to manage their exports. As such, the EMC purchases products from the domestic manufacturer, takes title, and assumes trading risks. The EMC may carry a manufacturer's complete product line or select products, and it may have exclusive rights to sell on behalf of a manufacturer in specific foreign markets.

EMCs generally have product, country, and regional specialization. Selling in its own name offers the EMC the opportunity to reap greater profits as it reduces the domestic firm's risk while increasing its own risk. The burden of the merchandise acquired provides a major motivation to complete the international sale

---

[1] FITA, Federation of International Trade Associations Web site, accessed February 11, 2003; Nelson T. Joyner, "How to Find and Use an Export Management Company." http://www.fita.org

successfully. The domestic firm selling to an EMC is in a comfortable position of having sold its merchandise and received money without having to deal with the complexities of the international markets. On the other hand, the domestic firm has no control over the export price and/or marketing strategy. Consequently, it is unlikely to gather much international expertise and therefore relegates itself to some extent to remaining a purely domestic firm.

The EMC as agent. In this case, the EMC acts as a sales representative of the domestic manufacturer with exclusive or nonexclusive rights to sell the products or product line in select markets. The EMC's primary responsibility is to develop foreign marketing and sales strategies and establish contacts abroad. The EMC is paid a commission on export sales. Since the EMC does not share in the profits from the sale, it depends heavily on a high volume of sales on which to charge a commission. It may therefore be tempted to take on as many products and as many clients as possible in order to obtain a high volume of sales. The risk in this is that the EMC can spread itself too thin and cannot adequately represent all the clients and products it carries. This risk is particularly great with small EMCs.

In addition to international activities, this type of EMC must concentrate a substantial amount of effort on the development of domestic clients. These clients often are exactly the firms that are unwilling to commit major resources to their export marketing efforts. Many times they must be convinced that it is worthwhile to consider export activities.

EMCs that have specific expertise (e.g., language capabilities, previous exposure, or specialized contacts) are typically the most successful and useful in aiding clients. By sticking to their expertise and representing only a limited number of clients, such agent services can be quite valuable.

Compensation of the EMC. What an EMC charges depends on services performed, the country served, the product or products involved, and the extent of involvement by the firm itself:

1. An EMC primarily operating as a commission agent gets a commission ranging from 10 percent for consumer products to 15 percent for industrial products.
2. An EMC can act as a merchant, buying products outright from manufacturers, asking for the best domestic discount plus an extra discount for the export activities performed. If the extra discount is not granted, the EMC will have to mark up the price to the buyer to accommodate the additional costs of exporting.
3. EMCs also charge for additional export services, such as participating in

trade fairs or special events, including additional payment of related marketing costs.

In one way or another, exporters must pay an EMC for the international marketing effort conducted on their behalf. This compensation can be in the form of fees (as indicated above) and/or cost-sharing or lower prices that can result in profits for the EMC. Otherwise, despite promises, the EMC may simply add the firm and product name only to its product offering and do nothing to achieve market penetration. Manufacturers need to be aware of this cost and the fact that EMCs do not offer a free ride. Depending on the complexity of the

---

EXHIBIT 4.1. Using an EMC: 10 Steps to International Success

1. **Prepare a Global Marketing Strategy**—An initial product consultation will help us determine if your product is ready to go global.
2. **Identify the most viable countries and distribution channels for your product**—This could be done relatively quickly; thus, saving you a lot of time, effort and money that could be spent if you attempt to blanket the world all at once while expecting distribution through all channels.
3. **Provide market specific data including customs rules, regulations and duties**—Our history and experience in many different product categories has allowed us to build a strong logistics database for each territory.
4. **Allocate specialized resources and trained personnel to handle specific research, sales and international customer service**—Our experts each specialize in a certain field and in a certain part of the world because we want to offer you the most specific information and results possible.
5. **Customization of the product for international distribution**—The current offer could be one that translates well to the rest of the world. Nevertheless, in the cases in which it does not, we help you create one that will.
6. **Maximize Industry contacts and strategic alliances in every market**—We find ways to be creative with our strategic planning and always strive to work with the widest distribution channels available in each market.
7. **Generate Product Sales**—After a standard testing period, we begin to generate on-going sales at the stage where the campaign is well-established in the country.
8. **Manage, coordinate and monitor the export process**—Complete logistical management includes freight forwarding, commercial invoice preparation, customs clearance, etc.
9. **Coordinate and Manage payments, financial transactions and collections prior to shipment**—We work on a cash-in-advance basis or on an irrevocable letter of credit and the details are always arranged with you—the supplier, prior to the product launch.
10. **Allow your business to maximize export sales without an increase in overhead**—We are your international sales department without taking space in your office. Our "fee for service" is a standardized, mutually agreed-upon commission.

© 2002 Mercury Global, Inc. All Rights Reserved. Courtesy, Jeff Mandell, CFO, Mercury Global.

product and the necessity to carry out developmental research, promotion, and service, manufacturers must be prepared to part with some portion of the potential international profitability to compensate the EMC for its efforts.

An exporter seeking services from an EMC can consult The Federation of International Trade Associations (FITA) Website (www.fita.org). This organization provides a Directory of Export Management Companies . In order to be listed in this directory, an EMC must have at least one verifiable exclusive agreement with a U.S. manufacturer. The exporter can carefully examine the areas of expertise of the listed EMCs and match its needs with their expertise.

Webb-Pomerene Associations

One form of export intermediary particular to the United States is the Webb-Pomerene association. The major feature of the Webb-Pomerene Act, also known as the Export Trade Act of 1918, is to enable competing domestic firms to form cooperative export associations to develop export markets. U.S. exporters can form these associations, known as Webb-Pomerene Export Associations (WPEAs), to engage in exporting and combine the costs of export marketing operations, using mechanisms such as market allocation, quota fixing, and selection of exclusive distributors and brokers.[2] The intent of Congress was to put U.S. exporters at legal and competitive parity with foreign firms. However, these associations must take care not to engage in activities that would reduce competition and thus violate antitrust laws in the United States.

In practice the Webb-Pomerene Act did not provide the legal basis to fully bypass antitrust laws. The Federal Trade Commission (FTC), which administers the Act, has placed limitations on the use of Webb-Pomerene Export Associations due to uncertainty in the application of antitrust laws. Under the provisions of the Act, "export trade" was defined as "trade or commerce in goods, wares, and merchandise exported from the United States." The Act further indicated that "the words 'export trade' did not include the production, manufacture, or selling for consumption and resale in the domestic market" (U.S.Code Collection, Title 15, Chapter 2, Subchapter II, Sec. 61). Due to these restrictions, WPEAs are more suited for exporters with relatively homogeneous products, such as raw materials, where the separations of domestic and export-related costs are readily determined. This is not the case with heterogeneous products (differentiated products such as manufactures) where the separation of such costs is not easily determined. Consequently, the effectiveness of WPEAs has not been substantial. At their peak from 1930 to 1934, fifty associations accounted for about 12 percent of

---

[2] Federal Trade Commission, "Export Associations." Washington, D.C.: Federal Trade Commission, 1963.

U.S. exports. By 2000, only 12 associations were active and accounted for less than 1 percent of U.S. exports.[3] In addition, it appears that most of the members are not the small and medium-sized firms that the Act was initially intended to assist but rather are the dominant representatives of their respective industries. Moreover, the creation of the new U.S. antitrust exemption vehicle such as the Export Trading Company Act of 1986 made it possible for many WPEAs to reregister with the government under the new mechanism.[4]

Export Trading Companies

While the types of intermediaries described above provide valuable services to the export community, an export trading company can provide the most complete range of export-related services. Export trading companies (ETCs) are service firms with expertise in the distribution and transportation areas, and are involved in many areas of export marketing and sales, such as market analysis, documentation, legal and financial services and other pre- and post-sale services. Their worldwide networks and subsidiaries provide these services for firms that wish to tap significant foreign markets.

Most well-known export trading companies today operate primarily in Japan, Brazil, and South Korea. The concept was originated by the European trading houses such as the Fuggers and was soon formalized by the monarchs. Hoping to expand their imperial powers and wealth, kings chartered traders to form corporate bodies that enjoyed exclusive trading rights and protection. Examples of such early trading companies are the East India Company. Today the most famous trading companies are the sogoshosha of Japan. Names like Sumitomo, Mitsubishi, Mitsui, and C. Itoh have become household words around the world.

Four major reasons are given for the success of Japanese sogoshosha. First, by concentrating in obtaining and disseminating information about market opportunities and by investing huge funds in the development of information systems, these firms now have the mechanisms and organizations in place to gather, evaluate, and translate market information into business opportunities. Second, economies of scale permit them to take advantage of their vast transportation volume to obtain preferential treatment by, for example, negotiating transportation rates or even opening up new transportation routes. Third, these firms serve large international markets, not only in Japan but also around the world, and can benefit from opportunities for barter trade. Finally, sogoshosha have access to

---

[3] Federal Trade Commission, "Web Pomerene Export Associations: A 50 Year Review," U.S. Government Printing Office, 1967.

[4] James F. Mongoven, "Federal Trade Commission," a personal interview in Washington DC on Apr. 6, 2000).

vast quantities of capital, both within Japan and in international capital markets. They can therefore carry many transactions that are larger and riskier than is palatable or feasible for other firms.

For many decades, the emergence of trading companies was commonly believed to be a Japan-specific phenomenon. In particular, Japanese cultural factors were cited as a reason why such intermediaries could operate successfully only from that country. In 1975, however, trading companies were established by government declaration in Korea. The intent was to continue Korea's export-led growth in a more efficient fashion. With the new legislation, the Korean government tied access to financing and government contracts to the formation of trading companies. By 1981, the major trading companies of Korea (such as Hyundai, Samsung, and Daewoo) were handling 43 percent of Korea's total exports. Similarly, the Brazilian government stimulated the creation of trading companies by offering preferential financing arrangements. Within a short time, these Brazilian firms dramatically increased their activities and accounted for almost 20 percent of total Brazilian exports. Also, the government of Turkey devised special incentives to develop export trading companies that resulted within a few years in such trading companies accounting for 46 percent of Turkey's exports.

The U.S. trading company. As observed above, many countries actively courted the international trading company format to promote export-led growth. In these countries, export merchants are able to combine export marketing efforts and offer their exports through the export trading company system. Due to antitrust considerations, U.S. companies were not able to work in such combinations to further their export activities.

The Export Trading Company Act of 1982 was enacted to stimulate U.S. exports of goods and services. Its main feature is to provide protection from antitrust legislation. The Act offers exporters the opportunity to engage in joint export activities by forming export trading companies that are freer of antitrust constraints. The Act permits companies to obtain advance antitrust certification through the Department of Commerce that issues a certificate that allows a company limited antitrust exemption. Similarly, the Act allows bank holding companies to invest and own export trading companies, thus enhancing the financing capabilities of the export trading company.[5]

Export trading companies are considered one-stop agents and provide the exporter with one additional service other than marketing services: extending financing to suppliers (seller or exporter) and to the buyer in the foreign country. Export trading companies can provide hundreds of small firms with new market

---

[5] Export Trading Company Act of 1982. Public Law 97-290, 97th Congress, Oct. 8, 1982.

opportunities, market research, and export-related services such as processing export orders, transportation, and documentation. Its most distinguishable feature is its financing services. Export trading companies differ from EMCs and Webb-Pomerene Associations in this respect: by providing financing of supplier and buyer, the export trading company can contribute significantly to the capabilities of the export sector, as these organizations can draw new exporters into the field. The benefits to the exporter are many. The export trading company can buy and sell products on its own account and provide the mechanism for an increased level of exports while relieving the small and medium-sized firms from the risks involved in market development. The full range of integrated services includes financing, market analysis, sales and distribution, shipping and documentation, insurance, and promotion. These services can be an important determinant in insuring firms to enter the export field and help in their successful market penetration.

The greatest disadvantage of the export trading company is that services may be too specialized for an exporting firm's particular needs. The marketing expertise may not fit the exporter's product and market needs. The key variable in the decision to use an export trading company is control. The exporter must decide upon the level of control desired in a particular market on a country/product basis and compare the cost of services provided by the export trading company against the desired level of control a firm may want on its own marketing activities.

Exporters looking for information about Export trading companies can consult the Office of Export Trading Company Affairs. This office was created as part of the Export Trading Act of 1982. It promotes the use of export trading companies and the development of joint export ventures, including joint ventures by U.S. firms that are competitors in the domestic market. It administers two programs: The *Export Trade Certificate of Review* program which assists companies in providing antitrust protection for a variety of export activities including joint ventures; and the *myEXPORTS* program that is a multimedia advertising tool to help U.S. firms advertise their exports worldwide.[6]

The Foreign Freight Forwarder

Freight forwarders are specialized transportation intermediaries who are an integral part of international trade and commerce. The freight forwarder provides a highly specialized facilitating function between the exporter and railroads, ocean shipping companies, airlines, and so on. They work in the port areas and arrange

---

[6] Office of Export Trading Affairs Web site (http://www.ita.doc.gov/td/oetca), accessed July 18, 2003.

for all the details of exportation and customs clearance. The freight forwarder's services make it possible for inexperienced firms to engage in exporting, even with little knowledge of the complexity and formality of export procedures. Many small and medium-sized exporters located far from export sites can rely on freight forwarders to move their goods to shipping docks or terminals and dispatch the shipments on their behalf via ocean or air. Freight forwarding can be conducted by an independent person or firm. However, performing forwarding activities on one's own behalf is not freight forwarding as it is commonly known. The primary function of the freight forwarder is to arrange for the transportation of the goods to be delivered to the port of exportation. They also provide additional services such as custom brokerage, warehousing, packaging, and insurance. The services provided by the freight forwarder are:

1. Provides prior to the movement of the goods and with information supplied by the exporter about the nature of the shipment, a shipping quotation for the designated term of sale (freight charges, port use fees if applicable, insurance costs, etc.) as well as possible alternatives for shipment in different shipping companies, and books cargo space for shippers.
2. Provides the documentation necessary to complete customs regulations prior to the time when the cargo is loaded on board a shipping vessel to ensure the proper export clearance procedures.
3. Prepares all shipping documents correctly and in accordance with the stipulation of the export order.
4. Obtains all other necessary documentation for import clearance, such as certificate of origin, consular invoice, etc., required by the country of destination and which must be obtained in the exporting country, duly signed by the proper authorities.
5. Obtains insurance coverage when so requested by buyer or seller under the terms of the export order.
6. Handles all the banking details on behalf of the exporter when an export order calls for payments through a letter of credit or on collection basis.

The freight forwarder is paid according to the number and level of services provided. In some countries, freight forwarders are required to be licensed. The United States dropped this requirement in 1966. However, freight forwarders must conform to regulatory practices. They usually are bonded.

Freight forwarders may be classified according to the kind of mode they specialize in. *Foreign freight forwarder* is the term used for forwarders who perform the functions required for international shipments. Some freight forwarders specialize in consolidating small shipments into full container loads. These are called *consolidating freight forwarders.* These consolidating services are becoming very important in the export trade as today most export shipments move in container ships.

In choosing the services of a freight forwarder, the exporter should seek the services of established, financially sound, and competent foreign freight forwarders. It must be remembered that forwarders take possession of the goods while in transit to the shipping point. When acting in this capacity, the forwarder is acting as an agent of the exporter. Consequently, is very important that exporters carefully choose the firm that will act on their behalf. A reputable, competent, and financially sound agent should be carefully chosen for the best results.

Summary

In addition to exporting, other possibilities for export market entry or expansion are the use of intermediaries. Firms with suitable products but reluctant to enter into exporting may use intermediaries to enter export markets. Typical intermediaries are export management companies, Webb-Pomerene Export Associations, and export trading companies. For the export market entry to be successful, various export functions need to be performed. Export intermediaries can take on these functions. For the arrangement to be viable, however, a proper fit between the exporter's product and marketing service needs and the export intermediary competency must exist. Similarly, such services entail additional costs in exporting. The major disadvantage of such intermediaries is that they may take on more clients or more diverse functions than they are staffed to perform.

The foreign freight forwarder is an important transportation intermediary service provider who specializes in assisting exporters in transportation logistics from warehouse to port of exportation. Freight forwarders are an important link in the export function.

CHAPTER 5

Financial Environment

You need to understand those business forces you can't control. At the top of any list of uncontrollable forces is the financial environment in which you operate. **But if you** analyze that environment carefully and understand it in terms of the company's ability to operate within its demands, you will have the ability to get the financial support your marketing program needs to be successful. Key to such understanding is awareness of the types of financial risk, knowledge of how a fiscally sound credit policy is developed, knowledge of the different sources of financing, and the key factors in managing foreign exchange risk. With this understanding you will be able to weather the financial crises that confront every business from time to time. This chapter will focus on the financial concerns of the exporter and the support it can obtain in securing a contract, getting paid, and avoiding risk.

Credit Policy

Every exporter's primary concern is to get paid for the goods shipped or service rendered. Before a particular order is received, you should have already formulated a policy on the acceptable degree of risk and preferable terms. The extent of credit offered is determined by: (1) firm-specific factors such as size, experience in international trade, and capacity for financing transactions; (2) market characteristics, such as degree of economic development and availability of means of payment; and (3) factors relating to the particular transaction such as the amount of payment and the need for protection, terms offered by competition, the relative strength and attractiveness of the trading partner, and the type of good or service involved (for example, perishables or custom solutions).

The development of a credit policy requires teamwork between the exporter's marketing and finance personnel and its commercial banks. To get the best assistance, most companies need access to larger banks that provide a full range of finance, insurance, and advisory services. These include regional banks, with which a company maintains day-to-day relationships, and money-center banks, which typically provide more sophisticated and broader services.

Financing has to be understood as a marketing tool. Export finance managers may not have time to listen to marketers and understand the kind of financing terms that are needed to make sales or to work with the more complicated solutions needed. This can be overcome by helping the marketing personnel better understand financing options and by allowing marketers to communicate their needs directly to the banks. Action to accomplish this may include regular roundtable discussions between marketers and bankers and trips abroad by teams of marketers and finance people working together to understand the sale and financing package from start to finish. The goal is to seek and provide the kind of financing that wins business.

Once established, the credit policy should help the exporter (1) determine the extent of risk to be absorbed; (2) explore new ways of financing exports; and (3) prepare for a changing environment in terms of types of risk encountered.

Types of Financial Risk

Developments halfway around the world can destroy even the most carefully made credit decisions in the blink of an eye. In addition to macrodevelopments causing nonpayment, the buyer may go out of business before paying the seller. The major types of financial risk are commercial risk, political risk, foreign exchange risk, and other risks such as those related to inflation.

The term *commercial risk* refers primarily to the degree of likelihood that an overseas buyer will not pay a bill—default—or will take an unacceptably long time to pay it. Inability of a business to pay its bills (commercial default) usually results from deterioration of conditions in the buyer's market, fluctuations in demand, unanticipated competition, or technological changes. The range of specific reasons may include:

1. Internal changes, such as the death of a key person. For example, many importing entities are heavily dependent on the owner-operator.
2. The buyer loses a key customer. With an increase in mergers and acquisitions, buyers dependent on key accounts may be vulnerable.
3. Unexpected difficulty experienced by the buyer in meeting operating expenses. For example, the importer's final product might fall under price controls while input prices might not be controlled in a high-inflation market.

4. Natural disasters, such as floods and industrial accidents.
5. Slow payment by government customers.

All of these risks can emerge in a domestic environment as well, but the geographic and psychological distances to international markets make the risks more severe and more difficult to anticipate.

Political risk is completely beyond the control of either the buyer or the seller. For example, the foreign buyer may be willing to pay, but the government may use every means to delay payment as far into the future as possible. In addition to foreign exchange transfer delay, which has the most direct impact on a transaction, other political risks include war, revolution, or similar hostilities; unforeseen withdrawal or nonrenewal of license to export or import; requisition, expropriation, confiscation, or intervention in the buyer's business by a government authority; transport or insurance changes caused by interruption or diversion of shipments and certain other government acts that prevent or delay payment beyond the control of either the buyer or seller.

Foreign exchange risk refers to the effects of fluctuating exchange rates. The choice of the currency to be used to pay the bill depends largely on the bargaining positions of the buyer and the seller as well as on the accepted business practices in the industry or region. However, if the price quotation is not in the seller's currency, the seller must be prepared to use foreign exchange forward markets to protect itself against possible losses resulting from unfavorable changes in the value of the payment received.

Sources of Financing

Except in the case of larger companies that may have their own financing entities, most exporters support their customers abroad in securing appropriate financing. Export financing terms (interest rates and length of financing) can significantly affect the total cost for both the exporter and the importer. Consider, for example, two competitors for a $1 million sale. Exporter A offers an 8 percent interest rate over a 10-year payment period, while B offers 9 percent for the same term. Over 10 years, the difference in interest is $55,000. In many cases, buyers will award a contract to the provider of more attractive credit and overlook differences in quality and price.

Financing assistance is available from both the private and public sectors. The exporter should assess not only domestic programs but those in other countries. For example, Japan and Taiwan have import financing programs that provide exporters added potential in penetrating these significant markets.

It is necessary to identify the type of financing needed. *Trade financing* refers to financing of individual transactions where the provider of the financing collects the sales proceeds and secures repayment of any loan. If an exporter cannot wait for payment, *foreign accounts receivable financing* is available. Exporters may also need *financing for market development activities*, which may include expenses to start and expand exporting capacity and for marketing-related activities, such as trade show participation. In many of these cases, the private and public sectors interact to develop solutions for exporters.

Commercial Banks

Commercial banks provide trade financing depending on their relationship with the exporter, the nature of the transaction, the country of the borrower, and the availability of export insurance, which means first-rate credit risks only, which in turn means that many would-be U.S. exporters can't get assistance from these banks. Furthermore, some U.S. banks do not see international trade finance as part of their core competence. Although the situation has improved in recent years, exporters still continue to complain about lack of export financing as it pertains to developing countries, financing high technology, or lending against foreign receivables. Many exporters complain that banks will not deal with them "without a guarantee from the EX-IM Bank of rock-solid collateral, such as property and/or equipment."

However, as the share of international sales and reach of companies increases, banking relationships become all the more important, a fact that is also noted by banks themselves. Many banks offer enhanced services, such as electronic services, which help exporters monitor and expedite their international transactions to customers who do a certain amount of business with them. As with all suppliers, the more business done with a bank, the higher the level of service, usually at a better price. As the relationship builds, the bankers feel more comfortable about the exporter's business and are more likely to go out of their way to help, particularly with difficult transactions. Also, some banks have come to specialize in certain areas, usually areas of interest to their customers and/or operating region. For example, Silicon Valley Bank in San Jose finances fledgling technology exporters, while Capitol Bank in Los Angeles provides export and import financing to companies doing business in Taiwan and South Korea. It is clear that the development of an effective credit policy requires teamwork between the company's marketing and finance staffs and its bankers.

In addition to using the types of services provided, the bank's overseas reach is important. Reach is a combination of the bank's own network of facilities and correspondent relationships. While money-center banks can provide the greatest amount of coverage through their own offices and staff, they still use correspondents in regions outside the main banking or political centers of foreign markets.

For example, Citibank has a worldwide correspondent network of 5,000 institutions in addition to its facilities in more than 100 countries.

Some banks have formed alliances to extend their reach to markets that their customers are entering. Wachovia, a super-regional bank based in North Carolina, has developed relationships with global banks that have strong correspondent networks in emerging markets. Regional banks, such as Bank One, which have no intention of establishing branches abroad, rely only on strong alliances with foreign banks, which can provide a competitive advantage to exporters because of their home-country connections and their strong global networks. For example, Commerzbank, Germany's third largest bank, has branches in the Far East, Latin America, South America, and Eastern Europe to support its international trade financing activities in the NAFTA area. Regardless of the arrangement, the bank's own branches or correspondents play an important role at all stages of the international transaction, from gathering market intelligence about potential new customers to actually processing payments. Additional services include reference checks on customers in their home markets and suggestions for possible candidates to serve as intermediaries.

Forfaiting and Factoring

Forfaiting provides the exporter with cash at the time of the shipment. In a typical forfait deal, the importer pays the exporter with bills of exchange or promissory notes guaranteed by a leading bank in the importer's country. The exporter can sell them to a third party (for example, Citicorp) at a discount from their face value for immediate cash. The sale is without recourse to the exporter, and the buyer of the notes assumes all the risks. The discount rate takes into account the buyer's creditworthiness and country, the quality of the guaranteeing bank, and the interest cost over the term of the credit.

The benefits to the exporter are the reduction of risk, simplicity of documentation (because the documents used are well known in the market), and 100 percent coverage, which official sources such as export-import banks do not provide. In addition, forfaiting does not involve either content or country restrictions, which many of the official trade financing sources may have. The major complaints about forfaiting center on availability and cost. Forfaiting is not available where exporters need it most, that is, the high-risk countries. Furthermore, it is usually a little more expensive than public sources of trade insurance.

Certain companies, known as *factoring houses*, purchase an exporter's receivables for a discounted price (2 to 4 percent less than face value). Two common arrangements exist: (1) cash in advance, or discount factoring, in which the factor issues an advance of funds against the exporter's receivables; and (2) collection factoring, in which the factor pays the exporter, less a commission charge, when receivables are due (usually regardless of the importer's ability to pay). Factors not only buy receivables but also provide the exporter with a complete financial package that combines credit protection, accounts receivable bookkeeping, and collection services to eliminate many of the challenges that come with doing business overseas. Arrangements are typically with recourse, leaving the exporter ultimately liable for repaying the factor in case of a default. Some factors accept export receivables without recourse but require a large discount.

A dozen major players, most of which are subsidiaries of major banks, dominate the industry. Leaders include the CIT Group, 80 percent owned by Dai-Ichi Kangyo Bank of Japan and 20 percent owned by Chase Manhattan, and Bank of America Commercial Finance/Factoring, which has won the President's "E" Award for its excellence in export service. However, with the increase in companies looking for factoring services, independent factors are also emerging. Factors can be found through the Commercial Finance Association or through marketing facilitators whose clients use factors.

Although the forfaiting and factoring methods appear similar, they differ in four significant ways:

1. Factors usually want a large percentage of the exporter's business, while most forfaiters work on a one-shot basis.
2. Forfaiters work with medium-term receivables (over 180 days to 5 years), while factors work with short-term receivables.
3. Factors usually do not have strong capabilities in the developing countries, but since forfaiters usually require a bank guarantee, most are willing to deal with receivables from these countries.
4. Forfaiters work with capital goods, factors typically with consumer goods.

Official Trade Finance

Official financing can take the form of either a loan or a guarantee, including credit insurance. In a loan, the government, through an export credit agency (ECA), provides funds to finance the sale and charges interest on those funds at a stated fixed rate. The government lender accepts the risk of a possible default. In a guarantee, a private-sector lender provides the funds and sets the interest rate, with the government assuring that it will reimburse the lender if the loan is unpaid. The government is providing not funds but rather risk protection. The programs provide assurance that the governmental agency will pay for a major portion of the loss should the foreign buyer default on payment. The advantages are significant:

1. Protection in the riskiest part of an exporter's business (foreign sales receivables).

EXHIBIT 5.1. Standard ECA Guarantee.

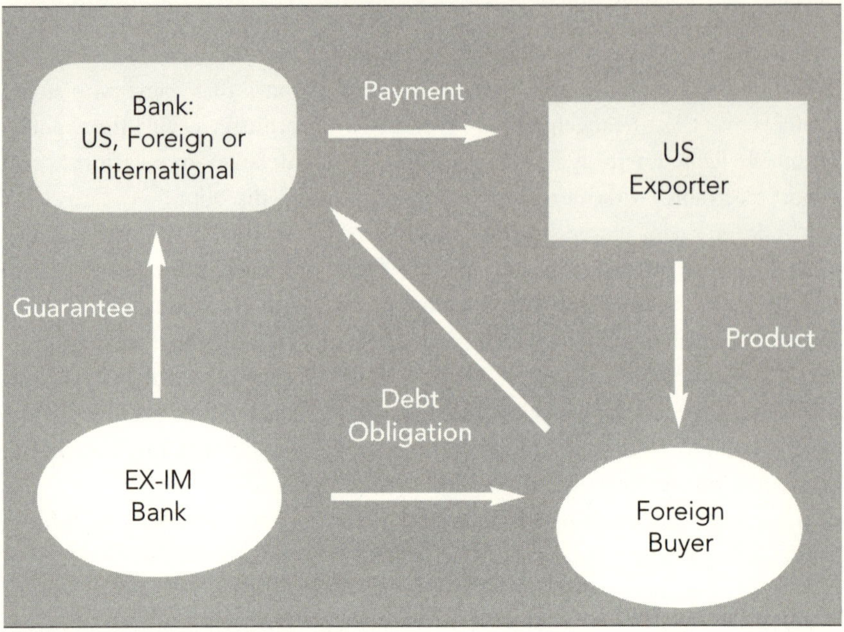

SOURCE: Courtesy: David Chavern.

2. Protection against political and commercial risks over which the exporter does not have control.
3. Encouragement to exporters to make competitive offers by extending terms of payment.
4. Broadening of potential markets by minimizing exporter risks.
5. The possibility of leveraging exporter accounts receivable.
6. Through the government guarantee, the opportunity for commercial banks to remain active in the international finance arena.

The standard ECA process is summarized in Exhibit 5.1.

Because credit has emerged as an increasingly important component in export selling, governments of most industrialized countries have established entities that insure credit risks for exports. Officially supported export credit agencies, such as the French Coface or German Hermes, are organizations whose central purpose is to promote national trade objectives by providing financial support for national exports. ECAs benefit from varying degrees of explicit or implicit support from national governments. Some ECAs are divisions of government trade missions. Other ECAs operate as autonomous or even private institutions, but most require a degree of recourse to national government support.

The Export-Import Bank of the United States (Ex-Im Bank) was created in 1934 and established as an independent U.S. government agency in 1945. The purpose of the bank is "to aid in financing and facilitating exports." Since its inception, Ex-Im Bank has supported more than $400 billion in U.S. export sales. The Ex-Im Bank supports short-, medium-, and long-term financing to creditworthy international customers (both in the private and public sectors) as well as working capital guarantees to U.S. exporters. Special initiatives exist for environmental exports, small business, and lending directly to municipalities in certain countries.

The data and examples in Exhibit 5.2 highlight the programs available for exporters—pre-export, short-term, medium-term, and long-term. One of the greatest impediments small businesses experience in attempting to fulfill export

EXHIBIT 5.2. Examples of Ex-Im Projects

EXPORTS	APPROPRIATE PROGRAM	EXAMPLE
Pre-export	Working Capital Guarantee	Pragmatic Environmental Solutions of Roanoke, Virginia, received a $100,000 loan from Suntrust Bank that enabled it to make an export sale of pollution control equipment to Wren Oil Co. of Australia.
Short-term	Export Credit Insurance	Wildflower International of Santa Fe, New Mexico, expanded its export sales of software to Mexico, Israel, and Saudi Arabia by offering 90- and 180-day open account credit terms in insuring them with Ex-Im.
Medium-term	Guarantees	Senstar Capital Group provided a 4-year $400,000 loan to Ecopreneur, S.A. of Buenos Aires to purchase water treatment equipment from six U.S. small-business water-treatment suppliers.
Long-term	Direct loans	$49.7 million loan to sponsor Ormat Leyte Co., Ltd. to build, own, and operate four geothermal plants in the Philippines with significant inputs from U.S. suppliers.

SOURCE: Examples courtesy of Craig O'Connor.

orders is a lack of working capital to build necessary inventory for the export order. If the local bank is reluctant to make such financing available (because the exporter might have reached its borrowing limit, for example), the Working Capital Guarantee program is available.

The ability to offer financing or credit terms is often critical in competing for, and winning, export contracts. Increasingly, foreign buyers expect suppliers to offer open account or unsecured credit terms rather than requiring letters of credit, which may be expensive. Yet for small exporters, extending credit terms to foreign customers may represent an unacceptable risk, especially when the exporter's bank is unwilling to accept foreign receivables as collateral for working lines of credit. The solution is export credit insurance, wherein, for a reasonable premium, an institution (e.g., an insurance company or an ECA) guarantees payment to the seller if the buyer defaults. Five major players, which account for more than 75 percent of the world market, dominate the short-term credit-insurance business: Coface, Euler, Gerling, Hermes, and NCM.

Ex-Im Bank also guarantees to provide repayment protection for private-sector loans to creditworthy buyers of U.S. goods and services. Guarantees, both for the medium and long term, are backed in full by the U.S. government. The fee schedule is determined by country risk and repayment terms of the transaction. Medium-term (not to exceed seven years) guarantees are typically used by commercial banks that do not want exposure in a certain country or that have reached their internal exposure limit in a given country. For long-term guarantees, projects are usually large (in excess of $100 million), and commercial banks may not want such exposure for long periods of time in one country or in a particular industry sector. Ex-Im may act as a direct lender to the foreign buyer. The majority (typically 85 percent or more) of the project must be U.S.-produced goods and services.

In addition to the ECAs, other public-sector supporters exist as well. In the United States, the Overseas Private Investment Corporation (OPIC) offers investment guarantees comparable to those offered by the Ex-Im Bank to manufacturers who wish to establish facilities in less-developed countries, either by themselves or as a joint venture with local capital. The programs involve either (1) direct loans, (2) loan guarantees to U.S. institutional lenders, or (3) political risk insurance against currency inconvertibility, expropriation or takeover, and physical damage resulting from political strife. The Agency for International Development (AID) administers most of the foreign economic assistance programs of the United States and since many of them require that purchases be made from the United States, exporters can use this support mechanism. The U.S. Department of Agriculture's Commodity Credit Corporation (CCC) operates export credit guarantee programs to provide agricultural exporters or financial institutions a guarantee that they will be repaid for export financing to foreign buyers. The Small Business Administration (SBA) has two programs to assist small businesses in starting export operations: the working capital program and the international trade loan program.

In addition to country-specific entities, the exporter will find it worthwhile to monitor the activities of multilateral institutions such as the United Nations and the World Bank Group as well as regional development banks (such as the Inter-American Development Bank and the Asian Development Bank). They specialize in financing investment activities and can provide valuable leads for future business activity. In a typical year, the United Nations purchases $3 billion of goods and services with 12 percent going to U.S. companies. For example, Igloo Corp. annually sells $200,000 worth of picnic coolers to the United Nation's Children's Fund for the transportation of temperature sensitive vaccines in tropical climates.

Managing Foreign Exchange Risk

Unless the exporter and the importer share the same currency (as is the case in the 12 countries of the European Union), exchange rate movements may harm one or the other of the parties. This is exchange risk. Exchange risk is the result of fluctuation of currency value due to changes in economic conditions or, in unusual situations, from a revaluation or devaluation of a currency by a central bank. Assume that a U.S. importer bought $250,000 worth of goods from a German company which agreed to accept U.S. dollars for payment in 90 days. At the time of the quotation the exchange rate for $1 was 1.00, whereas at the time of payment, it had changed to 0.97. This means that the German exporter, instead of receiving 250,000, winds up with 242,500.

If the price is quoted in the exporter's currency, the exporter will get exactly the price it wants but may lose some sales because the price is not in the buyer's currency. The exporter who really needs the sale should price the sale in the importer's currency and assume the exchange risk. Some exporters, if they are unable to secure payment in their own currency, try to minimize the risk by negotiating shorter terms of payment, such as 10 or 15 days instead of 30 or 60 days.

The Foreign Exchange Market

The foreign exchange market is the market for currencies; that is, the physical and institutional structure through which money is exchanged for that of another country, the rate of exchange between currencies is determined, and foreign exchange transactions are physically completed. The participants in this market are

EXHIBIT 5.3. Foreign Exchange Rates

	USD	EUR	JPY	GBP	CHF	CAD	AUD	HKD
HKD	7.7838	9.7242	0.0713	14.5439	6.1666	5,8338	6.0231	
AUD	1.2923	1.6145	0.0118	2.4147	1.0238	0.9686		0.166
CAD	1.3342	1.669	0.0122	2.493	1,057		1.0324	0.1714
CHF	1.2622	1.5769	0.0116	2.3585		0.946	0.9767	0.1622
GBP	0.5352	0.6686	0.0049		0.424	0.4011	0.4141	0.0688
JPY	109.11	136.311		203.872	86.4409	81.7763	84.4293	14.0177
EUR	0.8004		0.0073	1.4956	0.6341	0.5999	0.6194	0.1028
USD		1.2493	0.0092	1.8685	0.7922	0.7495	0.7738	0.1285

SOURCE: http://www.bloomberg.com, accessed February 27, 2004.

banks, governments, speculators, as well as individuals and firms conducting transactions.

The price of one currency in terms of another is the *exchange rate*. Daily exchange rates such as those indicated in Exhibit 5.3 are available through media such as *The Financial Times* and online services such as Bloomberg. The exporter, however, has to contact a bank's foreign-exchange trader for a firm quote. Both spot and forward transactions are made in the market. The market for selling and buying on the current day is the *spot market*. The settlement can take up to two days, in some countries even longer. The market for contracts on subsequent periods of 30, 90, or 180 days is called the *forward market*. Forward contracts for lesser-used currencies are not readily available, and for unstable currencies, they are quite expensive. Some of the currencies are free-floating—i.e., their values determined by market forces—while some are pegged to other currencies (such as the HK$ to the U.S.$ at a rate of 7.78).

Two types of approaches to protect against currency-related risk are: (1) risk shifting, such as foreign currency contractual hedging, and/or (2) risk modifying, such as manipulating prices and other elements of a marketing strategy. When invoicing in foreign currencies, an exporter cannot insulate itself from the problems of currency movements, but it can at least know how much it will eventually receive by using the mechanism of the forward exchange market. In essence, the exporter gets a bank to agree to a forward rate at which it will buy the foreign currency the exporter will receive when the importer makes payment. The rate is expressed as either a premium or a discount on the current spot rate. The risk still remains if the exchange rate does not move as anticipated, and the exporter may be worse off than if it had not bought forward.

Although forward contracts are the most common foreign currency contractual hedge, other financial instruments and derivatives, such as currency options and futures, are available. An option gives the holder the right to buy or sell foreign currency at a pre-specified price on or up to a pre-specified date. The difference between the currency options market and the forward market is that the transaction in the former gives the participant the right to buy or sell, whereas a transaction in the forward market entails a contractual obligation to buy or sell. This means that if an exporter does not have any or the appropriate amount of currency when the contract comes due, it would have to go into the foreign exchange markets to buy the currency, potentially exposing itself to major losses if the currency has appreciated in the meanwhile. The greater flexibility in the options contract makes it more expensive, however.

The currency futures market is conceptually similar to the forward market; that is, to buy futures on the British pound sterling implies an obligation to buy in the future at a pre-specified price. However, the minimum transaction sizes are considerably smaller on the futures market. Forward quotes apply to transactions of $1 million or more, whereas on the futures market transactions will typically be well below $100,000. The market, therefore, allows relatively small firms engaged in international trade to lock in exchange rates and lower their risk. Forward contracts options, and futures are available from banks, the Chicago Mercantile Exchange and the Philadelphia Stock Exchange.

The marketing approaches to dealing with foreign-exchange challenges are discussed in the pricing chapter. These vary from short-term changes in pricing to long-term changes such as shifting production or sourcing bases.

Dealing with Financial Crises

A series of financial crises have hit promising emerging markets. The devaluation of the Mexican peso in 1994, the Asian crisis of July 1997, the Russian ruble collapse of 1998, the fall of the Brazilian real in August 1999, and the Argentine default of 2001 have all challenged exporters and their interest in these markets. In Argentina, for example, the supply of most foreign-made goods was choked off.

Changes in the economic environment affect both consumers and marketers. Consumer confidence is eroded and marketers have to weigh their marketing strategies carefully. Some of these adjustments are summarized in Exhibit 5.4. For example, Deere & Co. would sell its farm equipment in Argentina only if payment was in US$ or to customers with bank accounts abroad. Michelin changed its marketing positioning from "expensive, but worth it" to "surprisingly affordable" in Asian markets affected by the crisis. Unilever reduced the size of its ice-cream packs, making them cheaper, and the use of premiums (such as buy three, get one free).

EXHIBIT 5.4. Customer and Marketer Adjustment to Financial Crises

CUSTOMER ADJUSTMENT TO FINANCIAL HARDSHIP	MARKETER ADJUSTMENT TO FINANCIAL HARDSHIP
• **General reactions** Reduce consumption and wastefulness More careful decision-making More search for information	• **Marketing-mix strategies** Withdraw from weak markets Fortify in strong markets Acquire weak competitors Consider youth markets Resale market for durables
• **Product adjustments** Necessities rather than luxuries Switch to cheaper brands or generics Local rather than foreign brands Smaller quantities/packages	• **Product strategies** Prune weak products Avoid introducing new products in gaps Flanker brands Augment products with warranties Adaptive positioning
• **Price adjustments** Life-cycle costs—durability/value Emphasis on economical prices	• **Pricing strategies** Improve quality while maintaining price Reduce price while maintaining quality Consider product life-cycle pricing
• **Promotion adjustments** Rational approach Reduced attraction to gifts Information rather than imagery	• **Promotion strategies** Maintain advertising budget Focus on print media Assurances through rational appeals Expert endorsements Advisory tone Customer loyalty programs Train sales force to handle objections
• **Shopping adjustments** Increased window shopping Preference for discount stores Fewer end-of-aisle purchases	• **Distribution strategies** Location is critical Sell in discount and wholesale centers Prune marginal dealers Alternative channels

SOURCE: Compiled from Swee Hoon Ang, Siew Meng Leong and Philip Kotler, "The Asian Apocalypse: Crisis Marketing for Consumers and Businesses," *Long Range Planning* 33(February 2000): 97–119.

Summary

The financial dimensions of a transaction are an important marketing tool for the exporter. This requires a good understanding of the various types of financing alternatives available as well the workings of the foreign exchange market. To help the exporter with financial risk, both the private and public sectors (often in unison) have established programs. Foreign exchange risk is present any time an exporter is to receive payment in a currency other than its own. Various contractual methods exist in handling this challenge. When financial crises emerge, exporters are advised to make various adjustments to ensure long-term competitiveness in a market hard-hit by a crisis.

CHAPTER 6

The Role of Government in International Trade

Political and legal factors play a critical role in export activities. Apart from specific technical circumstances that often lead governments to become involved in international trade and marketing, the political environment in most countries tends to provide general support of the country's firms. For example, a government may work to reduce trade barriers or increase trade opportunities through bilateral and multilateral negotiations. Often, however, governments also impose restrictions on international trade with specific rules and regulations. Such regulations are frequently political in nature and are based on the fact that governments see commerce as only one of several international objectives, such as foreign policy and national security.

Transnational Institutions Affecting World Trade

The World Trade Organization (WTO)

The World Trade Organization has its origins in the General Agreement of Tariffs and Trade (GATT), to which it became the successor organization in January of 1995. In order to better understand the WTO, a brief review of the GATT is appropriate. The GATT began in 1947 as a set of rules for nondiscrimination, transparent procedures, and settlement of disputes in international trade. One of the most important tools is the Most-Favored Nation (MFN) clause, which calls for each member country to grant every other member country the most favorable treatment it accords to any other country with respect to imports and exports. In effect, MFN is the equal opportunity clause of international trade. Over time, the GATT sponsored successive rounds of international trade negotiations with a key focus on reducing high tariffs.

In spite of, or perhaps because of, its successes, GATT became less effective over time. For example, the average U.S. tariff rate fell from 26 percent in 1946 to an average of 5.4 percent in 2001. Further reductions are therefore unlikely to have a major impact on world trade. Most imports already either enter the United States duty free or are subject to low tariffs.

Many nations developed new tools for managing and distorting trade flows, nontariff tools that were not covered under GATT rules. Examples are "voluntary agreements" to restrain trade, bilateral or multilateral special trade agreements such as the multifiber accord that restricts trade in textiles and apparel, and other nontariff barriers. Also, GATT, which was founded by 24 like-minded governments, was designed to operate by consensus. With a membership of 148, this consensus rule often led to a stalemate of many GATT activities.

In January of 1995 a new institution, the World Trade Organization, became the umbrella organization responsible for the GATT, the General Agreement on Trade in Services (GATS), agreements on trade-related aspects of intellectual property rights (TRIPS), and trade-related investment measures (TRIMS), and a broad variety of international trade and investment accords.

In 2001, new trade negotiations were initiated in the city of Doha, Qatar (the "Doha Round"). The aim was to further implement trade liberalization and to help impoverished and developing nations. Examples include trade in agricultural goods, antidumping regulations, and electronic commerce.

The International Monetary Fund (IMF)

The International Monetary Fund (IMF), conceived in 1944 at Bretton Woods in New Hampshire, was designed to provide stability for the international monetary framework and for fixed exchange rates between countries.

The result of using the U.S. dollar as the main world currency was a glut of dollar supplies in the 1960s. This forced the United States to abandon the gold standard and devalue the dollar and resulted in flexible or floating exchange rates in 1971. Today, the IMF continues to contribute toward providing international liquidity, helping to manage sovereign debt, and facilitating international trade.

The World Bank

The World Bank, whose official name is the World Bank Group, was initially formed in 1944 to aid countries suffering from the destruction of war. After completing this process most successfully, it has since taken on the task of aiding world development. With more and more new nations emerging during the twentieth century, the bank has made major efforts to assist fledgling economies to participate in a modern economic trade framework. More recently, the bank has begun to actively address the debt and poverty problems of the developing world.

Economic Integration

Regional changes have also taken place, based on the notion that trade between countries needs to be encouraged. Of particular importance was the formation of economic blocs that integrated the economic and political activities of nations.

European Integration. The most important integration has been the European Union (EU), where the freedom of movement for products, services, people, and capital has led to more intense competition among companies. These factors and the establishment of a common currency—the Euro—have created more efficiencies and consolidation of firms across industries and across countries. Firms in "Euroland" enjoy cheaper transaction costs and reduced currency risks, and consumers and businesses experience more price transparency and increased price-based competition.

The integration has important implications for firms within and outside Europe. There are substantial benefits for those firms already operating in Europe. These firms gain because their operations in one country can now be freely expanded into others and their products may be freely sold across borders. In a borderless Europe of 25 nations, firms have access to approximately 460 million consumers. Substantial economies of scale in production and marketing are possible. The extent of these economies of scale depends on the ability of the exporters to find pan-regional segments or to homogenize tastes across borders through promotional activity.

Exporters need to worry about maintaining their competitive position and continued access to the market. Small and mid-sized U.S. companies account for more than 60 percent of U.S. exports to the EU. Their success during times of high dollar value was based on the relationships they had developed with their customers. Companies with a physical presence may be in a better position to assess and take advantage of new market developments. Internet systems provider WatchGuard Technologies almost doubled its staff in Europe, from 12 to 20 in 2002, in the wake of September 11 and increasing concern about viruses. In some industries, exporters do not see a reason either to be in Europe at all or to change from exporting to more involved modes of entry. Machinery and machine tools, for example, are in great demand in Europe, but exporters in these industries say they have little reason to manufacture there.

North American Integration. North American integration efforts also gained momentum and attention. What started as a trading pact between two close and economically well-developed allies has been expanded to include Mexico, with long-term plans calling for further additions. However, North American integration is for purely economic reasons; there are no constituencies for political integration.

The North American Free Trade Agreement (NAFTA) represents a free market with 390 million consumers and a total output of over $13 trillion. The pact marked a bold departure: Never before have industrialized countries created such a massive free trade area with a developing-country neighbor. Controversy has centered on the gains and losses for the United States and Mexico. Proponents argue that the agreement gives U.S. firms access to a huge pool of relatively low-cost Mexican labor at a time when demographic trends are resulting in labor shortages in many parts of the United States. At the same time, many new jobs are created in Mexico. The agreement gave firms in both countries access to millions of additional consumers, and the liberalized trade flows resulted in higher economic growth in both countries.

Opposition to NAFTA centers on issues relating to labor and the environment. Unions in particular worry about job loss to Mexico, given its lower wages and work standards; some estimate that 6 million U.S. workers are vulnerable to migration of jobs. Similarly, any expansion of NAFTA is perceived as a threat.

Trade among Canada, Mexico, and the United States has increased by 50 percent since NAFTA took effect, exceeding $621 billion in 2003. Thirty reforms have turned Mexico into an attractive market in its own right. Mexico's gross domestic product has been expanding by more than 3 percent every year since 1989, and exports to the United States have doubled since 1986 to $143 billion in 2003. By institutionalizing the nation's turn to open its markets, the free trade agreement has attracted considerable new foreign investment ($85 billion since NAFTA began). The United States has benefited from Mexico's success. U.S. exports to Mexico ($101.3 billion) surpass those to Japan at $51.6 billion. While Mexico's surplus of $1.3 billion in 1994 had turned to a deficit of $30.0 billion in 2003, these imports have helped Mexico's recovery and will, therefore, strengthen NAFTA in the long term. Furthermore, U.S. imports from Mexico have been shown to have much higher U.S. content than imports from other countries. Cooperation between Mexico and the United States is expanding beyond trade and investment. Among the U.S. industries to benefit are computers, autos and auto parts, and petrochemicals.

Despite U.S. fears of rapid job loss if companies send business south of the border, recent studies have declared the job gain or loss almost a washout. The good news is that free trade will create higher-skilled and better-paying jobs in the United States as a result of growth in exports. As a matter of fact, jobs in U.S. exporting firms tend to pay 10 to 15 percent more than the jobs they have replaced. Losers have been U.S. manufacturers of auto parts, furniture, and household glass; sugar, peanut, and citrus growers; and seafood and vegetable producers. The U.S. Department of Labor has certified 316,000 jobs as threatened or lost due to trade with Mexico and Canada. At the same time, the U.S. economy has added some 20 million jobs in the years since NAFTA. The fact that job losses have been in more heavily unionized sectors has made these losses politically charged.

Outsourcing of lower-skilled jobs is an unstoppable trend for developed economies such as the United States. However, NAFTA has given U.S. firms a way of taking advantage of lower cost labor while still keeping close links to U.S. suppliers. Mexican assembly plants get 82 percent of their parts from U.S. suppliers, while factories in Asia are using only a fraction of that. Without NAFTA, entire industries might be lost to Asia rather than just the labor-intensive portions.

Integration in Latin America. Before the signing of the U.S.-Canada Free Trade Agreement, all the major trading bloc activity had taken place elsewhere in the Americas. However, none of the activity in Latin America has been hemispheric; that is, Central America had its structures, the Caribbean nations had theirs, and South America had its own different forms. However, for reasons both political and economic, these attempts have never fully reached their set objectives. In a dramatic transformation, these nations sought free trade as a salvation from stagnation, inflation, and debt. In response to these developments, Brazil, Argentina, Uruguay, and Paraguay set up a common market called Mercosur (Mercado Commun del Sur). Despite their own economic challenges and disagreements over trade policy, the Mercosur members and the two associate members, Bolivia and Chile, have agreed to economic convergence targets similar to those the EU made as a precursor to the Euro. These are in areas of inflation, public debt, and fiscal deficits. Bolivia, Colombia, Ecuador, Peru, and Venezuela, in turn, have formed the Andean Common Market (ANCOM).

Many Latin nations are realizing that if they do not unite, they will become increasingly marginal in the global market. Their ultimate goal is a free trade zone from Point Barrow, Alaska, to Patagonia under a framework called the Free Trade Area of the Americas (FTAA). The argument is that free trade throughout the Americas would channel investment and technology to Latin nations and give U.S. firms a head start in those markets.

Integration in Asia. While European and North American arrangements have been driven by political will, market forces may force more formal integration on Asian politicians.

European and American markets are significant for the Asian producers, and some type of organization or bloc may be needed to maintain leverage and balance against the two other blocs. Given that much of the Asian trade growth is from intraregional trade, having common understandings and policies will become necessary. Future integration will most likely use the frame of the most established arrangement in the region, the Association of Southeast Asian Nations (ASEAN).

Australia proposed the Asia Pacific Economic Cooperation (APEC) as an annual forum. The proposal calls for ASEAN members to be joined by Australia, New Zealand, Japan, South Korea, Canada, Chile, Mexico, and the United States. Economic integration has also taken place on the Indian subcontinent. Seven nations of the region (India, Pakistan, Bangladesh, Sri Lanka, Nepal, Bhutan, and the Maldives) launched the South Asian Association for Regional Cooperation (SAARC). Cooperation has been limited to relatively noncontroversial areas, such as agriculture and regional development, and has been hampered by political disagreements.

Integration in Africa and the Middle East. Africa's economic groupings range from currency unions among European nations and their former colonies to customs unions between neighboring states. In addition to wanting to liberalize trade among members, African countries want to gain better access to European and North American markets for farm and textile products. Given that most of the countries are too small to negotiate with the other blocs, alliances have been the solution. Sixteen West African nations attempted to create a megamarket large enough to interest investors from the industrialized world and reduce hardship through economic integration.

The objective of the Economic Community of West African States (ECOWAS) was to form a customs union and eventually a common market. Although many of its objectives have not been reached, its combined population of 160 million represents the largest economic entity in sub-Saharan Africa. Other entities in Africa include the Common Market for Eastern and Southern Africa (COMESA); la Communiauté Economiques d'États de l'Afrique or the Economic Community of Central African States (CEEAC); the Southern African Customs Union; the Southern African Development Community (SADC); and some smaller, less globally oriented blocs, such as the Economic Community of the Great Lakes Countries, the Mano River Union, and the East African Community (EAC).

Countries in the Arab world have made some progress in economic integration. The Arab Maghreb Union ties together Algeria, Libya, Mauritania, Morocco, and Tunisia in northern Africa. The Gulf Cooperation Council (GCC) is one of the most powerful of all trade groups. The per capita income of its six member states (Bahrain, Kuwait, Oman, Qatar, Saudi Arabia, and the United Arab Emirates) is well over $15,000. A listing of the major regional trade agreements is provided in Exhibit 7.1.

EXHIBIT 6.1. Major Regional Trade Agreements

AFTA	ASEAN Free Trade Area Brunei, Indonesia, Laos, Malaysia, Myanmar, Philippines, Singapore, Thailand, Vietnam
ANCOM	Andean Common Market Bolivia, Colombia, Ecuador, Peru, Venezuela
APEC	Asia Pacific Economic Cooperation Australia, Brunei, Canada, Chile, Cina, Hong Kong, Indonesia, Japan, Malaysia, Mexico, New Zealand, Papua New Guinea, Peru, Philippines, Russia, Singapore, South Korea, Taiwan, Thailand, Vietnam, United States
CACM	Central American Common Market Costa Rica, El Salvador, Guatemala, Honduras, Nicaragua
CARICOM	Caribbean Community Antigua and Barbuda, Bahamas, Barbados, Belize, Dominica, Grenada, Guyana, Jamaica, Montserrat, St. Kitts-Nevis, St. Lucia, St. Vincent and the Grenadines, Suriname, Trinidad-Tobago
ECOWAS	Economic Community of West African States Benin, Burkina Faso, Cape Verde, Gambia, Ghana, Guinea, Guinea-Bissau, Ivory Coast, Liberia, Mali, Mauritania, Niger, Nigeria, Senegal, Sierra Leone, Togo
EFTA	European Free Trade Association Iceland, Liechtenstein, Norway, Switzerland
EU	European Union Austria, Belgium, Denmark, Finland, France, Germany, Greece, Ireland, Italy, Luxembourg, Netherlands, Portugal, Spain, Sweden, United Kingdom
GCC	Gulf Cooperation Council Bahrain, Kuwait, Oman, Qatar, Saudi Arabia, United Arab Emirates
LAIA	Latin American Integration Association Argentina, Bolivia, Brazil, Chile, Colombia, Cuba, Ecuador, Mexico, Paraguay, Peru, Uruguay, Venezuela
MERCOSUR	Southern Common Market Argentina, Brazil, Paraguay, Uruguay
NAFTA	North American Free Trade Agreement Canada, Mexico, United States
SAARC	South Asian Association for Regional Cooperation Bangladesh, Bhutan, India, Maldives, Nepal, Pakistan, Sri Lanka
SACU	Southern African Customs Union Botswana, Lesotho, Namibia, South Africa, Swaziland

For information, see http://www.aseansec.org; http://www.apec.org; http://www.caricom.org; http://www.eurunion.org; http://www.mercosur.org.uy; and http://www.nafata-sec-alena.org

Economic Integration and the Export Manager

Regional economic integration creates opportunities and potential problems for the exporter. It may have an impact on a company's entry mode by favoring direct investment because one of the basic rationales of integration is to generate favorable conditions for local production and intraregional trade. By design, larger markets are formed to create more opportunity. Because of harmonization efforts, regulations may be standardized, thus positively affecting the exporter.

The exporter must, however, make integration assessments and decisions from four points of view. The first task is to envision the outcome of the change. Change in the competitive landscape can be dramatic if scale opportunities can be exploited in relatively homogeneous demand conditions. This is usually the case for industrial goods, consumer durables (such as cameras and watches), and professional services.

Second, the exporter will then have to develop a strategic response to the new environment to maintain a sustainable long-term competitive advantage. For example, those companies already located in an integrated market should fill in gaps in their product/market portfolios through acquisitions or alliances to create a regional or global company. In many scale industries, such as automobiles or mobile communications, two or three giants may try to dominate blocs in the twenty-first century. Firms with weak positions will have to create alliances for market entry and development with established firms or leave the market altogether if they cannot remain competitive because of new competition.

Third, most changes require reorganization. Authority will have to become more centralized to execute regional programs. In staffing, focus will have to be on individuals who understand the subtleties of consumer behavior across markets and are therefore able to evaluate similarities and differences between and among cultures and markets. In developing systems for the planning and implementation of regional programs, adjustments have to be made to incorporate views throughout the organization. For example, the introduction of the Euro has meant increased coordination in pricing compared to the relative autonomy in price setting enjoyed by country organizations in the past.

Fourth, economic integration creates its own powers and procedures similar to those of the EU commission and its directives. The exporter is not powerless to influence both of them; as a matter of fact, a passive approach may result in competitors gaining an advantage or may put the company at a disadvantage. Often, policymakers rely heavily on the knowledge and experience of the private sector to carry out their work. Influencing change will therefore mean providing industry information, such as test results, to the policy community.

Export Promotion

Many countries provide export assistance to their firms. Key reasons for such assistance are the national need to earn foreign currency, the encouragement of domestic employment, and the increase in domestic economic activity.

Government support can be designed to annul unfair foreign practices, increase market transparency (and therefore contribute to the better functioning of markets), or, in the interest of long-term national competitiveness, help overcome the short-term orientation of firms. Areas where governments typically provide assistance to their exporters are shown in Exhibit 6.2.

The U.S. Department of Commerce provides companies with an impressive array of data on foreign trade and marketing developments. Its Commercial Ser-

EXHIBIT 6.2. Sources of Export Information and Advice

- Information and advisory services for new-to-exporting firms

Production Support
- Production planning and product modification advice for firms that have decided to export

Marketing Support
- Market information
- Market research
- Find customers and representatives (networking)
- Display products at:
  - Trade fairs
  - Exhibitions
  - Trade centers
  - Delegation visit
- Feasibility studies
- Negotiating assistance

Finance and Guarantees
- Export credit guarantees against:
  - Political risks
  - Commercial risks
- Direct loans
- Interest subsidies
- Rediscounting
- Currency exchange permits
- Insurance
- Tax incentives
- Subsidies

SOURCE: Lisa A. Elvey, "Export Promotion and Assistance: A Comparative Analysis." International Perspectives on Trade Promotion and Assistance. Eds. S. Tamer Cavusgil and Michael Czinkota. Quorum Books: Westport, CT, 1990.

vice provides U.S. businesses with information and market assistance. Efforts are made to coordinate the activities of diverse federal agencies. A national network of export assistance centers has been created, capable of providing one-stop shops for exporters in search of export counseling and financial assistance. In addition, an official interagency advocacy network was created that helps U.S. companies win overseas contracts for large government purchases abroad. A variety of agencies have formed the Trade Promotion Coordination Committee in order to continue to improve services to U.S. exporters. A listing of these agencies together with their Web sites is provided in the appendix to this chapter, so that readers can obtain the most up-to-date information about trade policy changes and export assistance.

A new focus has come about in the area of export financing. Policymakers have increasingly recognized that U.S. business may be placed at a disadvantage if it cannot meet the subsidized financing rates of foreign suppliers. The Export-Import Bank of the United States, charged with the new mission of aggressively meeting foreign export-financing conditions, in recent years has offered mixed aid credits. These take the form of loans composed partially of commercial interest rates and partially of highly subsidized developmental aid interest rates. The bank has also launched a major effort to reach out to smaller-sized businesses and assist in their export success.

Tax legislation that once inhibited the employment of Americans by U.S. firms abroad is now more favorable to U.S. firms. In the past, U.S. nationals living abroad were fully subject to U.S. federal taxation. Because the cost of living abroad can often be quite high—rent for a small apartment can easily approach the range of $6,000-plus per month—this tax structure often imposed a significant burden on U.S. citizens abroad and kept U.S. companies from sending their employees abroad. However, now the tax code allows up to $80,000 (in 2002) to remain tax-free. Americans breathe easier and in their work they may specify the use of U.S. products and thus enhance the competitive opportunities of U.S. firms. One other U.S. export promotion development was the passage of the Export Trading Company Act. Intended to be the U.S. response to Japanese sogoshoshas (international trading firms), this legislation permits firms to work together to form export consortiums. The basic idea was to provide the foreign buyer with a one-stop shopping center in which a group of U.S. firms could offer a variety of complementary and competitive products. It exempts U.S. firms from current antitrust statutes and permits banks to cooperate in the formation of these ventures through direct capital participation and the financing of trading activities. So far, it appears that the legislation may not have provided sufficient incentive for banks, export service firms, or exporters to participate. Banks simply may find domestic profit margins to be more attractive and safe; export service firms may be too small; and exporters themselves may be too independent to participate in such consortia.

Home Country Political and Legal Environment

Exporters cannot afford to ignore home country policies and regulations. Many laws and regulations may not be designed specifically to address export transactions, yet they can have a major impact on a firm's opportunities abroad. The cost of domestic safety regulations may significantly affect the pricing policies of firms in their export marketing efforts. For example, U.S. legislation that created the Environmental Superfund required payment by chemical firms based on their production volume, regardless of whether the production is sold domestically or internationally. As a result, these firms are at a disadvantage internationally when exporting their commodity-type products because they must compete against foreign firms that are not required to make such a payment in their home countries and therefore have a cost advantage.

Governments usually provide general support for the export marketing efforts of the country's firms. For example, a government may work to reduce trade barriers or to increase trade opportunities through bilateral and multilateral negotiations. Such actions will affect individual firms to the extent that they improve the international climate for free trade.

Often, however, governments also have specific rules and regulations restricting export trade. Such regulations are frequently political in nature and are based on the fact that governments believe commerce to be only one objective among many, such as foreign policy and national security. Four main areas of governmental activities are of major concern to the exporter here: export controls, import controls, embargoes or trade sanctions, and the regulation of international business behavior. The terms *trade sanctions* and *embargoes* as used here refer to governmental actions that distort the free flow of trade in goods, services, or ideas for decidedly political reasons.

Export Controls

Many nations have export control systems, which are designed to deny or at least delay the acquisition of strategically important goods by adversaries. Most of these systems make controls the exception, rather than the rule, with exports considered to be independent of foreign policy. The United States, however, differs substantially from this perspective in that exports are considered to be a privilege rather than a right, and exporting is seen as an extension of foreign policy.

The legal basis for export controls varies across nations. For example, in Germany armament exports are covered in the so-called War Weapons List, which is

Determinants for Export Controls

- National Security
- Foreign Policy
- Short Supply
- Nuclear Nonproliferation

Decision Steps in the Export Licensing Process

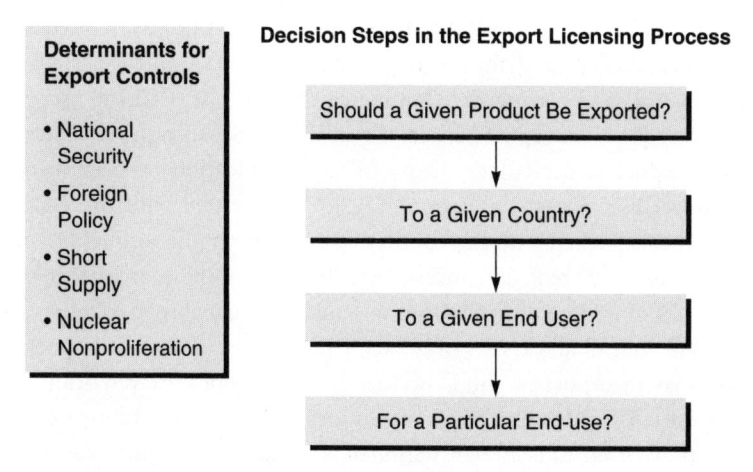

Should a Given Product Be Exported?
↓
To a Given Country?
↓
To a Given End User?
↓
For a Particular End-use?

EXHIBIT 6.3. The U.S. Export Control System

a part of the War Weapons Control Law. The German Export List covers the exports of other goods. The Joint List of the European Union then controls dual-use items, which are goods useful for both military and civilian purposes.

Most products exported from the United States do *not* require specific approval from the U.S. government. Most export transactions involved products that move under NLR conditions, which stand for "no license required." NLR provides blanket permission to export. Products can be freely shipped to most trading partners provided that neither the end user nor the end use involved are considered sensitive.

The majority of products that require a license are listed in the Commerce Control List (CCL), administered by the Department of Commerce, or the U.S. Munitions List (USML), administered by the State Department. The CCL includes products for export and re-export that have commercial use but also may have possible military applications. These are called "dual use" products and are, therefore, subject to export controls. Products listed in the USML include defense products, services, and related technologies. The U.S. government controls exports of these products and evaluates each request for export on a case-by-case basis. The U.S. also restricts exports to several countries, but exports may be permitted under export licenses. Each license request is considered on the basis of the product to be exported, the country of destination, the end-user, and the end-use.[1] Control determinants and the steps in the decision process are summarized in Exhibit 6.3.

---

[1] Export America Technical Advice Article Archive, www.bxa.doc.gov/factsheet, accessed 10/30/2003.

It is the exporter's responsibility to obtain an export license, if needed. The exporter must determine if their product fits an Export Control Classification Number (ECCN) and consult the Commerce Control List (CCL) to ascertain if the product requires an export license. If that is the case, then the exporter must request the export license. After an export license application has been filed, government specialists match the commodity to be exported with the CCL. The product is then matched with the country of destination, the recipient company and the end use. If there is no concern regarding any of these, an export license, which consists of written authorization to send a product abroad, is issued.

U.S. laws control all exports of goods, services, and ideas. It is important to note here that an export of goods occurs whenever goods are physically transferred from the United States. Services and ideas, however, are deemed exported whenever transferred to a foreign national, regardless of location. Permitting a foreign national from a controlled country to have access to a highly sensitive computer program in the United States is, therefore, considered an export activity.

A New Environment for Export Controls

The attacks of terrorists have again highlighted the importance of export controls. Restricting the flow of materials can be crucial in avoiding the development of weapons of mass destruction; restricting technology can limit the ability to target missiles; and restricting the flow of funds can inhibit funding of terrorist training.

Nowadays, quite a number of countries want chemical and nuclear weapons and the technology to make use of them. Major change has also resulted from the increased foreign availability of high-technology products. The broad availability makes any denial of such products more difficult to enforce. If a nation does control the exports of widely available products, it imposes a major competitive burden on its firms.

Increasingly, goods are dual-use, meaning that they are commercial products that have potential military applications. Examples are exported trucks that can be used to transport troops or the exports of supplies to a pesticide factory that, some years later, is revealed to be a poison gas factory. It is difficult enough to define weapons clearly. It is even more problematic to achieve consensus among nations regarding dual-use goods.

Conflicts can result from the desire of nations to safeguard their own economic interests. Due to different industrial structures, these interests vary across nations. For example, Germany, with a strong world market position in machine tools, motors, and chemical raw materials, will think differently about controls than a country such as the United States, which sees computers as an area of competitive advantage.

The terrorist attacks on Washington, D.C. and New York have led to a renewal of international collaboration in export control. The practicality and sensibility of policies are being scrutinized in light of the dangers of proliferation and international terrorism. The role of export controls and their sophistication can therefore be expected to increase.

Embargoes and Sanctions

The terms *trade sanctions* and *embargoes* as used here refer to governmental actions that distort the free flow of trade in goods, services, or ideas for decidedly adversarial and political, rather than strictly economic, purposes. The intent is to bring commercial interchange to a complete halt. Unilateral imposition of sanctions, however, tends to have major negative effects on the firms in the country that is exercising sanctions.

In the U.S., the Treasury Department is the agency responsible for implementing and regulating the economic and trade sanctions. The exporter is often caught in this political Web and loses business as a result. Frequently, firms try to anticipate sanctions based on their evaluations of the international political climate. Even when substantial precautions are taken, firms may still suffer substantial losses due to contract cancellations. However, this is the price of one's government's support for an open global trading and investing environment.

Regulation of International Business Behavior

Home countries may implement special laws and regulations to ensure that the international business behavior of their firms is conducted within the legal, moral, and ethical boundaries considered appropriate. The definition of appropriateness may vary from country to country and from government to government. Therefore, such regulations, their enforcement, and their impact on firms can differ substantially among nations.

Several major areas in which nations attempt to govern the export marketing activities of its firms are boycotts, whereby firms refuse to do business with someone, often for political reasons; antitrust measures, wherein firms are seen as restricting competition; and corruption, which occurs when firms obtain contracts with bribes rather than through performance. Arab nations, for example, have developed a blacklist of companies that deal with Israel. Even though enforcement of the blacklisting has decreased, some Arab customers still demand from their suppliers assurances that the source of the products purchased is not Israel and that the company does not do any business with Israel. The goal of these actions clearly is to impose a boycott on business with Israel. The U.S. government in turn, because of U.S. political ties to Israel, has adopted a variety of laws to prevent U.S. firms from complying with the Arab boycott. These laws include a provision to deny foreign income tax benefits to companies that comply with the boycott and also require notification of the U.S. government in case any boycott requests are received. U.S. firms that comply with the boycott are subject to heavy fines and denial of export privileges.

The second area of regulatory activity affecting export marketing efforts of firms is antitrust law. These can apply to the international operations of firms as well as to domestic business. In the European Union, for example, the commission watches closely when any firm buys an overseas company, engages in a joint venture with a foreign firm, or makes an agreement with a competing firm. The commission evaluates the effect these activities will have on competition and has the right to disapprove such transactions.

A third area in which some governments regulate export marketing actions concerns bribery and corruption. U.S. laws against bribery and corruption affect U.S. firms operating overseas. In many countries, payments or favors are a way of life, and "a greasing of the wheels" is expected in return for government services. In the past, many companies doing business internationally routinely paid bribes or did favors for foreign officials in order to gain contracts. Based on the argument, contracts won through bribes do not reflect competitive market activity. The Foreign Corrupt Practices Act was passed in the U.S., making it a crime for U.S. firms to bribe a foreign official to obtain business.

The problem is one of the ethics versus practical needs and also, to some extent, of the amounts involved. For example, it may be difficult to draw the line between providing a generous tip and paying a bribe in order to speed up a business transaction. Many business exporters argue that the United States should not apply its moral principles to other societies and cultures in which bribery and corruption are endemic. If they are to compete internationally, these exporters argue, they must be free to use the most common methods of competition in the host country. Particularly in industries that face limited or even shrinking markets, such stiff competition forces firms to find any edge possible to obtain a contract.

On the other hand, applying different standards to management and firms, depending on whether they do business abroad or domestically, is difficult to envision. Also, bribes may open the way internationally—including compliance with foreign expectations—to outright bribery and corruption. To assist the exporter in this task, revisions were made in the 1988 Trade Act to clarify the applicability of the Foreign Corrupt Practices legislation. These revisions clarify when an exporter is expected to know about violation of the act, and a distinction is drawn between the facilitation of routine governmental actions and governmental policy decisions. Routine actions concern issues, such as obtaining permits and licenses, processing governmental papers, such as visas and work orders, providing mail and phone service, and loading and unloading cargo.

Policy decisions refer mainly to situations in which obtaining or retaining contracts is at stake. One researcher differentiates between functional lubrication and individual greed. With regard to functional lubrication, he reports the "express fee" charged in many countries, which has several characteristics: the amount is small, it is standardized, and it does not stay in the hands of the official who receives it but is passed on to others involved in the processing of the documents. The express service is available to anyone, with few exceptions. By contrast, in the process driven by "individual greed," the amount depends on the individual official and is for the official's own personal use. Although the facilitation of routine actions is not prohibited, the illegal influencing of policy decisions can result in the imposition of severe fines and penalties.

Key underlying dimensions of all these issues are export and corporate virtue, vision, and veracity. Unless the world can believe in what exporters say they do, and trust the global activities of exporters, it will be hard, if not impossible, to forge a global commitment between those doing the marketing and the ones being marketed to. It is, therefore, of vital interest to exporters to ensure that corruption, bribery, lack of transparency, and the misleading of consumers, investors, and employees are systematically relegated to the history books where they belong. It will be the extent to which openness, responsiveness, long-term thinking, and truthfulness rule that will determine the degree of freedom for exporters.

Host Country Political and Legal Environment

The host country's legal and political environment affects the export marketing operations of firms in a variety of ways. The exporter must understand the country in which the firm operates so that he or she is able to work within the existing parameters and can anticipate and plan for changes that may occur. Firms usually prefer to conduct business in a country with a stable and friendly government, but such governments are not always easy to find. Exporters must therefore continually monitor the government, its policies, and its stability to determine the potential for political change that could adversely affect corporate operations.

There is political risk in every nation, but the range of risks varies widely from country to country. Political risk is defined as the risk of loss when trading with or investing in a given country caused by changes in a country's political structure or policies, such as tax laws, tariffs, expropriation of assets, or

EXHIBIT 6.4. Exposure to Political Risk

Contingencies May Include:	Loss May Be the Result of:	
	The actions of legitimate government authorities	Events caused by factors outside the control of government
The involuntary loss of control over specific assets without adequate compensation	• Total or partial expropriation • Forced divestiture • Confiscation • Cancellation or unfair calling of performance bonds	• War • Revolution • Terrorism • Strikes • Extortion
A reduction in the value of a stream of benefits expected from the foreign-controlled affiliate	• Nonapplicability of "national treatment" • Restriction in access to financial, labor, or material markets • Controls on prices, outputs, or activities • Currency and remittance restrictions • Value-added and export performance requirements	• Nationalistic buyers or suppliers • Threats and disruption to operations by hostile groups • Externally induced financial constraints • Externally imposed limits on imports or exports

SOURCE: José de la Torre and David H. Neckar, "Forecasting Political Risks for International Operations," in H. Vernon-Wortzel and L. Wortzel, *Global Strategic Management: The Essentials*, 2nd ed. (New York: John Wiley and Sons, 1990), 195. Copyright © 1990 John Wiley and Sons. Reprinted by permission of John Wiley and Sons, Inc.

restriction in repatriation of profits. For example, a company may suffer from such loss in the case of tightened foreign exchange availability, or from increased credit risk if the government changes policies to make it difficult for the company to pay creditors. In general, political risk is lowest in countries that have a history of stability and consistency.

Political risk tends to be highest in nations that do not have this sort of history. Three major types of political risk can be encountered: ownership risk, which exposes property and life; operating risk, which refers to interference with the ongoing operations of a firm; and transfer risk, which is mainly encountered when attempts are made to shift funds between countries. Political risk can be the result of government action, but it can also be outside the control of government. The types of risks that are most likely to affect exporters are operating and transfer risks. The type of actions and their effects are classified in Exhibit 6.4.

A major political risk in many countries involves conflict and violent change. An exporter will want to think twice before conducting business in a country in which the likelihood of such change is high. When internal political conflict occurs, the economic climate deteriorates, and importing firms may be precluded from or have difficulty in obtaining foreign exchange to pay for their purchases.

This can cause a disruption in business activities, sometimes temporary, sometimes long term, but always unprofitable. Clearly the exporter should carefully monitor these types of activities in countries where they are likely to occur.

The exporter must also worry about price controls. In many countries, domestic political pressures can force governments to control the prices of imported products or services, particularly in sectors that are considered to be highly sensitive from a political perspective, such as food or health care. If a foreign firm is involved in these areas, it is a vulnerable target of price controls because the government can play on its people's nationalistic tendencies to enforce the controls. Particularly in countries that suffer from high inflation and frequent devaluations, the exporter may be forced to choose between absorbing price differentials or getting out of the market.

Exporters face political and economic risk whenever they conduct business overseas, but there may be ways to lessen the risk. Obviously, if a new government that is dedicated to the removal of all foreign influences comes into power, a firm can do little. In less extreme cases, however, exporters can take actions to reduce the risk if they understand the root causes of the host country policies. Most important is the understanding and appreciation of the country's history, political background, and culture before making a long-term investment decision. Also, a high degree of sensitivity by a firm and its employees to country-specific approaches and concerns are important dimensions that help a firm to blend into the local landscape rather than stand out as a foreign object.

In this discussion of the political environment, laws have been mentioned only to the extent that they appear to be the direct result of political changes. However, each nation has laws regarding marketing, and the exporter must understand their effects on the firm's efforts.

Legal Differences and Restraints

Countries differ in their laws as well as in their use of the laws. From an international business perspective the two major legal systems worldwide can be categorized into common law and code law. Common law is based on tradition and depends less on written statutes and codes than on precedent and custom. Common law originated in England and is the system of law found today in the United States.

Code law is based on a comprehensive set of written statutes. Countries with code law try to spell out all possible legal rules explicitly. Code law is based on Roman law and is found in the majority of the nations of the world. In general, countries with the code law system have much more rigid laws than those with the common law system. In the latter, courts adopt precedents and customs to fit the cases, allowing the exporter a better idea of the basic judgment likely to be rendered in new situations. Although widely different in theory, the practical differences between code law and common law and their impact on the exporter are often relatively small. For example, many common law countries, including the United States, have adopted commercial codes to govern the conduct of business.

Host countries may adopt a number of laws that affect exports. To begin with, there can be laws affecting the entry of goods, such as tariffs and quotas. Also in this category are antidumping laws, which prohibit below-cost sales of products, and laws that require export and import licensing. In addition, many countries have health and safety standards that may, by design or by accident, restrict the entry of foreign goods. Japan, for example, has particularly strict health standards that affect the import of pharmaceuticals. Rather than accepting test results from other nations, the Japanese government insists on conducting its own tests, which are time consuming and costly. It claims that these tests are necessary to take into account Japanese peculiarities. Yet some importers and their governments see these practices as thinly veiled protectionist barriers.

Other laws may be designed to protect domestic industries and reduce imports. For example, Russia charges a 20 percent value-added tax on most imported goods; assesses high excise taxes on goods such as cigarettes, automobiles, and alcoholic beverages; and provides a burdensome import licensing and quotas regime for alcohol and products containing alcohol to depress Russian demand for imports. Even when no laws exist, the exporter may be hampered by regulations. For example, in many countries, governments require a firm to join the local chamber of commerce or become a member of the national trade association. These institutions, in turn, may have internal regulations that set standards for the conduct of business and may be seen as quite confining to the exporter.

Finally, the enforcement of laws may have a different effect on national and on foreign exporters. For example, the simple requirement that an executive has to stay in a country until a business conflict is resolved may be a major burden for the exporter.

Influencing Politics and Laws

To succeed in a market, the exporter must be able to deal with the intricacies of national politics and laws. Although a full understanding of another country's legal and political system will rarely be possible, the firm must be aware of the importance of this system and will work with people who do understand how to operate within it.

Many areas of politics and law are not immutable. Viewpoints can be modified or even reversed, and new laws can supersede old ones. Therefore, existing political and legal restraints do not always need to be accepted. To achieve change, however, there must be some impetus for it, such as the clamors of a constituency. Otherwise, systemic inertia is likely to allow the status quo to prevail.

The exporter has various options. One approach may be to simply ignore prevailing rules and expect to get away with it. Pursuing this option is a high-risk strategy because of the possibility of objection and even prosecution. A second, traditional option is to provide input to trade negotiators and expect any problem areas to be resolved in multilateral negotiations. The drawback to this option is, of course, the quite time-consuming process involved.

A third option involves the development of coalitions or constituencies that can motivate legislators and politicians to consider and ultimately implement change. This option can be pursued in various ways. One direction can be the recasting or redefinition of issues. Often, specific terminology leads to conditioned though inappropriate responses. For example, before China's accession to the World Trade Organization in 2001, the country's trade status with the United States was highly controversial for many years. The U.S. Congress had to decide annually whether to grant "Most Favored Nation" (MFN) status to China. The debate on this decision was always very contentious and acerbic and was often framed around the question why China deserved to be treated the "most favored way." Lost in the debate was the fact that the term "most favored" was simply taken from WTO terminology and indicated only that trade with China would be treated like that with any other country. Only in late 1999 was the terminology changed from MFN to NTR, or "normal trade relations." Even though there was still considerable debate regarding China, the controversy about special treatment had been eliminated.

Beyond terminology, exporters can also highlight the direct linkages and their cost and benefit to legislators and politicians. For example, the exporter can explain the employment and economic effects of certain laws and regulations and demonstrate the benefits of change. Including indirect linkages can enlarge the picture. Suppliers, customers, and distributors can be asked to participate in delineating to decision makers the benefit of change.

Many countries and companies have been effective in their lobbying in the United States. The number of U.S. lobbyists working on behalf of foreign entities is estimated to be in the thousands. As an example, Brazil has held on average nearly a dozen contracts per year with U.S. firms covering trade issues. Brazilian citrus exporters and computer manufacturers have hired U.S. legal and public relations firms to provide them with information on relevant U.S. legislative activity. U.S. firms also have representation in Washington, DC, as well as state capitols. Often, however, these same U.S. companies are much less adept at ensuring proper representation abroad.

Although representation of the firm's interests to government decision makers and legislators is entirely appropriate, the exporter must also consider any potential side-effects. Major questions can be raised if such representation becomes very strong. In such instances, short-term gains may be far outweighed by long-term negative repercussions if the exporter is perceived as exerting too much political influence

The International Environment

In addition to the politics and laws of both the home and the host countries, the exporter must consider the overall international political and legal environment. Relations between countries can have a profound impact on firms trying to do business internationally.

International Politics. The effect of politics on export marketing is determined by both the bilateral political relations between home and host countries and the multilateral agreements governing the relations among groups of countries.

The government-to-government relationship can have a profound effect, particularly if it becomes hostile. The premier example is perhaps U.S.-Iranian relations following the 1979 Iranian revolution. Although the internal political and legal changes in the aftermath of that revolution would certainly have affected export marketing in Iran, the deterioration in U.S.-Iranian political relations that resulted from the revolution had a significant impact. U.S. firms were injured not only by physical damage caused by the violence but also by the anti-American feelings of the Iranian people and their government. The clashes between the two governments completely destroyed any business relationships, regardless of corporate feelings or agreements on either side. It took more than 20 years to reopen governmental dialogue between the two countries.

The Helms-Burton Act presented a more recent example of government-to-government conflict. Passed in response to the shooting down of two unarmed small planes by the Cuban Air Force, this U.S. legislation granted individuals the right to sue, in U.S. courts, subsidiaries of those foreign firms that had invested in properties confiscated by the Cuban government in the 1960s. In addition, managers of these firms were denied entry into the United States. Many U.S. trading partners strongly disagreed with this legislation. In response, Canada proposed suing U.S. firms that had invested in properties taken from royalists in 1776, and the European Union threatened to permit European firms to counter sue subsidiaries of U.S. firms in Europe and to deny entry permits to U.S. executives.

But international political relations do not always have harmful effects on international exporters. If bilateral political relations between countries improve, business can benefit. A good example is the recasting of the political map of Europe. Countries such as Hungary, Poland, and the Czech Republic that decades ago were members of the Soviet bloc are now full-fledged members of the European Union. Activities such as selling computers, which would have been considered treasonous then, are now routine. The exporter needs to be aware of political currents worldwide and attempt to anticipate changes in the international political environment, good or bad, so that his or her firm can plan for them.

International Law. International law plays an important role in the conduct of international business. Although no enforceable body of international law exists, certain treaties and agreements respected by a number of countries profoundly influence international business operations. The World Trade Organization (WTO) defines internationally acceptable economic practices for its member nations. Although it does not directly affect individual firms, it does influence them indirectly by providing a more stable and predictable international market environment.

A number of efforts have been made to simplify the legal aspects of business procedures. Firms wanting to patent their products in the past had to register them separately in each country in order to have protection. In response to the chaos and expense of such procedures, several multilateral simplification efforts have been undertaken. European countries have been at the forefront of such efforts with the European Patent Convention and the Community Patent Convention.

Similar efforts have been undertaken with regard to trademarks so that firms can benefit from various multilateral agreements. The two major international conventions on trademarks are the International Convention for the Protection of Industrial Property and the Madrid Arrangement for International Registration of Trademarks. Several regional conventions include the Inter-American Convention for Trademark Protection and a similar agreement in French West Africa. In addition to multilateral agreements, bilateral treaties and conventions affect firms. The United States, for example, has signed bilateral treaties of friendship, commerce, and navigation (FCN) with a wide variety of countries. These agreements generally define the rights of U.S. firms doing business in the host country. They normally guarantee that the host country will treat the U.S. firms in the same manner in which domestic firms are treated. Although these treaties provide for some stability, they can be canceled when relationships worsen.

Other Aspects of the Locus of Control. International agreements are also critical when it comes to jurisdictional disputes. If a conflict occurs between contracting parties in two different countries, a question arises concerning which country's laws will be followed. Sometimes the contract will contain a jurisdictional clause, which settles the matter. If not, the parties to the dispute can follow either the laws of the country in which the agreement was made or those of the country in which the contract will have to be fulfilled. Deciding on the laws to be followed and the location to settle the dispute are two different decisions. As a result, a dispute between a U.S. exporter and a French importer could be resolved in Paris with the resolution based on New York State law.

The parties to a business transaction can also choose either arbitration or litigation. Litigation is usually avoided for several reasons. It often involves extensive delays and is very costly. In addition, firms may fear discrimination in foreign countries. Companies therefore tend to prefer conciliation and arbitration because these processes result in much quicker decisions.

Arbitration. International trade disputes are not matters of law but of fact. Trade disputes arise in the natural course of business activities, and many differences may be ultimately decided through court action. In trade disputes, however, litigation may not be the best way to solve a dispute because it is time-consuming and expensive. The exporter may find that obtaining relief under the law requires conducting litigation in the importer's country. Language barriers, distance, and lack of familiarity with foreign laws are some factors that can contribute to an expensive and time-consuming process. To avoid such problems, the exporter can rely on voluntary settlement of disputes through arbitration. Any dispute arising from an international transaction may be subject to arbitration, that is, a person chosen by the parties or by an appointed statutory authority can settle a dispute or case in controversy.

Arbitration is increasingly playing an important role in trade disputes and for that purpose, the American Arbitration Association has developed standard arbitration clauses for inclusion in written contracts in order to settle disputes effectively and at a low cost. The principal arbitration agency in the United States is the American Arbitration Association. It maintains a nationwide system of arbitration tribunals and panels, as well as reciprocal agreements with foreign organizations, such as the International Chamber of Commerce in Paris and many chambers of commerce worldwide.

Arbitration can give the exporter a cheaper way to settle disputes under principles that are understood by the litigants. Enforcing arbitrational awards, however, may sometimes be difficult. In order to help solve these problems, forty countries signed the United Nations Convention of the Recognition and Enforcement of Foreign Arbitrational Awards, which was initially certified by 45 countries. This agreement binds the signatory countries to respect the arbitrational awards, simplifying the requirement of recognition and enforcement of arbitrational awards.[2]

---

[2] Marta Ortiz-Buonafina, *Profitable Export Marketing, A Strategy for U.S. Business* (1992), Washington, D.C., University Press of America, pp.57–58.

Summary

To improve the trade environment and expand trade activities, the WTO, the IMF, and the World Bank were founded. In addition, several economic blocs such as the EU, NAFTA, and Mercosur were formed. Many of these organizations have been very successful in their mission, yet new realities of the trade environment demand new types of action.

The political and legal environment in the home country, the environment in the host country, and the laws and agreements governing relationships among nations are all important to the exporter. Compliance with them is mandatory in order to do business abroad successfully. Such laws can control exports and imports both directly and indirectly and can also regulate the international business behavior of firms, particularly in the areas of boycotts, antitrust, corruption, and ethics.

To avoid the problems that can result from changes in the political and legal environment, the exporter must anticipate changes and develop strategies for coping with them. Whenever possible, the manager must avoid being taken by surprise and thus not let events control business decisions.

In the final analysis, a firm conducting business internationally is subject to the vagaries of political and legal changes and, if not attuned to them, can lose business as a result. The best the manager can do is to be aware of political influences and laws and strive to adapt to them as far as possible.

Appendix A. The Sales Contract

After negotiating the export order, a legally enforceable agreement or sales contract may be required before an export transaction can begin. This situation arises when the product is complex and product specifications, delivery time, and size of the transaction require specific obligations from both buyer and seller.

The exporter should carefully prepare the sales contract that meets negotiated conditions. The following considerations should be included in drawing up a sales contract:

- The Proposal. To avoid possible communication problems, the contract should be clear, and the product or service being sold should be described in direct and concise language. The use of technological jargon should be limited, unless a glossary of terms is included in the sales contract. It is important to make sure that the buyer has a clear understanding of what the sales contract involves. In order to establish each party's responsibility, a listing of what the seller will provide under the resulting contract and the buyer's corresponding responsibilities should be provided.

- Terms of the Contract. In international sales, it is customary to use fixed price contracts. Under a fixed contract, the parties agree at the time of the offering the contract price of the goods and services to be rendered, regardless of the actual cost to the seller at the time of performing the contract. Consequently the seller should be very careful to specify the time period for which the fixed prices are valid, as well as delivery terms (FOB, CIF, etc.).
- Payment. The seller of the goods must establish if the foreign buyer has the financial assets in the seller's currency to pay for the goods, unless otherwise stipulated. Payment arrangement should be outlined so that no question arises as to the actions that must taken in order to entitle the seller to payment by the buyer.
- Choice of Law. There is no universal set of laws regulating international trade *and* contracts today. It is, therefore, very important for the exporter to specify the governing law that would apply in constructing the rights and obligations of the parties. Exporters, when possible, should select their own state law as the controlling law of the parties. This will greatly facilitate handling any legal problems arising from breach of contract.
- Arbitration. An export sales contract should include a provision calling for the settlement of all disputes under the Rules of Conciliation and Arbitration of the International Chamber of Commerce. Arbitration has, for the most part, proven itself a relatively economical and efficient means of resolving differences arising between parties to an international sales contract.[3]

Appendix B. Members of the U.S. Trade Promotion Coordination Committee (TPCC)

Information on both individual TPCC agency programs and the National Export Strategy is available on the Internet. The TPCC's official repository of export promotion information is the National DataBank available from STAT-USA. Information about individual TPCC agency programs can be obtained by using the following Internet addresses:

- Agency for International Development (http://www.usaid.gov)
- Council of Economics Advisors (http://www.whitehouse gov/cea)
- Department of Agriculture (http://www.fas.usda.gov)
- Department of Commerce (http://www.ita.doc.gov)

---

[3] Op. Cit, pp. 176–177.

- Department of Defense (http://www.defenselink.mil)
- Department of Energy (http://www.osti.ov)
- Department of Interior (http://www.doi.gov)
- Department of Labor (http://www.dol.gov)
- Department of State (http://www.state.gov)
- Department of Transportation (http://www.dot.gov)
- Department of the Treasury (http://www.ustreas.gov)
- Environmental Protection Agency (http://www.epa.gov)
- Export-Import Bank of the United States (http://www.exim.gov)
- National Trade Data Bank (http://www.stat-usa.gov)
- National Economic Council (http://www.whitehouse.gov/nec)
- Office of Management and Budget (http://www.whitehouse.gov/omb/circulars)
- Office of the U.S. Trade Representative (http://www.ustr.gov)
- Overseas Private Investment Corporation (htttp://www.opic.gov)
- Small Business Administration (http://www.sba.gov)
- U.S. Trade and Development Agency (http://www.tda.gov)

Source: *National Export Strategy,* Fourth Annual Report to the United States Congress, U.S. Government Printing Office, October 1996, p. 54.

CHAPTER 7

Export Market Choice and Development

Market choice and development are an integral part of every successful company's strategic planning process and the fundamental cornerstone of a sound marketing strategy. Many see the global markets as the exclusive realm of large multinational companies with a global reach, but that view is shortsighted. Overlooked is the fact that thousands of smaller-sized firms have been fueling U.S. export growth, which has supported the economy in times of limited domestic growth.

Exporting is one of the many market expansion and growth activities virtually every firm can pursue. Actually, it is similar to looking for new customers in the next town, the next state, or on the other coast. The only difference is that national borders are crossed. And exporting offers opportunity for economies of scale: By expanding its markets to reach and serve customers abroad, a firm can produce more and do so more efficiently. As a result, the firm may achieve lower costs and higher profits both at home and abroad. Export markets are potential sources of new business that cannot be ignored.

This chapter describes some of the growth and profit opportunities that exporting represents to the firm, particularly smaller firms. Issues concerning growth and expansion, market definition, and segmentation that influence export marketing strategy and are closely tied to a firm's export planning process are explored.

Choosing and Developing a Market

The first step in formulating an export marketing strategy involves evaluating opportunities in order to define which market(s) are the most attractive. The process entails matching the firm's products and capabilities with a particular country market. Then the exporter must decide how to develop potential opportunity into a profitable one; that is, decide which strategy best serves the company's interests. When a firm decides to enter exporting reactively, that is, as a result of an unsolicited order from abroad, the choice of the export market is a given. Nevertheless, entering this type of export activity without further examination of the country market is shortsighted. The firm should evaluate the nature of the opportunity with an evaluation of the country's socioeconomic and regulatory environments to determine if, in fact, the unsolicited order is worth pursing as a viable opportunity or a simply one-shot deal.

On the other hand, if the firm decides to enter exporting proactively, it must evaluate market opportunities that are relevant to the firm and its capabilities and offer the proper product-market fit that is both a growth opportunity and profitable to the firm in the long run.

In either case, the exporter should make a country-market choice based on various dimensions of product-market fit. Moreover, the analysis should go beyond the broader country market analysis and into the assessment of specific target markets within the country.

Export Market Potential and Market Growth

When evaluating different target markets, you need to focus on determining how much demand exists for a given product (market potential) given the parameters that define the target market. In other words, you must define the number of consuming units (be they individual consumers, households, business firms, etc.) and purchasing power. Similarly, you also need to evaluate the growth of the particular market, that is, the number of consuming units that can enter the market in the foreseeable future. In order to properly evaluate the market potential of an export market, it is necessary to evaluate such factors as current market size, potential market growth, market accessibility, economic stability, and political climate. A sample checklist for evaluating potential export markets is presented in Exhibit 7.1.

Once the exporter has decided on the country market to serve and the target market potential, then he is in a position to delineate the strategic alternatives that can serve as the basis for a comprehensive and focused export marketing strategy. The strategic planning process allows the exporter to understand what needs to be done in order to serve identified target market segments and further define the type of information needed to develop the export marketing strategy.

The Strategic Planning Process

Given the opportunities and challenges presented by new markets, a firm's decision-makers should engage in strategic planning to match markets with products and other company resources more effectively and efficiently and to strengthen the company's long-term competitive advantage. While the process

EXHIBIT 7.1. Evaluating Export Market Potential

COUNTRY	PRODUCT
Current Market Size:	Population Total GNP Local Production of the Product Import of the Product U.S. Exports of the Product
Market Growth Rate:	Population Total GNP U.S. Export of the Product Domestic Consumption of the Product
Market Accessibility:	Import Duties and Tariffs Number of Sales Representatives available Pricing Methods and Credit Terms Promotional Practices
Economic Stability:	Balance of Payments Foreign currency reserves Availability of U.S. dollars Foreign Exchange Performance in past 6 months
Political Climate:	Non-tariff barriers Favorable attitude towards imports Favorable attitude towards U.S. Political Stability
Geographic Factors:	Distance to country Cultural differences Availability of Transportation Services

SOURCE: Adapted from "Checklist for Evaluating Potential Markets," www.tradeport.org, accessed 3/2/00.

has been summarized as a sequence of steps in Exhibit 12.2, many of the stages can occur simultaneously. Furthermore, feedback as a result of evaluation and control may restart the process at any stage. See Exhibit 7.2.

It has been shown that, for internationally committed exporters, formal strategic planning contributes to both financial performance and nonfinancial objectives. These benefits include raising the efficacy of growth opportunities, cost reduction efforts, and improving product quality and market share performance. Internally, these efforts increase cohesion and improve on understanding different units' points of view.

EXHIBIT 7.2. Export Strategy Formulation

```
            Assessment and Adjustment of Core Strategy
   Market/Competitive Analysis          Internal Analysis
                              ↓
                  Formulation of Global Strategy
   Choice of Competitive Strategy    Choice of Target Countries and
                                     Segments
                              ↓
              Development of Global Marketing Program
                              ↓
                          Implementation
   Organizational Structure              Control
```

The authors appreciate the contributions of Robert M. Grant in the preparation of this figure.

Internal Analysis

Organizational resources determine a company's capacity for establishing and sustaining competitive advantage within export markets. Industrial giants "with deep pockets" may be able to establish a presence in any market they wish, while more thinly capitalized companies may have to move cautiously. Human resources is a similarly important checkpoint when considering market expansion.

This analysis begins with a rigorous assessment of the organization's ability to export to the markets (country or region) under consideration as well as an assessment of the product's readiness to face the new competitive environment. In many cases this means focusing on certain products and leaving others at home. For example, Nokia, the world's largest manufacturer of mobile phones, started its rise in the industry when a decision was made at the company in 1992 to focus on digital cellular phones and to sell off dozens of other product lines (such as personal computers, automotive tires, and toilet tissue). By focusing its efforts on this line, the company was able to bring new products to market quickly, build scale economies into its manufacturing, and concentrate on its customers, thereby communicating a commitment to their needs.

Formulating the Export Marketing Strategy

The first step in the formulation of an export strategy is the choice of competitive strategy to be employed, followed by the choice of country markets to be entered or to be penetrated further.

Choice of competitive strategy. In dealing with export markets, the export manager has three general choices of strategies, as shown in Exhibit 7.3 (1) cost leadership, (2) differentiation, or (3) focus. A focus strategy is defined by its emphasis on a single market segment within which the orientation may be toward either low cost or differentiation. Any one of these strategies can be pursued on a single-market or on a regional basis. Similarly, the exporter may decide to mix and match strategies as a function of market or product dimensions.

In pursuing cost leadership, the exporter offers an identical product or service at a lower cost than the competition. This often means investment in scale economies and strict control of costs, such as overhead, and logistics. Differentiation, whether it is industry-wide or focused on a single market, takes advantage of the exporter's real or perceived uniqueness on elements such as product design or after-sales service. It should be noted, however, that a low-price, low-cost strategy does not imply a commodity situation. Although Japanese, U.S., and European technical standards differ, mobile phone manufacturers like Motorola and Nokia design their products to be as similar as possible to hold down manufacturing costs. As a result, they can all be made on the same production line, allowing the manufacturers to shift rapidly from one model to another to meet changes in demand and customer requirements.

In the case of IKEA, the low-price approach is associated with a clear positioning and unique brand image focused on a clearly defined target market audience of "young people of all ages." Similarly, exporters who opt for high differentiation cannot forget to monitor costs. One common denominator of consumers around the world is their quest for value for their money. With the availability of information increasing and levels of education improving, customers are poised to demand even more of their suppliers.

Most exporters combine high differentiation with cost containment to enter markets and to expand their market shares. Flexible manufacturing systems using

EXHIBIT 7.3. Competitive Strategies

		Source of Competitive Advantage	
		Low Cost	Differentiation
Competitive Scope	Industry-wide	Cost Leadership	Differentiation
	Single Segment	Focus	

SOURCE: Michael Porter, *Competitive Advantage: Creating and Sustaining Superior Performance* (New York: Free Press, 1998), chapter 1.

mostly standard components and total quality management measures that reduce the occurrence of defects are allowing exporters to offer an increasing amount of customized products while at the same time saving on costs.

Export Country-Market Choice

An export strategy does not apply solely to global or regional markets. Every country and every market segment represents critical choices regarding the allocation of a company's resources.

The usual approach in exporting is to start with one country and then move into neighboring areas and then regional areas. Many exporters use multiple levels of regional groupings to follow the organizational structure of the company.

Various portfolio models have been proposed as tools for this analysis. They typically involve two measures—internal strength and external attractiveness. As indicators of internal strength, the following variables have been used: relative market share, product fit, contribution margin, and market presence, which would incorporate the level of support by constituents as well as resources allocated by the company itself. Country attractiveness has been measured using market size, market growth rate, number and type of competitors, and governmental regulation, as well as economic and political stability.

An example of such a matrix is provided in Exhibit 7.4. The 3x3 matrix on country attractiveness and company strength is applied to the European markets. Applying the model to export activities, markets in the invest/grow position will require continued commitment by management in market research and development, investment in distribution and storage facilities, and the training of personnel at the country level. In cases of relative weakness in growing markets, the exporter's position may have to be strengthened (through acquisitions or strategic alliances) or a decision to leave the market may be necessary. It is critical that those involved in the planning process consider potential competitors and their impact on the markets should they enter. For example, rather than license software for their next-generation mobile phones from Microsoft, the largest makers (with a combined market share of 80 percent of the mobile hand-set market) established a software consortium called Symbian to produce software of their own. This will allow the participants to try out many different designs without having to start from scratch every time or be dependent on a potential competitor.

Export Market Growth and Expansion

Like all business executives, exporters need to consider and evaluate different growth and market expansion strategies. One useful tool to help visualize the

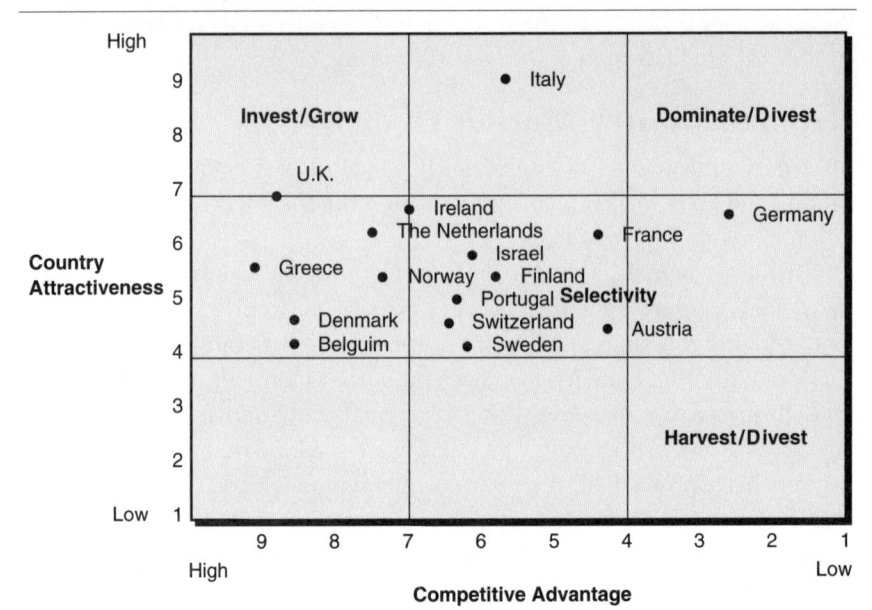

EXHIBIT 7.4. Example of a Market-Portfolio Matrix

```
High
       9                              • Italy
              Invest/Grow                              Dominate/Divest
       8
              U.K.
       7      •
                           • Ireland
       6              • The Netherlands      • Germany
Country          • Greece    • Israel   • France
Attractiveness 5           • Norway • Finland
                           • Portugal  Selectivity
                      • Denmark  • Switzerland  • Austria
       4              • Belguim    • Sweden

       3
                                              Harvest/Divest
       2

Low    1
          9    8    7    6    5    4    3    2    1
         High                                      Low
              Competitive Advantage
```

SOURCE: Adapted from Gilbert D. Harrell and Richard O. Kiefer, "Multinational Market Portfolios in Global Strategy Development," *International Marketing Review* 10 (no. 1, 1993): 60–72.

different way that a firm can achieve growth objectives is the Ansoff Product-Market Growth Matrix (Exhibit 7.5). The vertical axis represents opportunities for growth, either in existing markets or in multiple markets. The horizontal axis shows the allocation of resources either on existing products or through the development or acquisition of new products for new markets. The matrix provides four different fundamental marketing strategies: market penetration, market development, product development, and diversification, which, when applied to export activities, yield the following:

- *Export Market Penetration*: This strategy pursues growth through the sale of one or several existing products in export markets, seeking market segments where product/market fit is very similar to that of the exporting country using product extension. The product is marketed in much the same way as in the domestic market. The strategy is to tap the market share that is consistent with the company's financial resources and capabilities.
- *Export Market Development*: This strategy pursues growth through the diversification of the markets, either through the sale of existing products in more than one export market or seeking product/market fit with product

EXHIBIT 7.5. Export Product-Market Growth Matrix

		EXPORT PRODUCT DEVELOPMENT	
		Existing Products	New Products
EXPORT MARKET DEVELOPMENT	Existing Markets	Market Penetration	Product Development
	New Markets	Market Development	Diversification

SOURCE: Based on I.H. Ansoff, "Strategies for Diversification," *Harvard Business Review*, 30 (September-October 1957): 113–124.

standardization. Product adjustment is followed where cultural variation and regulatory factors makes it necessary.
- *Export Product Development:* This strategy pursues growth through the diversification of product offerings and selling new products in existing markets, developing the strategy that best fits the market. Product adjustments are pursued to tap specific market segments or niche marketing and product standardization is pursued to improve a product's performance or extend the firm's product line. New variations of a product are also pursued.
- *Export Diversification:* This strategy pursues the expansion of market coverage as well as looking for opportunities with new products and new markets. Product development includes standardization as well as product adjustment to pursue new market segments within and across export markets. Standardization is emphasized to tap cross-cultural market segments in global markets.[1]

Concentration versus Diversification

When choosing country markets, a company must make decisions beyond those relating to market attractiveness and company position. A market expansion policy will determine the allocation of resources among various markets. The basic alternatives are *concentration* on a small number of markets and *diversification*, which is characterized by growth in a relatively large number of markets. Expansion strategy is determined by market-, mix-, and company-related factors, listed

---

[1] I.H. Ansoff, "Strategies for Diversification," *Harvard Business Review*, 30 (September-October 1957): 113–124, and M.R. Solomon and E.W Stuart, *Marketing*, Third Edition, New Jersey: Prentice Hall, 2002: 41–42.

EXHIBIT 7.6. Factors Affecting the Choice between Concentration and Diversification Strategies

FACTOR	DIVERSIFICATION	CONCENTRATION
MARKET		
Market growth rate	Low	High
Sales stability	Low	High
Sales response function	Decreasing	Increasing
Extent of constraints	Low	High
MARKETING		
Competitive lead time	Short	Long
Spillover effects	High	Low
Need for product adaptation	Low	High
Need for communication adaptation	Low	High
Economies of scale in distribution	Low	High
Program control requirements	Low	High

SOURCE: Adapted from Igai Ayal and Jehiel Zif, "Marketing Expansion Strategies in Multinational Marketing," *Journal of Marketing* 43 (Spring 1979): 89.

in Exhibit 7.6. Market-related factors determine the attractiveness of the market in the first place. With high and stable growth rates only in certain markets, the firm will likely opt for a concentration strategy, which is often the case for innovative products early in their life cycle. If demand is strong worldwide, as the case may be for consumer goods, diversification may be attractive. If markets respond to marketing efforts at increasing rates, concentration will occur; however, when the cost of market share points in any one market becomes too high, marketers tend to begin looking for diversification opportunities.

The uniqueness of the product offering with respect to competition is also a factor in expansion strategy. If lead time over competition is considerable, the decision to diversify may not seem urgent. Very few products, however, afford such a luxury. Finally, the objectives and policies of the company itself will guide the decision-making on expansion. If extensive interaction is called for with intermediaries and clients, efforts are most likely to be concentrated because of resource constraints.

For the exporter, three factors should determine country selection:

1. The stand-alone attractiveness of a market (e.g., China in consumer products due to its size).
2. Global strategic importance (e.g., Finland in shipbuilding due to its lead in technological development in vessel design).

3. Possible synergies (e.g., entry into Latvia and Lithuania after success in the Estonian market given the market similarities).

Market Segmentation

Effective use of market segmentation—that is, the recognition that groups within markets differ sufficiently to warrant individual marketing mixes—allows exporters to take advantage of the benefits of standardization, such as economies of scale and consistency in positioning, while addressing the unique needs and expectations of a specific target group. This approach means looking at markets on a country basis to identify intramarket segments to tailor export marketing to the specific country markets and on a global, or regional, basis for intermarket segments for the standardization of marketing programs.

The emergence of intermarket segments that span many country markets is already evident in the world marketplace. Global exporters have successfully targeted the teenage segment, which is converging as a result of common tastes in sports and music fueled by their computer literacy and travels abroad. Furthermore, a media revolution is creating a common fabric of attitudes and tastes among teenagers. Today, satellite TV and global network concepts such as MTV are both helping create this segment and providing global exporters access to the teen audience around the world.

For example, Reebok used a global ad campaign to launch its Instapump line of sneakers in the United States, Germany, Japan, and 137 other countries. Given that teenagers around the world are concerned with social issues, particularly environmentalism, Reebok has introduced a new ecological climbing shoe made from recycled and environmentally sensitive materials. Similarly, two other distinct segments have been detected to be ready for a pan-regional approach. One includes trendsetters who are wealthier and better educated and tend to value independence, refuse consumer stereotypes, and appreciate exclusive products. The second one includes Europe's businesspeople, who are well-to-do, regularly travel abroad, and have a taste for luxury goods.

The greatest challenge for the exporter is the choice of an appropriate base for the market segmentation effort. The objective is to arrive at a grouping or groupings that are substantial enough to make economic and strategic sense. Demographic segmentation for consumer and intermediate markets is very useful in more developed countries because population and business statistics are readily available. Psychographic segmentation is still sparsely used due to the sophistication needed to make it helpful. Using a combination of demographic and psychographic techniques, however, may produce more meaningful results.

Bases should be related to environmentally based variables (see Exhibit 7.7). Product-related bases include the degree to which products are culture-based,

EXHIBIT 7.7. Export Segments Based on Cultural Values

SEGMENT	CHARACTERISTICS	GEOGRAPICS
Strivers	More likely to be men; place more emphasis on material and professional goals	One-third of people in developing Asia; one-quarter in Russia and developed Asia
Devouts	22 percent of adults; women more than men; tradition and duty are paramount	Africa, Asia, Middle East; least common in Europe
Altruists	18 percent of adults; larger portion of females; interested in social issues and welfare of society; older	Latin America and Russia
Intimates	15 percent of population; personal relationships and family take precedence	Europeans and North Americans
Fun Seekers	12 percent of population; youngest group	Disproportionately more in developed Asia
Creatives	10 percent worldwide; strong interest in education, knowledge, and technology	Europe and Latin America

SOURCE: Tom Miller, "Global Segments from 'Strivers' to 'Creatives,'" *Marketing News,* July 20, 1998, 11. Reprinted with permission. See also http://www.roper.com.

which stage of the life cycle they occupy, consumption patterns, and attitudes toward product attributes (such as country of origin), as well as consumption infrastructure (for example, telephone lines for modems). However, there can be surprising exceptions. The growth of microwave sales, for example, has been surprising in low-income countries. Microwave ownership has become a matter of status, and buying them more of an emotional issue. Many consumers in these markets also want to make sure they get the same product as available in developed markets, thereby eliminating the need in many cases to develop market-specific products. Adjustments will have to made, however. For example, noticing that, for reasons of status and space, many Asian consumers put their refrigerators in their living rooms, Whirlpool makes refrigerators available in striking colors such as red and blue.

With promotion, customers' values and norms set the baseline for global versus regional vs. local solutions. The significant emphasis on family relationships among many Europeans and North Americans creates a multiregional segment that can be exploited by consumer goods and consumer-services exporters (such as car exporters or telecommunications service providers). On the pricing side, dimensions such as customers' price sensitivity may lead the exporter to go after segments that insist on high quality despite high price in markets where overall purchasing power may be low to ensure global or regional uniformity in the marketing approach. Affordability is a major issue for customers whose buying power may fall short for at least the time being. Offering only one option may exclude potential customers of the future who are not yet part of a targeted segment. Companies like Procter & Gamble and Gillette offer an array of products at different price points to attract them and to keep them as they move up the income scale.

As can be expected, firms go through different stages as they start exporting and, therefore, face different problems that require different strategies. Firms at an export awareness stage—partially interested in the international market—are primarily concerned with operational matters such as information flow and the mechanics of carrying out international business transactions. They understand that a totally new body of knowledge and expertise is needed and try to acquire it. Companies that have already had some exposure to international markets begin to think about tactical marketing issues such as communication and sales effort. Finally, firms that have reached the export adaptation phase are mainly strategy- and service-oriented, which is to say that they worry about longer-range issues such as service delivery and regulatory changes. Utilizing the traditional marketing concept, one can therefore recognize that increased sophistication in international markets translates into increased application of marketing knowledge on the part of the firm. The more they become active in international markets, the more the firm recognizes that strategic planning and a marketing orientation internationally is just as essential as it is in domestic markets.

Summary

The choice of an export strategy policy is a key decision in export marketing planning as it affects resource allocation and it leads to different levels of marketing effort. The market expansion strategy chosen leads to different marketing mix investments such as marketing channels of distribution, choice of market entry, promotional outlays and so on. Issues of available organizational resource, control, and risk tolerance are important determinants in the chosen strategy.

Exporters need to engage is strategic planning to better adjust to the realities of the international marketplace. In formulating an export strategy, the company needs to make choices about market and competitive strategy, concentration or diversification, and segmentation strategies. This may result in the choice of one segment across markets or the exploitation of multiple segments in which the company has a competitive advantage.

CHAPTER 8

Product Adjustments

How different is "different"? That isn't a trick question, although the answer can be tricky—and crucial to a company's success in exporting. Since meeting and satisfying customer needs and expectations is the key to all successful marketing, the exporter needs to identify and define market traits and potential to determine the amount of customization needed to make products appealing to a specific market and still profitable. Even if today's emerging market trends allow this assessment to take place regionally or even globally, both regulations and customer behavior differences require that these costs and revenue potentials and the severity of their impact be taken into consideration. Adapting to new markets should be seen globally, not just locally, but the total impact should be identified as clearly as possible.

This chapter discusses the influence of an array of both external and internal variables in export market product selection and development and shows how the export marketer should adjust the firm's product offering to the marketplace. A delicate balance has to be achieved between the advantages of standardization and those of localization to maximize export performance. The challenge of intellectual property violation will be focused on as a special concern. Exporters must be ready to defend themselves against theft of their ideas and innovations.

Product Variables

The core of a firm's international operations is the product or service. This product or service can be defined as the complex combination of tangible and intangible elements that distinguishes it from the other entities in the marketplace, as shown in Exhibit 8.1. The firm's success depends on how good its product or

Product Adjustments

EXHIBIT 8.1. Elements of a Product

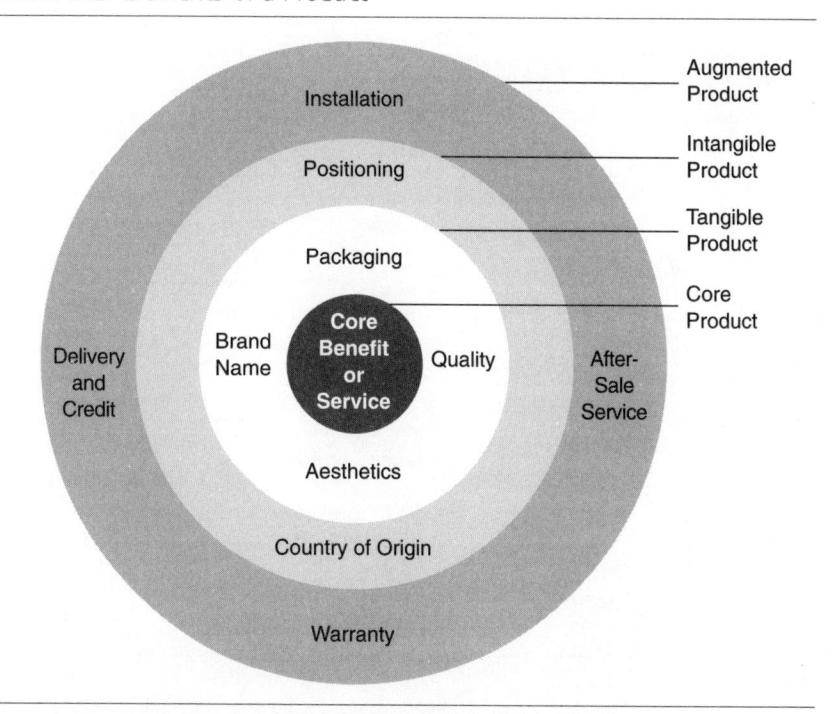

```
                    Installation                        Augmented
                                                        Product

                    Positioning                         Intangible
                                                        Product

                    Packaging                           Tangible
                                                        Product

            Brand       Core                            Core
Delivery    Name      Benefit    Quality    After-      Product
and                     or                  Sale
Credit                Service               Service

                    Aesthetics

                  Country of Origin

                    Warranty
```

SOURCE: Adapted from Philip Kotler, *Marketing Management*, 11th ed., 408. © 2003. Reprinted by permission of Pearson Education, Inc., Upper Saddle River, New Jersey.

service is and on how well the firm is able to differentiate the product from the offerings of competitors.

The extent to which a company needs to adjust a product should be determined by market research and feedback from buyers and/ or intermediaries abroad. To enter a market successfully, the exporter must be prepared to develop the proper product/market fit to conform to the market characteristics and the company's capabilities. Exhibit 8.2 provides an overview of each product element indicating the adjustment issues that may arise as well as relative cost. The bottom line in the decision to adjust or not is the actual cost of the adaptation versus market size and profit potential; in other words, "is it worth it?" The exporter must evaluate all costs, direct and indirect, involved in product adjustment. It may be a simple translation of an instruction manual to a complete re-engineering, from a very low cost to a very high one. Moreover, there are many types and degrees of adjustments that need to be considered in order to develop the proper product/market fit. The exporter must carefully evaluate the cost-profit tradeoff in terms of product line and market potential issues.

EXHIBIT 8.2. Elements of a Product: Adjustment Issues

ELEMENTS	COMPONENTS	ADJUSTMENT ISSUE	RELATIVE COSTS
Core Product	Basic Benefits	Same primary benefit or "customized" benefits?	N to H
	Physical Product	Re-engineering required?	M to VH
Tangible Product	Features	Decrease or Increase?	L to H
	Quality	Downgrade or Upgrade?	L to H
	Package	Change size or appearance?	L to H
		Change package material for climatic/geographic conditions?	M
	Labeling	Change labeling?	M to L
	Brand	Same brand or either modified or new brand?	N to H
Intangible Product	Price	Cost or market driven?	M to H
		With price escalation?	M to H
	Credit	Extend credit?	H
	Positioning	Same for all markets or customize to each market?	M to H
Augmented Product	Warranty	Partial or Full?	L to H
	Repair & Maintenance	Offer it directly or indirectly through foreign-based intermediaries?	H to M
	Installation	Offer it directly or indirectly through foreign-based intermediaries?	H to L
	Delivery	Determined by delivery terms	
	Customer Service	Direct support or through foreign-based intermediaries?	H to L
	Produce Use Instructions	Leave as is or translate?	L

N - None
L - Low
M - Moderate
H - High
V - Very High

To the potential buyer, a product is a complete cluster of value satisfactions. A customer attaches value to a product in proportion to its perceived ability to help solve problems or meet needs. This will go beyond the technical capabilities of the product to include intangible benefits sought. In Latin America, for example, great value is placed on products made in the United States. If packaging is localized, then the product may no longer have the "Hecho en EEUU" ("made in USA") appeal that motivates customers to choose the product over others, especially over local competitors.

In some cases, customer behavior has to be understood from a broader perspective. For example, while Chinese customers may view Japanese products quite positively regarding their quality, historic animosity toward Japan may prevent them from buying Japanese goods or cause them to prefer goods from other sources. Given such dramatic variation from market to market, careful assessment of product dimensions is called for.

Standardization versus Adaptation

The first question, after the internationalization decision has been made, is whether to standardize or adapt. A firm has four basic alternatives in approaching international markets:

1. Sell the product as is in the international marketplace.
2. Modify products for different countries and/or regions.
3. Design new products for foreign markets.
4. Incorporate all the differences into one product design and introduce a global product.

Different approaches for implementing these alternatives exist. For example, a firm may identify only target markets where products can be marketed with little or no modification. A large consumer products exporter may have in its product line for any given markets global products, regional products, and purely local products.

The overall advantages and drawbacks of standardization versus adaptation are summarized in Exhibit 8.3. The benefits of standardization—that is, selling the same product worldwide—are cost savings in production and marketing. In addition to these economies of scale, many point to economic integration as a driving force in making markets more unified. As a response to integration efforts around the world, especially in Europe, many international exporters are indeed standardizing many of their marketing approaches, such as branding and packaging, across markets. Similarly, having to face the same competitors in the major markets of the world will add to the pressure of having a worldwide

EXHIBIT 8.3. Standardization versus Adaptation

FACTORS ENCOURAGING STANDARDIZATION	FACTORS ENCOURAGING ADAPTATION
• Economies of scale in production • Economies in product R&D • Economies in marketing • "Shrinking" of the world marketplace/economic integration • Global competitions	• Differing use conditions • Government and regulatory influences • Differing consumer behavior patterns • Local competition • True to the marketing concept

approach to international marketing. However, in most cases, demand and usage conditions vary sufficiently to require some changes in the product or service itself.

Although product standardization is generally increasing, there are still substantial differences in company practices, depending on the products marketed and where they are marketed. As shown in Exhibit 8.4, industrial products such as steel, chemicals, and agricultural equipment tend to be less culturally

EXHIBIT 8.4. Strategic Adaptation to Foreign Markets

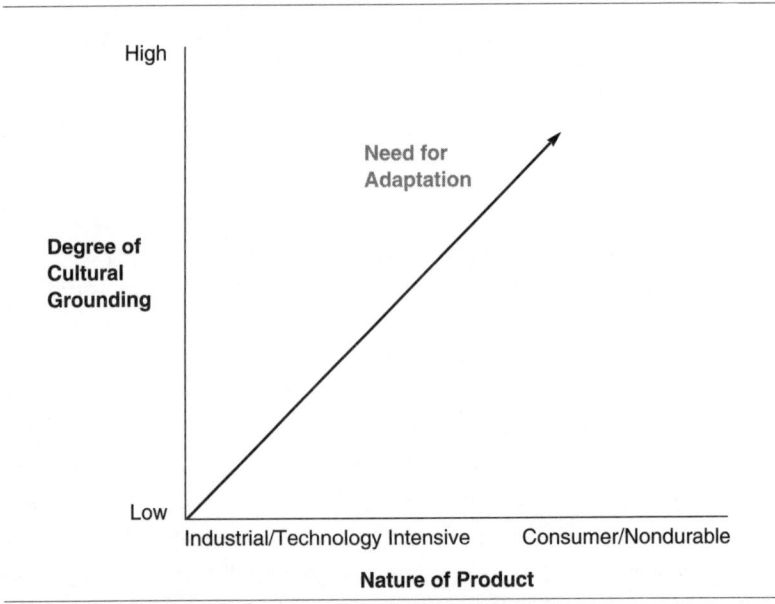

[Graph: Y-axis "Degree of Cultural Grounding" from Low to High; X-axis "Nature of Product" from Industrial/Technology Intensive to Consumer/Nondurable; diagonal arrow labeled "Need for Adaptation" rising from lower-left to upper-right]

SOURCES: Adapted from W. Chan Kim and R.A. Mauborgne, "Cross-Cultural Stragegies," *Journal of Business Strategy* 7 (Spring 1987): 31; and John A. Quelch and Edward J. Hoff, "Customizing Global Marketing," *Harvard Business Review* 64 (May–June 1986): 92–101.

grounded and warrant less adjustment than consumer goods. Similarly, exporters in technology-intensive industries such as scientific instruments or medical equipment find universal acceptability for their products. Within consumer products, luxury goods and personal care products tend to have high levels of standardization while food products do not.

Adaptation needs in the industrial sector may exist even though they may not be overt. As an example, capacity performance is seen from different perspectives in different countries. In some countries, like Germany, the performance specifications of a German product must be precise. In the United States, however, the safety factor can vary within specific ranges as long as safety is not compromised.

Consumer goods generally require product adaptation because of their higher degree of cultural grounding. The amount of change introduced in consumer goods depends not only on cultural differences but also on economic conditions in the target market. Low incomes may cause pressure to simplify the product to make it affordable in the market. For example, Unilever learned that low-income Indians, usually forced to settle for low-quality products, wanted to buy high-end detergents and personal care products but could not afford them in available formats. In response, the company developed extremely low-cost packaging material and other innovations that allowed the distribution of single-use sachets costing the equivalent of pennies rather than the $5 regular-sized containers. Having the same brand in both product formats builds long-term loyalty for the company.

Beyond the dichotomy of standardization and adaptation exist other approaches. The exporter may design and introduce new products for foreign markets in addition to the firm's relatively standardized "flagship" products and brands. Some of these products developed specifically for foreign clients may later be introduced elsewhere, including in the domestic market. For example, IKEA introduced sleeper sofas in the United States to cater to local tastes but has since found demand for the concept in Europe as well.

Increasingly, companies are attempting to develop global products by incorporating rating differences regionally or worldwide into one basic design. This is not pure standardization. For example, to develop a standard in the United States and use it as a model for other markets is dramatically different from obtaining inputs from the intended markets and using the data to create a standard. What is important is that adaptability is built into the product around a standardized core. For example, IBM makes more than 20 different keyboards for its relatively standardized personal computers to adjust to language differences in Europe alone. The exporter attempts to exploit common denominators, but local needs must be considered from product development to the eventual marketing of the product.

Factors Affecting Adaptation

In deciding the form in which the product is to be marketed abroad, the firm should consider three sets of factors: (1) the market(s) that have been targeted, (2) the product and its characteristics, and (3) company characteristics, such as resources and policy. For most firms, the key question linked to adaptation is whether the effort is worth the cost involved—in adjusting production runs, stock control, or servicing, for example—and the investigative research involved in determining, for example, features that would be most appealing.

For most firms, the expense of modifying products should be moderate. In practice, this may mean, however, that the expense is moderate when modifications are considered and acted on, whereas modifications are considered but rejected when the projected cost is substantial. Studies on product adaptation show that the majority of products have to be modified for the international marketplace one way or another. Changes typically affect packaging, measurement units, labeling, product constituents and features, usage instructions, and, to a lesser extent, logos and brand names.

There is no panacea for resolving questions of adaptation. Many firms are formulating decision-support systems to aid in product adaptation, and some consider every situation independently. Exhibit 8.5 provides a summary of the factors that determines the need for either mandatory or discretionary product adaptation. All products have to conform to the prevailing environmental condi-

EXHIBIT 8.5. Factors Affecting Product-Adaptation Decisions

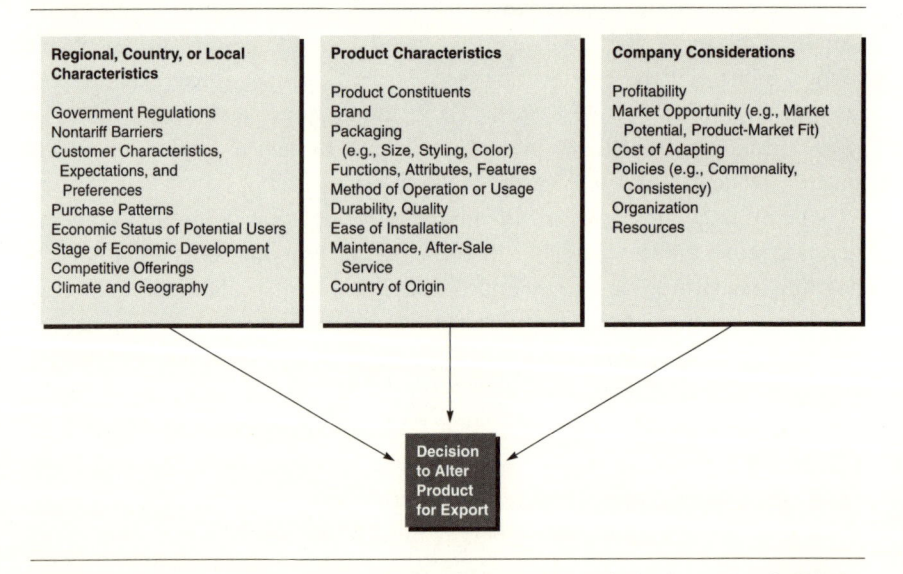

Regional, Country, or Local Characteristics	Product Characteristics	Company Considerations
Government Regulations Nontariff Barriers Customer Characteristics, Expectations, and Preferences Purchase Patterns Economic Status of Potential Users Stage of Economic Development Competitive Offerings Climate and Geography	Product Constituents Brand Packaging (e.g., Size, Styling, Color) Functions, Attributes, Features Method of Operation or Usage Durability, Quality Ease of Installation Maintenance, After-Sale Service Country of Origin	Profitability Market Opportunity (e.g., Market Potential, Product-Market Fit) Cost of Adapting Policies (e.g., Commonality, Consistency) Organization Resources

↓

Decision to Alter Product for Export

SOURCE: Adapted from V. Yorio, *Adapting Products for Export* (New York: Conference Board, 1983): 7.

tions, over which the exporter has no control. These relate to legal, economic, and climatic conditions in the market. Further adaptation decisions are made to enhance the exporter's competitiveness in the marketplace. This is achieved by matching competitive offers, catering to customer preferences, and meeting demands of local distribution systems.

The adaptation decision will also have to be assessed as a function of time and market involvement. The more exporters learn about local market characteristics in individual markets, the more they are able to establish similarities and, as a result, standardize their marketing approach. This market insight will give the exporters legitimacy with the local representatives in developing a common understanding of the extent of standardization versus adaptation.

The Market Environment

Government regulations often present the most stringent requirements. Some of the requirements may serve no purpose other than political (such as protection of domestic industry or response to political pressures). Because of the sovereignty of nations, individual firms need to comply but can influence the situation by lobbying, directly or through their industry associations, for the issue to be raised during trade negotiations. Government regulations may be spelled out, but firms need to be ever vigilant in terms of changes and exceptions.

Sweden was the first country in the world to enact legislation against most aerosol sprays on the grounds that they may harm the atmosphere. The ban, which went into effect January 1, 1979, covers thousands of hair sprays, deodorants, air fresheners, insecticides, paints, waxes, and assorted sprays that use Freon gases as propellants. It does not apply to certain medical sprays, especially those used by people who suffer from asthma although economic integration usually reduces discriminatory governmental regulation, and some national environmental restrictions may stay in place. For example, a ruling by the European Court of Justice let stand Danish laws that require returnable containers for all beer and soft drinks. These laws seriously restrict foreign brewers, whose businesses are not on a scale large enough to justify the logistics system necessary to handle returns. A poll of 4,000 European companies found that burdensome regulatory requirements (e.g., need to ensure that products confirm to national requirements) affecting exports made the United Kingdom the most difficult market to trade with in the EU.

Government regulations are probably the single most important factor contributing to product adaptation and, because of bureaucratic red tape, often the most cumbersome and frustrating factor to deal with. In some cases, government regulations have been passed and are enforced to protect local industry from competition from abroad. *Nontariff barriers* include product standards, testing or approval procedures, subsidies for local products, and bureaucratic red tape. The nontariff barriers affecting product adjustments usually concern elements outside the core product. For example, France requires the use of the French language in any offer, presentation, or advertisement, whether written or spoken, in instructions for use, and in specification or guarantee terms for goods or services, as well as for invoices and receipts.

Because nontariff barriers are usually in place to keep foreign products out and/or to protect domestic producers, getting around them may be the toughest single problem for the international exporter. The cost of compliance with government regulations is high. The U.S. Department of Commerce estimates that a typical machine manufacturer can expect to spend between $50,000 and $100,000 a year on complying with foreign standards. For certain exports to the European Union, that figure can reach as high as $200,000. As an example, Mack International has to pay $10,000 to $25,000 for a typical European engine certification. Brake system changes to conform to other countries' regulations run from $1,500 to $2,500 per vehicle. Wheel equipment changes will cost up to $1,000 per vehicle. Even with these outlays and the subsequent higher price, the company is still able to compete successfully in the international marketplace.

Small companies with limited resources may simply give up in the face of seemingly arbitrary harassment. For example, product testing and certification requirements have made the entry of many foreign companies into Japanese markets quite difficult, if not impossible. Japan requires testing of all pharmaceutical products in Japanese laboratories, maintaining that these tests are needed because the Japanese may be physiologically different from Americans or Swiss. Similarly, foreign ski products were kept out because Japanese snow was somehow unique. Many exporters, rather than try to move mountains of red tape, have found ways to accommodate Japanese regulations.

With a substantial decrease in tariff barriers, nontariff forms of protectionism have increased. On volume alone, agriculture dominates the list. The United States and the EU have fought over beef produced with the aid of hormones. Although it was declared safe for consumption by UN health authorities, the Europeans have banned the importation of such beef and demand appropriate labeling as a pre-condition for market entry. In a similar debate, an international trade agreement was reached in 2000 that requires the labeling of genetically modified food in the world market. This will mean that U.S. farmers have to separate the increasingly controversial foods from the overall supply.

One way to keep a particular product or producer out of a market is to insist on particular standards. Since the EU chose ISO 9000 as a basis to harmonize varying technical norms of its member states, some of its trading partners have accused it of erecting a new trade barrier against outsiders. ISO 9000 refers to a series of guidelines on quality management and system control elements.[1] These standards offer a uniform way of determining whether manufacturing plants and service organizations implement and document sound quality procedures. The ISO itself does not administer or regulate these standards; that job is left to the 143 countries that have voluntarily adopted them. The feeling that ISO registration is a trade barrier comes from the Europeans' earlier start and subsequent control of the program. Of the 570,616 registrations made by 2001, Europe accounts for 269,950, while North American companies have reached 50,894. Growth has been dramatic in the United States, from about 500 companies in 1992 to over 37,000 at present. Studies show that over half the U.S. companies with ISO 9000 registration have fewer than 500 employees, and one-quarter have fewer than 150. There is no legal requirement to adopt the standards; however, many agree that it makes good business sense to adopt them. In many instances, ISO 9000 standards are becoming a condition for doing business around the world. This is especially true for products for which there are safety or liability issues, or that require exact measurements or calibration, such as medical or exercise equipment.

The exporter must bear in mind that these standards can also serve as a nontariff barrier if advanced nations impose their own requirements and systems on developing countries that often lack the knowledge and resources to meet such conditions. Similarly, since the adoption rate has increased more rapidly in the last few years to 36,765 in 2001, with Europe accounting for 49.62 percent and North America for 7.35 percent of the total, ISO 9000 is a fact of life in world markets. A company can be recognized as being compliant with ISO standards by being audited by independent qualified auditors. A list of companies that meet ISO requirements can be obtained by visiting the following Web site: http://www.iso9000directory.com.

Product decisions of consumer product exporters are especially affected by local behavior, tastes, attitudes, and traditions—all reflecting the exporter's need to gain customers' approval. This group of variables is critical in that it is the most difficult to quantify but is nevertheless essential in making a go/no-go decision. Three groups of factors determine cultural and psychological specificity in relation to products and services: consumption patterns, psychosocial characteristics, and general cultural criteria. The types of questions asked in Exhibit 8.6 should be answered and systematically recorded for every product under consideration. Use of the list of questions will guide the international exporter through the analysis, ensuring that all the necessary points are dealt with before a decision is made. Because Brazilians are rarely breakfast eaters, Dunkin' Donuts is

---

[1] For more information of ISO 9000, go to http://www,fastresponse.com/iso.html.

EXHIBIT 8.6. Cultural and Psychological Factors Affecting Product Adaptations

I. Consumption Patterns
   A. Patterns of Purchase
      1. Is the product or service purchased by relatively the same consumer income group from one country to another?
      2. Do the same family members motivate the purchase in all target countries?
      3. Do the same family members dictate brand choice in all target countries?
      4. Do most consumers expect a product to have the same appearance?
      5. Is the purchase rate the same regardless of the country?
      6. Are most of the purchases made at the same kind of retail outlet?
      7. Do most consumers spend the same amount of time making the purchase?
   B. Pattern of Usage
      1. Do most consumers use the product or service for the same purpose or purposes?
      2. Is the product or service used in different amounts from one target area or country to another?
      3. Is the method of preparation the same in all target countries?
      4. Is the product or service used along with other products or services?

II. Psychosocial Characteristics
   A. Attitudes toward the Product or Service
      1. Are the basic psychological, social, and economic factors motivating the purchase and use of the product the same for all target countries?
      2. Are the advantages and disadvantages of the product or service in the minds of consumers basically the same from one country to another?
      3. Does the symbolic content of the product or service differ from one country to another?
      4. Is the psychic cost of purchasing or using the product or service the same, whatever the country?
      5. Does the appeal of the product or service for a cosmopolitan market differ from one market to another?
   B. Attitudes toward the Brand
      1. Is the brand name equally known and accepted in all target countries?
      2. Are customer attitudes toward the package basically the same?
      3. Are customer attitudes toward pricing basically the same?
      4. Is brand loyalty the same throughout target countries for the product or services under consideration?

III. Cultural Criteria
      1. Does society restrict the purchase and/or use of the product or service to a particular group?
      2. Is there a stigma attached to the product or service?
      3. Does the usage of the product or service interfere with tradition in one or more of the targeted markets?

SOURCE: Adapted from Steuart Henderson Britt, "Standardizing Marketing for the International Market," *Columbia Journal of World Business* 9 (Winter 1974): 32–40. Copyright © 1974 Columbia Journal of World Business. Reprinted with permission.

marketing doughnuts in Brazil as snacks and desserts and for parties. To further appeal to Brazilians, the company makes doughnuts with local fruit fillings like papaya and guava. Campbell Soup Company failed in Brazil with its offerings of vegetable and beef combinations, mainly because Brazilians prefer the dehydrated products of competitors such as Knorr and Maggi; Brazilians could use these products as soup starters but still add their own flair and ingredients. The only way of solving this problem is through proper customer testing, which can be formidably expensive for a company interested only in exports.

Often, no concrete product changes are needed, only a change in the product's positioning. Positioning refers to consumers' perception of a brand as compared with that of competitors' brands, that is, the mental image that a brand, or the company as a whole, evokes. For example, Gillette has a consistent image worldwide as a masculine, hardware, and sports-oriented company. A brand's positioning, however, may have to change to reflect the differing lifestyles of the targeted market.

The influence of culture is especially of concern where society may restrict the purchase of the product, or when the product or one of its features may be subject to a stigma. A symbol in packaging may seem fully appropriate in one culture yet be an insult elsewhere. Dogs, for example, were alleged to have eaten one of Mohammed's regiments and therefore are considered signs of bad luck and uncleanliness in parts of North Africa. A U.S. cologne manufacturer discovered this after launching a product featuring a man and his dog in a rural setting.

Management must take into account the present stage of economic development of the overseas market. As a country's economy advances, buyers are in a better position to buy and to demand more sophisticated products and product versions. With broad country considerations in mind, the firm can determine potentials for selling certain kinds of products and services. This means managing affordability in a way that makes the exporter's products accessible. Similarly, economic conditions will affect packaging in terms of size and units sold in a package. In developing markets, products such as cigarettes and razor blades are often sold by the piece so that consumers with limited incomes can afford them. Soft drink companies have introduced four-can packs in Europe, where cans are sold singly even in large stores. On the other hand, products oriented to families, such as food products, appear in larger sizes in developing markets. Pillsbury packages its products in six- and eight-serving sizes for developing countries, whereas the most popular size in the North American market is for two.

Monitoring competitors' product features, as well as determining what has to be done to meet and beat them, is critical. Competitive offerings may provide a baseline against which the firm's resources can be measured—for example, what it takes to reach a critical market share in a given competitive situation. An analysis of competitors' offerings may reveal holes in the market or suggest avoiding certain market segments. American Hospital Supply, a Chicago-based producer of medical equipment, adjusts its product in a preemptive way by making products that are hard to duplicate. As a result, the firm achieved increases of about 40 percent per year in sales and earnings in Japan over a ten-year period. The products are so specialized that it would be hard for Japanese firms to duplicate them on a mass production basis.

In many markets, the exporter is competing with global players and local manufacturers and must overcome traditional purchasing relationships and the certainty they provide. What is needed is a niche-breaking product that is adjusted to local needs. TeleGea has had success in Japan because its technology (which has been adjusted to support Asian languages) automates the service-fulfillment process for telecom companies, cutting their delivery costs more than 30 percent.

Climate and Geography

Climate and geography will usually have an effect on the total product offering: the core product; tangible elements, mainly packaging; and the augmented features. Some products, by design, are vulnerable to the elements. The product itself has to be protected against longer transit times and possibly for longer shelf life; on the other hand, care has to be taken that no non-allowed preservatives are used. One firm experienced this problem when it tried to sell Colombian guava paste in the United States. Because the packaging could not withstand the longer distribution channels and the longer time required for distribution, the product arrived in stores in poor condition and was promptly taken off the shelves. If a product is exposed to a lot of sunshine and heat as a result of being sold on street corners, as may be the case in developing countries, exporters are advised to use special varnishing or to gloss the product wrappers. Without this, the coloring may fade and make the product unattractive to the customer.

Product Characteristics

Product characteristics are the inherent features of the product offering, whether actual or perceived. The inherent characteristics of products and the benefits they provide to consumers in the various markets make certain products good candidates for standardization, others not. Consumer nondurables, such as food products, generally show the highest amount of sensitivity toward differences in national tastes and habits. Consumer durables, such as cameras and home electronics, are subject to far more homogeneous demand and more predictable adjustment (for example, adjustment to a different technical system in television sets and videotape recorders). Industrial products tend to be more shielded from cultural influences.

However, substantial modifications may sometimes be required—in the telecommunications industry, for example—as a result of government regulations and restraints. The exporter must make sure products do not contain ingredients that might be in violation of legal requirements or religious or social customs. As an example, DEP Corporation, a Los Angeles manufacturer with $19 million annual sales of hair and skin products, takes particular pains to make sure that no Japan-bound products contain formaldehyde—an ingredient commonly used in the United States but illegal in Japan. When religion or custom determines consumption, ingredients may have to be replaced in order for the product to be acceptable. In Islamic countries, for example, animal fats have to be replaced by ingredients such as vegetable shortening.

Branding

Brand names convey the image of the product or service. The term *brand* refers to a name, term, symbol, sign, or design used by a firm to differentiate its offerings from those of its competitors. Brands are one of the most easily standardized items in the product offering; they may allow further standardization of other marketing elements such as promotional items. The brand name is the vocalizable part of the brand, the brand mark the nonvocalizable part (for example, Camel's "camel").

The brand mark may become invaluable when the product itself cannot be promoted but the symbol can be used. For example, Marlboro cannot be advertised in most European countries because of legal restrictions on cigarette advertising; however, Philip Morris features advertisements showing only the Marlboro cowboy, who is known throughout the world. Unfortunately, most brands do not have such recognition. The term *trademark* refers to the legally protected part of the brand, indicated by the symbol ®. Increasingly, international markets have found their trademarks violated by counterfeiters who are illegally using or abusing the brand name of the exporter.

The exporter has a number of options in choosing a branding strategy. The exporter may choose to be a contract manufacturer to a distributor (the generics approach) or to establish national, regional, or worldwide brands. The use of standardization in branding is strongest in culturally similar markets; for example, for U.S. exporters this means Canada and the United Kingdom. Standardization of product and brand do not necessarily move hand in hand; a regional brand may well have local features, or a highly standardized product may have local brand names.

The establishment of worldwide brands is difficult; how can a consumer exporter establish world brands when it sells 800 products in more than 200 countries, most of them under different names? This is Gillette's situation. A typical example is Silkience hair conditioner, which is sold as Soyance in France, Sientel in Italy, and Silkience in Germany. Many companies have, however, massive standardization programs of brand names, packaging, and advertising. Standardizing names to reap promotional benefits can be difficult, because a particular name may already be established in each market and the action may raise objections from local constituents. Despite the opposition, globalizing brands presents huge opportunities to cut costs and achieve new economies of scale.

The psychological power of brands is enormous. Brands are not usually listed on balance sheets, but they can go further in determining success than technological breakthroughs by allowing the exporter to demand premium prices. Brand loyalty translates into profits despite the fact that favored brands may not be superior by any tangible measure. However, new brands may be very difficult and expensive to build in export markets, so the exporter may see more benefits in brand extension than adaptation, unless it is a mandatory adaptation. Brand extension also allows the exporter to take advantage of country-or-origin benefits.

If brand adaptation is required, the exporter must consider the fact that brand names often do not travel well. Semantic variations can hinder a firm's product overseas. Even the company name or the trade name should be checked out. To avoid problems with brand names in foreign markets, NameLab, a California-based laboratory for name development and testing, suggests these approaches:

1. Translation. When a brand needs to be translated to meet country regulations, a literal translation is called for. However, this may not translate the intended meaning of the brand name. In that case, transliteration, transparency, or transculture translations may be needed.
2. Transliteration. This is the translation of the brand name with the connotative meaning in the language. This requires the testing of an existing brand name for connotative meaning in the language of the intended market. Flick Pen Corporation, for example, would be perceived in France as a manufacturer of writing instruments for the police because the slang term "flic" connotes something between "cop" and "pig." In other instances, positive connotations are sought.
3. Transparency. This can be used to develop a new, essentially meaningless brand name to minimize trademark complexities, transliteration problems, and translation complexities. (Sony is an example.)
4. Transculture. This means using a foreign-language name for a brand.

Vodkas, regardless of where they originate, should have Russian-sounding names or at least Russian lettering, whereas perfumes should sound French. Brands are powerful marketing tools; for example, the chemicals and natural ingredients in any popular perfume retailing for $140 an ounce may be worth less than $3. In Korea, for example, Sprite has been renamed Kin, a native name. The same situation has emerged in Mexico, where local branding is required.

Packaging

Packaging serves three major functions: protection, promotion, and user convenience. The major consideration for the international exporter is making sure the product reaches the ultimate user in the form intended. Packaging will vary as a function of transportation mode, transit conditions, and length of time in transit. Because of the longer time that products spend in channels of distribution, firms in the international marketplace, especially those exporting food products, have had to use more expensive packaging materials and/or more expensive transportation modes. The solution of food processors has been to utilize airtight, reusable containers that reject moisture and other contaminants.

Pilferage is a problem in a number of markets and has forced companies to use only shipping codes on outside packaging. With larger shipments, containerization has helped alleviate the theft problem. An exporter should anticipate inadequate, careless, or primitive loading methods. The labels and loading instructions should be not only in English but also in the market's language as well as in symbols.

The promotional aspect of packaging relates mostly to labeling. The major adjustments concern bilingual legal requirements, as in the case of Canada (French and English), Belgium (French and Flemish), and Finland (Finnish and Swedish). Even when the same language is spoken across markets, nuances will exist requiring labeling adaptation. Governmental requirements include more informative labeling on products. Inadequate identification, failure to use the needed languages, or inadequate or incorrect descriptions printed on the labels may cause problems. If in doubt, a company should study foreign competitors labels.

Package aesthetics must be a consideration in terms of the promotional role of packaging. This mainly involves the prudent choice of colors and package shapes. African nations, for example, often prefer bold colors, but flag colors may be alternatively preferred or disallowed. Red is associated with death or witchcraft in some countries. Color in packaging may be faddish. White is losing popularity in industrialized countries because name brands do not want to be confused with generic products, usually packaged in white. Black, on the other hand, is increasingly popular and is now used to suggest quality, excellence, and "class."

Package shapes may serve an important promotional role as well. When Grey Goose, a French brand of vodka, researched its international market entry, the development of the bottle took center stage. The company finally settled on a tall (taller than the competition) bottle that was a melange of clear glass, frosted glass, a cutaway of geese in flight, and the French flag. Package size varies according to purchasing patterns and market conditions. For instance, a six-pack format for soft drinks may not be feasible in certain markets because of the lack of refrigeration capacity in households. Quite often, overseas consumers with modest or low discretionary purchasing power buy smaller sizes or even single units in order to stretch a limited budget.

Exporters are wise to monitor packaging technology developments in the world marketplace. A major innovation was in aseptic containers for fruit drinks and milk. Tetra Pak International, the $6.5-billion Swedish company, converted 40 percent of milk sales in Western Europe to its aseptic packaging system, which keeps perishables fresh for five months without refrigeration. The company claimed 5 percent of the fruit juice packaging market and 20 percent of the fruit drink market in the United States. Today, it markets its technologies in over 160 countries.

Finally, the consumer mandate for exporters to make products more environmentally friendly also affects the packaging dimension, especially in terms of the 4 Rs: redesign, reduce, recycle, and reuse. The EU has strict policies on the amounts of packaging waste that are generated and the levels of recycling of such materials. Depending on the packaging materials (20 percent for plastics and 60 percent for glass), producers, importers, distributors, wholesalers, and retailers are held responsible for generating the waste. In Germany, which has the toughest requirements, all packaging must be reusable or recyclable, and packaging must be kept to a minimum needed for proper protection and marketing of the product. Exporters to the EU must find distributors who can fulfill such requirements and agree how to split the costs of such compliance.

Appearance

Adaptations in product styling, color, size, and other appearance features are more common in consumer marketing than in industrial marketing. Color plays an important role in the way consumers perceive a product, and exporters must be aware of the signal being sent by the product's color. Color can be used for brand identification—for example, the yellow of Hertz, red of Avis, and green of National. Colors communicate in a subtle way in developed societies; they have direct meaning in more traditional societies.

Method of Operation and Usage

The product as it is offered in the domestic market may not be operable in the foreign market. One of the major differences faced by appliance manufacturers is electrical power systems. In some cases, variations may exist even within a country, such as Brazil. An exporter can learn about these differences through local government representatives or various trade publications such as the U.S. Department of Commerce publication Electric Current Abroad. However, exporters should determine for themselves the adjustments that are required by observing competitive products or having their product tested by a local entity.

Many complicating factors may be eliminated in the future through standardization efforts by international organizations and by the conversion of most countries to the metric system. Some companies have adjusted their products to operate in different systems, for example, VCR equipment that will record and play back on different color systems.

An exporter may also have to adapt the product to different uses. MicroTouch Systems, which produces touch-activated computer screens for video poker machines and ATMs, makes a series of adjustments in this regard. Ticket vending machines for the French subway need to be waterproof, since they are hosed down. Similarly, for the Australian market, video poker screens are built to take a beating because gamblers there take losing more personally than anywhere else.

The exporter should be open to ideas for new or different uses for the product being offered. New uses may substantially expand the market potential of the product. For example, Turbo Tek, Inc., which produces a hose attachment for washing cars, has found that foreign customers have expanded the product's functions. In Japan, Turbo-Wash is used for cleaning bamboo, and the Dutch use it to wash windows, plants, and the sidings of their houses. To capture these phenomena, observational research, rather than asking direct questions, may be the most appropriate approach. This is especially true in emerging and developing markets in order to understand how consumers relate to products in general and to the exporter's offer in particular.

Quality

Many Western exporters must emphasize quality in their strategies because they cannot compete on price alone. Many new exporters compete on value in the particular segments in which they have chosen to compete. In some cases, producers of cheaper Asian products have forced international exporters to reexamine their strategies, allowing them to win contracts on the basis of technical advantage. To maintain a position of product superiority, exporting firms must invest in research and development for new products as well as manufacturing methods.

Increasingly, many exporters realize that they have to meet international quality standards to compete for business abroad and to win contracts from multinational corporations. Foreign buyers, especially in Europe, are requiring compliance with international ISO 9000 quality standards. For example, German electronics giant Siemens requires ISO compliance in 50 percent of its supply contracts and is encouraging other suppliers to conform. This has helped eliminate the need to test parts, which saves time and money. DuPont began its ISO drive after losing a big European order for polyester films to an ISO-certified British firm. However, many exporters still have grave misunderstandings about the certification process and its benefits. Nevertheless, exporters are finding that it makes good business sense to adopt ISO standards. In many countries it is becoming a condition for doing business.[2]

Service

When a product sold overseas requires repairs, parts, or service, the problem of obtaining, training, and holding a sophisticated engineering or repair staff is not easy. If the product breaks down, and the repair arrangements are not up to standard, the image of the product will suffer. In some cases, products abroad may not even be used for their intended purpose and may thus require modifications not only in product configuration but also in service frequency. For instance, snowplows exported from the United States are used to remove sand from driveways in Saudi Arabia. Closely related to servicing is the issue of product warranties. Warranties not only are instructions to customers about what to do if the product fails within a specified period of time but also are effective promotional tools.

Country-of-Origin Effects

The country of origin of a product, typically communicated by the phrase "Made in (country)," has a considerable influence on the quality perceptions of a product. The manufacture of products in certain countries is affected by a built-in positive or negative stereotype of product quality. These stereotypes become important when significant dimensions of a product category are also associated with a country's image. For example, if an exporter has a positive match of quality and performance for its car exports, the country of origin should be a prominent feature in promotional campaigns. If there is a mismatch, the country of

---

[2] http://www.fastresponse.com/iso.html, accessed 8/23/2003.

origin may have to be hidden or the product sold with the help of prestigious partners whose image overshadows concerns about negative country-of-origin perceptions. This issue may be especially important to developing countries, which need to increase exports, and for importers, who source products from countries different from those where they are sold. In some markets, however, there may be a tendency to reject domestic goods and embrace imports of all kinds.

Country-of-origin effects lessen as customers become more informed. Also, as more countries develop the necessary bases to manufacture products, the origin of the products becomes less important. This can already be seen with so-called hybrid products (for example, a U.S. multinational company manufacturing the product in Malaysia). The argument has been made that with the advent of more economic integration, national borders become less important. However, many countries have started strategic campaigns to improve their images to promote exports and in some cases to even participate in joint promotional efforts. In some cases, this means the development of new positive associations rather than trying to refute past negative ones.

Company Considerations

Before launching a product in the international marketplace, the exporter needs to consider organizational capabilities as well as the nature of the product and the level of adaptation needed to accommodate various market-related differences between domestic and international markets. The issue of product adaptation most often climaxes in the question "Is it worth it?" The answer depends on the firm's ability to control costs, correctly estimate market potential, and finally, secure profitability, especially in the long term. While new markets, such as those in central Europe, may at present require product adaptation, some exporters may feel that the markets are too small to warrant such adjustments and may quite soon converge with western European ones, especially in light of their pending EU membership. While sales of a standard product may be smaller in the short term, long-term benefits will warrant the adoption of this approach. However, the question that used to be posed as "Can we afford to do it?" should now be "Can we afford not to do it?"

The decision to adapt should be preceded by a thorough analysis of the market. Formal market research with primary data collection and/or testing is warranted. From the financial standpoint, some firms have specific return-on-investment levels to be satisfied before adaptation (for instance, 25 percent), whereas some let the requirement vary as a function of the market considered and also the time in the market—that is, profitability may be initially compromised for proper market entry.

Most companies aim for consistency in their marketing efforts. This translates into the requirement that all products fit in terms of quality, price, and user perceptions. An example of where consistency may be difficult to control is in the area of warranties. Warranties can be uniform only if the use conditions do not vary drastically and if the company is able to deliver equally on its promise anywhere it has a presence.

A critical element of the adaptation decision has to be human resources, that is, individuals to make the appropriate decisions. Individuals are needed who are willing to make risky decisions and who know about existing market conditions. Many companies benefit from having managers from different (types of) countries, giving them the experience and the expertise to make decisions between standardization and adaptation.

Product Counterfeiting

Counterfeit goods are any goods bearing an unauthorized representation of a trademark, patented invention, or copyrighted work that is legally protected in the country where it is marketed. The International Trade Commission estimated that U.S. companies lose a total of $60 billion every year because of product counterfeiting and other infringement of intellectual property. Hardest hit are the most innovative, fastest-growing industries, such as computer software, pharmaceuticals, and entertainment. In 2001, the software, publishing, and distribution industries lost more than $10.97 billion due to software theft. Worldwide, more than 40 percent of all software is illegally copied, with the percentage rising to over 90 percent in countries such as Vietnam.

The practice of product counterfeiting has spread to high-technology products and services from the traditionally counterfeited products: high-visibility, strong brand name consumer goods. In addition, previously the only concern was whether a company's product was being counterfeited; now, companies have to worry about whether the raw materials and components purchased for production are themselves real. The European Union estimates that trade in counterfeit goods now accounts for 2 percent of total world trade. The International Chamber of Commerce estimates the figure at close to 5 percent. In general, countries with lower per capita incomes, higher levels of corruption in government, and lower levels of involvement in the international trade community tend to have higher levels of intellectual property violation.

Counterfeiting problems occur in three ways and, depending on the origin of the products and where they are marketed, require different courses of action.

Approximately 75 percent of counterfeit goods are estimated to be manufactured outside the United States, and 25 percent are either made in this country or imported and then labeled here. Problems originating in the United States can be resolved through infringement actions brought up in federal courts. The customs barrier should stop counterfeit products that originate overseas and that are marketed in the United States. Enforcement has been problematic because of the lack of adequate personnel and the increasingly high-tech character of the products. When an infringement occurs overseas, action can be brought under the laws of the country in which it occurs.

The sources of the largest number of counterfeit goods are China, Brazil, Taiwan, Korea, and India, which are a problem to the legitimate owners of intellectual property on two accounts: the size of these countries' own markets and their capability to export. For example, Nintendo estimates its annual losses to video-game piracy at $700 million, with the origin of the counterfeits mainly China and Taiwan. Countries in Central America and the Middle East are typically not sources but rather markets for counterfeit goods. Counterfeiting is a pervasive problem in terms not only of geographic reach but also of the ability of the counterfeiters to deliver products, and the market's willingness to buy them.

The first task in fighting intellectual property violation is to use patent application or registration of trademarks or mask works (for semiconductors). The rights granted by a patent, trademark, copyright, or mask work registration in the United States confer no protection in a foreign country. There is no such thing as an international patent, trademark, or copyright. Although there is no shortcut to worldwide protection, some advantages exist under treaties or other international agreements. These treaties, under the World Intellectual Property Organization (WIPO), include the Paris Convention for the Protection of Industrial Property, the Patent Cooperation Treaty, the Berne Convention for the Protection of Literary and Artistic Works, and the Universal Copyright Convention, as well as regional patent and trademark offices such as the European Patent Office. Applicants are typically granted international protection throughout the member countries of these organizations.

After securing valuable intellectual property rights, the international exporter must act to enforce, and have enforced, these rights. Four types of action against counterfeiting are legislative action, bilateral and multilateral negotiations, joint private sector action, and measures taken by individual companies.

In the legislative arena, the Omnibus Tariff and Trade Act of 1984 amended Section 301 of the Trade Act of 1974 to clarify that the violation of intellectual property rights is an unreasonable practice within the statute. The act also introduced a major carrot-and-stick policy: The adequacy of protection of intellectual property rights of U.S. manufacturers is a factor that will be considered in the designation of Generalized System of Preferences (GSP) benefits to countries. The United States has denied selected countries duty-free treatment on goods because of lax enforcement of intellectual property laws.

The Trademark Counterfeiting Act of 1984 made trading in goods and services using a counterfeit trademark a criminal rather than a civil offense, establishing stiff penalties for the practice. The Semiconductor Chip Protection Act of 1984 clarified the status and protection afforded to semiconductor masks, which determine the capabilities of the chip. Protection will be available to foreign-designed masks in the United States only if the home country of the manufacturer also maintains a viable system of mask protection. The Intellectual Property Rights Improvement Act requires the U.S. Trade Representative to set country-specific negotiating objectives for reciprocity and consideration of retaliatory options to assure intellectual property protection. The United States imposed punitive tariffs on $39 million of Brazilian imports to retaliate against Brazil's refusal to protect U.S. pharmaceutical patents.

The U.S. government is seeking to limit counterfeiting practices through bilateral and multilateral negotiations as well as education. A joint International Trade Administration and Patent and Trademark Office action seeks to assess the adequacy of foreign countries' intellectual property laws and practices, to offer educational programs and technical assistance to countries wishing to establish adequate systems of intellectual property protection, to offer educational services to the industry, and to review the adequacy of U.S. legislation in the area. Major legislative changes have occurred in the past few years in, for example, Taiwan and Singapore, where penalties for violations have been toughened. The WTO agreement includes new rules on intellectual property protection, under the Trade-Related Aspects of Intellectual Property Rights (TRIPS) agreement. Under them, trade-related intellectual property will enjoy 20 years of protection. More than 100 countries have indicated they will amend their laws and improve enforcement. Violators of intellectual property will face retaliation not only in this sector, but in others as well. Similarly, the NAFTA agreement provides extensive patent and copyright protection.

A number of private-sector joint efforts have emerged in the battle against counterfeit goods. In 1978, the International Anti-Counterfeiting Coalition was founded to lobby for stronger legal sanctions worldwide. The coalition consists of 375 members. The International Chamber of Commerce established the Counterfeit Intelligence and Investigating Bureau in London, which acts as a clearinghouse capable of synthesizing global data on counterfeiting.

In today's environment, companies are taking more aggressive steps to protect themselves. The victimized companies are losing not only sales but also goodwill in the longer term if customers believe they have the real product rather than a copy of inferior quality. In addition to the normal measures of registering trademarks and copyrights, companies are taking steps in product development to prevent knockoffs of trademarked goods. For example, new authentication materials in labeling are extremely difficult to duplicate.

Some companies, such as Disney, have tried to legitimize offenders by converting them into authorized licenses. These local companies would then be a part of the fight against counterfeiters because their profits would be the most affected by fakes. Many companies maintain close contact with the government and the various agencies charged with helping them. Computer makers, for example, loan testing equipment to customs officers at all major U.S. ports, and company attorneys regularly conduct seminars on how to detect pirated software and hardware. Other companies retain outside investigators to monitor the market and stage raids with the help of law enforcement officers. For example, when executives at WD-40 Co., the maker of an all-purpose lubricant, realized a counterfeit version of their product was being sold in China, they launched an investigation and then approached local authorities about the problem. Offending retailers were promptly raided and, in turn, led police to the counterfeiter.

The issue of intellectual property protection will become more important for the United States and the EU in future years. It is a different problem from what it was a decade ago, when the principal victims were manufacturers of designer items. Today, the protection of intellectual property is crucial in high technology, one of the strongest areas of U.S. competitiveness in the world marketplace. The ease with which technology can be transferred and the lack of adequate protection of the developers' rights in certain markets make this a serious problem.

Summary

Exporters may routinely exaggerate the attractiveness of international markets, especially in terms of their similarity. Despite the dramatic impact of globalization as far as market convergence is concerned, distances, especially cultural and economic, challenge the exporter to be vigilant. The international exporter must pay careful attention to variables that may call for an adaptation in the product offering. The target market will influence the adaptation decision through factors such as government regulation and customer preferences and expectations. The product itself may not be in a form ready for international market entry in terms of its brand name, its packaging, or its appearance. Some exporters make a conscious decision to offer only standardized products; some adjust their offerings by market.

Like the soft drink and packaged-goods exporters that have led the way, the newest exporters of world brands are producing not necessarily identical products, but recognizable products. As an example, the success of McDonald's in the world marketplace has been based on variation, not on offering the same product worldwide. Had it not been for the variations, McDonald's would have limited its appeal unnecessarily and would have been far more subject to local competitors' challenges.

Firms entering or participating in the international marketplace will certainly find it difficult to cope with the conflicting needs of the domestic and international markets. They will be certain to ask whether adjustments in their product offerings, if the marketplace requires them, are worthwhile. There are, unfortunately, no magic formulas for addressing the problem of product adaptation. The answer seems to lie in adopting formal procedures to assess products in terms of the markets' and the company's own needs.

The theft of intellectual property—ideas and innovations protected by copyrights, patents, and trademarks—is a critical problem for many industries and countries, accelerating with the pace of market globalization. Governments have long argued about intellectual property protection, but the lack of results in some parts of the world has forced companies themselves to take action on this front.

CHAPTER 9

Pricing

The pricing decision—setting the actual price of the product, the terms of sale, and terms of payment is a key decision for every business. The setting of export prices is complicated by factors such as increased distance from the markets, currency fluctuations, governmental policies such as duties, and typically longer and different types of channels of distribution. In spite of new factors influencing the pricing decision, the objective remains the same: to create demand for the exporter's offerings and to do so profitably in the long term. In achieving this, terms of sale and financing arrangements for export transactions are critical for two reasons: to establish the point where seller transfers title to buyer during the movement of the goods and to combat various types of risk in the transfer of funds from exporting to importing country. This chapter explores these issues.

Price Dynamics

Price is the only element of the marketing mix that is revenue generating; all the others are costs. It should therefore be used as an active instrument of strategy in the major areas of marketing decision-making. Price serves as a means of communication with the buyer by providing a basis for judging the attractiveness of the offer. It is a major competitive tool in meeting and beating close rivals and substitutes. Competition will often force prices down, whereas intracompany financial considerations have an opposite effect. Prices, along with costs, will determine the long-term viability of the enterprise.

Price should not be determined in isolation from the other marketing mix elements. It may be used effectively in positioning the product in the marketplace. For example, JLG, the world leader in self-propelled aerial work platforms used at construction sites, is able to charge premium prices because its products are powered by nonpolluting hydrogen fuel cells.

Similarly, pricing decisions cannot be made in isolation from the other functions of the firm. Effective financial arrangements can significantly support the marketing program if they are carefully formulated between the finance and marketing areas. Sales are often won or lost on the basis of favorable credit terms to the buyer. With large numbers of competent firms active in international markets, financing packages—often put together with the help of governmental support—have become more important. Customers abroad may be prepared to accept higher prices if they can obtain attractive credit terms.

Setting Export Prices

The setting of export price is a process of interaction of factors that are internal and external to the organization. Internal factors include the company's philosophy, goals, and objectives; the costs of developing, producing, and marketing the export product; and the nature of the exporter's product and industry. External factors relate to international markets in general or to a specific target market in particular and include such factors as customer, regulatory, competitive, and financial (mainly foreign exchange) characteristics.

A summary of the relationship between external and internal factors and the pricing dynamics is presented in Exhibit 9.1. External factors set the upper bound on the price, while internal factors determine the company's cost structure and therefore, set the limits of how low the price can be. The feasibility range for price setting established by demand, competition, costs, and legal considerations may be narrow or wide in a given situation (for example, the pricing of a commodity versus an innovation). Regardless of how narrow the gap allowed by these factors, however, pricing should never be considered a static element. The exporter's ultimate goal is to make the customer as inelastic as possible; i.e., the customer should prefer the exporter's offer even at a price premium.

As in all marketing decisions, the intended target market will set the basic premise for pricing. Factors to be considered include the importance of price in customer decision-making (in particular, the ability to pay), the strength of perceived price-quality relationships, and potential reactions to marketing-mix manipulation by exporters. The marketing mix must be planned to match the characteristics of the target market. Pricing will be a major factor in determining the desired level of marketing effort in the target country.

Export Pricing Objectives

The initial step in developing an export pricing strategy is to examine the pricing options available to the firm. This means establishing clear-cut objectives that relate the company's product to the environment and the target market. Pricing ob-

Pricing 143

EXHIBIT 9.1. Price Dynamics

EXTERNAL FACTORS

External Influences Affecting Pricing Decisions
1. Market-related factors
2. Industry-related factors
3. Demand conditions
    Target Market Definition
    Target Market Size
    Target Market Preferences

The price established by the exporter will lie between the upper limits set by environmental conditions, the company's cost structure as well as
1. Competitive Elements
2. Company Policies and Objectives in the Export Market
3. Company Competitive Advantages:
    Product Distinctiveness
    Channel of Distribution Structure
    Export-Related Services Provided, etc.

INTERNAL FACTORS

Internal Influences Defining Company Cost Structure
1. Export Marketing Strategy Mix
2. Company Characteristics
3. Management Attitudes

---

jectives do not stand in a vacuum but should be consistent and derived from overall company goals and objectives. Objectives provide well-defined guidelines that relate the role of price in the export marketing strategy and the firm's purpose in developing and exploiting an identified export market opportunity.

Objectives include profit maximization, market share, survival, percentage return on investment, and various competitive policies such as copying competitors' prices, following a particular competitor's prices, or pricing so as to discourage competitors from entering the market. For example, an exporter entering a new market may allow wholesalers and retailers above-normal profit margins to encourage maximum sales volume, geographic distribution, and loyalty.

Pricing objectives and prices should be flexible. Price changes are called for when a new product is launched, when a change occurs in overall market conditions (such as a change in the value of the billing currency), or when there is a change in the exporter's internal situation, such as costs of production. An exporter may elect not to change price even though the result may be lower profitability. However, if a decision is made to change prices, related changes must also be considered. For example, if an increase in price is required, it may at least initially be accompanied by increased promotional efforts. Price changes usually follow changes in the product's stage in the life cycle. As the product matures, more pressure will be put on the price to keep the product competitive despite increased competition and less possibility of differentiation.

With multiple-product pricing, the various items in the line may be differentiated by pricing them appropriately to indicate, for example, an economy version, a standard version, and the top-of-the-line version. One of the products in the line may be priced to protect against competitors or to gain market share from existing competitors. The other items in the line are then expected to make up for the lost contribution of such a "fighting brand."

Export Pricing Policies

Pricing policies follow from the overall objectives of the firm for a particular target market and reflect the general principles or rules that a firm follows in making pricing decisions. These policies represent the strategic course of action that the exporter selects after careful consideration of all the factors that affect pricing decisions, such as the firm's international commitment, its financial capabilities, and the environment in which it operates. Export pricing policies fit this general policy profile:

- *Penetration Pricing or low-margin pricing policy* is consistent with sales or market-share objectives. To enter and grow rapidly in a target market, the export firm needs to establish competitive prices in order to capture a segment of the market Prices must be set below competitors' prices. A penetration pricing policy can be formulated to generate increasing sales volume and satisfactory profit levels in the long run.

    Under this strategic option, the firm sacrifices short-term profits for the long-term objective of securing market share and growth. The underlying assumption in penetration pricing is a relatively high elasticity of demand. The exporter using penetration pricing must assume that demand for the product is sensitive to price changes and that a lower price can translate into a larger volume of sales, as consumers respond to a lower price strategy. This means that the exporter must have a thorough understanding of demand conditions in the export market and that the lower gross margin is enough to penetrate the market, given the product's quality, cost, competition, and elasticity of demand.
- *Skimming or high-margin pricing policy* is consistent with a profit-based objective. To enter a market and obtain targeted profit margins, the export firm needs to establish a price that will generate revenues required to reach profitability objectives. A high-margin policy means establishing the high-

est possible price, given the product's cost, quality, and competitive position. This usually entails a pricing strategy to position the product at the top level of competitive prices. Using this strategy, the firm sacrifices sales volume for higher profits. The underlying assumption is the relative inelasticity of demand. A high price is not expected to affect sales level significantly. An important consideration is the relative distinctiveness, uniqueness, or need for the product in the import market so that a high price does not imply loss of competitiveness in the target market.
- *Competitive or market-driven pricing policy* is usually directed at "meeting the competition" or "maintaining market stability. The exporter uses competitive prices as guidelines and sets prices accordingly. Any change in price is in response to price changes in the marketplace. Using this strategy allows the exporter to minimize competitive pressures and emphasize nonprice aspects of its export marketing mix. Firms usually follow this strategy when their financial position makes it impossible to compete on the basis of price. An important consideration of this policy is the size of a firm relative to the competition and the size of the target market.

Export pricing policies must reflect stated marketing and pricing objectives. Policies must be periodically evaluated, appraising the impact of price on the company's competitive position, sales, and profitability. Pricing policies such as skimming and penetration tend to evolve towards competitive pricing over time.

Export Pricing Strategies

Three general price-setting strategies in international marketing are standard worldwide price; dual pricing, which differentiates between domestic and export prices; and market-differentiated pricing. The first two approaches are cost-oriented methods that are relatively simple to establish and easy to understand. The third strategy is based on demand orientation and may thus be more consistent with the marketing concept. However, even the third approach has to acknowledge costs in the long term.

The standard worldwide price may be the same price regardless of the buyer (if foreign product or foreign marketing costs are negligible) or may be based on average unit costs of fixed, variable, and export-related costs.

In dual pricing, domestic and export prices are differentiated, and two approaches to pricing products for export are available: cost-driven and market-driven methods. If a cost-based approach is used, the exporter can choose between the cost-plus method and the marginal cost method. The cost-plus strategy is the true cost, fully allocating domestic and foreign costs to the product. Although this type of pricing ensures margins, the final price may be too high to be

EXHIBIT 9.2. Export Pricing Alternatives

PRODUCTION COSTS	STANDARD	COST PLUS	MARGINAL COSTS
Materials	2.00	2.00	2.00
Fixed costs	1.00	1.00	0.00
Additional foreign product costs	0.00	0.10	0.10
Production overhead	0.50	0.50	0.00
Total production costs	3.50	3.60	2.10
U.S. marketing costs	1.50	0.00	0.00
General and administrative	0.75	0.75	0.00
Foreign marketing	0.00	1.00	1.00
Other foreign costs	0.00	1.25	1.25
Subtotal	5.75	6.60	4.35
Profit margin (25 percent)	1.44	1.65	1.09
Selling price	7.19	8.25	5.44

SOURCE: Adapted from Lee Oster, "Accounting for Exporters," *Export Today* 7 (January 1991):28–33.

competitive. The alternative is a flexible cost-plus strategy, which allows for variations in special circumstances. Discounts may be granted, depending on the customer, the size of the order, or the intensity of competition.

Changes in prices may also be put into effect to counter exchange rate fluctuations. Despite these allowances, profit is still a driving motive, and pricing is more static as an element of the marketing mix. The marginal cost method considers the direct costs of producing and selling products for export as the floor beneath for prices. Fixed costs for plants, R&D, and domestic overhead as well as domestic marketing costs are disregarded. An exporter can thus lower export prices to be competitive in markets that otherwise might have been beyond access. On certain occasions, especially if the exporter is large, this may open a company to dumping charges, because determination of dumping may be based on average total costs, which are typically considerably higher than those produced by the marginal cost method. A comparison of cost-oriented methods is provided in Exhibit 9.2. Notice how the rigid cost-plus strategy produces the highest selling price by full-cost allocation.

Market-differentiated (or market-based) pricing calls for export pricing according to the dynamic conditions of the marketplace. For this pricing approach, the marginal cost strategy provides the cost floor, and prices change, sometimes frequently, due to changes in competition, exchange rate changes, or other environmental changes. The need for information and controls becomes crucial if this pricing alternative is used. Exporters are likely to use market-based pricing to gain entry or better penetration in a new market, ignoring many of the cost elements at least in the short term.

While most exporters, especially in the early stages of their internationalization, use cost-plus pricing, it usually does not lead to desired performance. It typically leads to pricing too high in weak markets and too low in strong markets by not reflecting prevailing market conditions. But as experience is accumulated, pricing eventually becomes more market-driven.

Overall, exporters see the pricing decision as a critical one, which means that it is typically taken centrally under the supervision of top-level management. In addition to product quality, correct pricing is seen as the major determinant of international marketing success.

Export-Related Costs

In preparing a quotation, the exporter must be careful to take into account and, if possible, include unique export-related costs. These are in addition to the normal costs shared with the domestic side. They include the following:

1. The cost of modifying the product for foreign markets.
2. Operational costs of the export operation: personnel, market research, additional shipping and insurance costs, communications costs with foreign customers, and overseas promotional costs.
3. Costs incurred in entering the foreign markets: tariffs and taxes; risks associated with a buyer in a different market (mainly commercial credit risks and political risks); and risks from dealing in other than the exporter's domestic currency—that is, foreign exchange risk.

The combined effect of both clear-cut and hidden costs results in export prices that far exceed domestic prices. The cause is termed *price escalation*. Four different export scenarios are compared with a typical domestic situation in Exhibit 9.3.

The first case is relatively simple, adding only the CIF (cost, insurance, freight) and tariff charges. The second adds a foreign importer and thus lengthens the foreign part of the distribution channel. In the third case, a value-added tax (VAT), such as those used within the European Union, is included in the calculations. This is imposed on the full export selling price, which represents the "value added" to or introduced into the country from abroad. In Italy, for example, where most food items are taxed at 2 percent, processed meat is taxed at 18 percent because the government wants to use the VAT to help reduce its trade deficit. The fourth case simulates a situation typically found in less-developed countries where distribution channels are longer. Lengthy channels can easily double the landed (CIF) price.

Complicating price escalation in today's environment may be the fact that price increases are of different sizes across markets. If customers are willing to

EXHIBIT 9.3. Export Price Escalation

INTERNATIONAL MARKETING CHANNEL ELEMENTS AND COST FACTORS	Domestic Wholesale-Retail channel	CASE 1 Same as Domestic with Direct Wholesale Import CIF/tariff	CASE 2 Same as 1 with Foreign Importer added to channel	CASE 3 Same as 2 with VAT added	CASE 4 Same as 3 with Local Foreign Jobber added to channel
Manufacturer's net price	6.00	6.00	6.00	6.00	6.00
+ Insurance and shipping cost (CIF)	—	2.50	2.50	2.50	2.50
= landed cost (CIF value)	—	8.50	8.50	8.50	8.50
+ Tariff (20 percent on CIF value)	—	1.70	1.70	1.70	1.70
= Importer's cost (CIF value + tariff)	—	10.20	10.20	10.20	10.20
+ Importer's margin (25 percent on cost)	—	—	2.55	2.55	2.55
+ VAT (16 percent on full cost plus margin)	—	—	—	2.04	2.04
= Wholesaler's cost (= importer's price)	6.00	10.20	12.75	14.79	14.79
+ Wholesaler's margin (33 1/3 percent on cost)	2.00	3.40	4.25	4.93	4.93
+ VAT (16 percent on margin)	—	—	—	.79	.79
= Local foreign jobber's cost (= wholesale price)	—	—	—	—	20.51
+ Jobber's margin (33 1/3 percent on cost)	—	—	—	—	6.84
+ VAT (16 percent on margin)	—	—	—	—	1.09
= Retailer's cost (= wholesale or jobber price)	8.00	13.60	17.00	20.51	28.44
+ Retailer's margin (50 percent on cost)	4.00	6.80	8.50	10.26	14.22
+ VAT (16 percent on margin)	—	—	—	1.64	2.28
= Retail price (what consumer pays)	12.00	20.40	25.50	32.41	44.94
Percentage price escalation over domestic		70%	113%	170%	275%
Percentage price escalation over Case 1			25%	59%	120%
Percentage price escalation over Case 2				27%	76%
Percentage price escalation over Case 3					39%

SOURCE: Helmut Becker, "Pricing: An International Marketing Challenge," in *International Marketing Strategy*, eds. Hans Thorelli and Helmut Becker (New York: Pergamon Press, 1980), 215.

Pricing

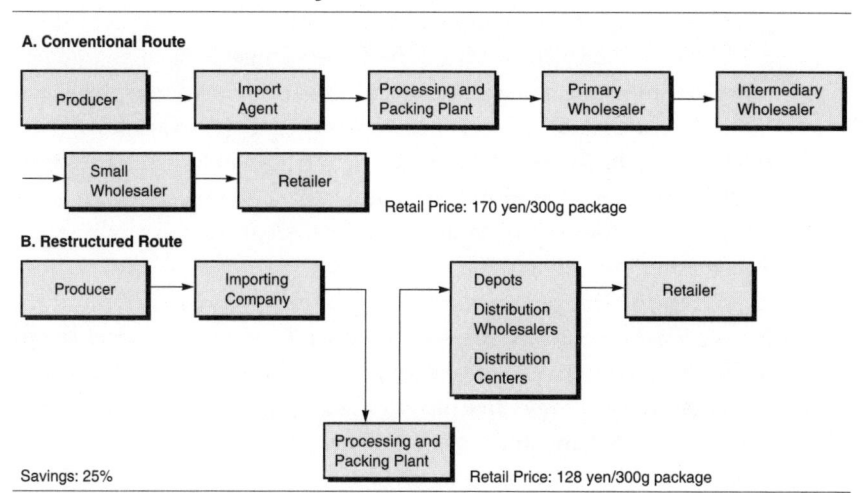

EXHIBIT 9.4. Distribution Adjustment to Decrease Price Escalation

A. Conventional Route

Producer → Import Agent → Processing and Packing Plant → Primary Wholesaler → Intermediary Wholesaler → Small Wholesaler → Retailer

Retail Price: 170 yen/300g package

B. Restructured Route

Producer → Importing Company → Depots / Distribution Wholesalers / Distribution Centers → Retailer

Processing and Packing Plant

Savings: 25%   Retail Price: 128 yen/300g package

SOURCE: From *International Marketing Strategy: Readings*, 1st edition by Michael R. Czinkota. © 1994. Reprinted with permission of South-Western, a division of Thomson Learning: http://www.thomsonrights.com.

shop around before purchasing, the problem of price differentials will make distributors unhappy and can result in a particular market's being abandoned altogether.

Price escalation can be overcome through creative strategies, depending on what the demand elasticities in the market are. Typical methods, such as the following, focus on cost cutting:

1. Reorganize the channel of distribution: The example in Exhibit 9.4, based on import channels for spaghetti and macaroni in Japan, shows how the flow of merchandise through the various wholesaling levels has been reduced to only an internal wholesale distribution center, resulting in savings of 25 percent and increasing the overall potential for imports. Shortening of channels may, however, bring about other costs such as demands for better discounts if a new intermediary takes the role of multiple previous ones.

2. Adapt the product: The product itself can be reformulated by including less expensive ingredients or unbundling costly features, which can be made optional. Remaining features, such as packaging, can also be made less expensive. If price escalation causes price differentials between markets, the product can be altered to avoid cross-border price shopping by customers. For example, Geochron alters its clocks' appearance from one region to another.

3. Use new or more economical tariff or tax classifications: In many cases, products may qualify for entry under different categories that have different charges levied against them. The exporter may have to engage in a lobbying effort to get changes made in existing systems, but the results may be considerable savings. For example, when the U.S. Customs Service ruled that multipurpose vehicles were light trucks and, therefore, subject to 25 percent tariffs (and not the 2.5 percent levied on passenger cars), Britain's Land Rover had to argue that its $56,000 luxury vehicle, the Range Rover, was not a truck.

    When the United States introduced a luxury tax (10 percent of the part of a car's price that exceeded $33,000), Land Rover worked closely with the U.S. Internal Revenue Service to establish that its vehicles were trucks (since trucks were free of such tax). Before it got its way, however, it had to make slight adjustments in the vehicle, since the IRS defines a minimum weight for trucks at 6,000 lbs. Land Rover's following year model weighed in at 6,019 lbs.

4. Assemble or produce overseas: In the longer term, the exporter may resort to overseas sourcing or, eventually, production. Through foreign sourcing, the exporter may accrue an additional benefit to lower cost: duty drawbacks. An exporter may be refunded up to 99 percent of duties paid on imported goods when they are exported or incorporated in articles that are subsequently exported within five years of the importation. Levi Strauss, for example, imports zippers from China that are sewn into the company's jackets and jeans in the United States. The amount that Levi's reclaims can be significant, because the firm uses a lot of zippers.

Of course good accounting is an essential of every business, and exporting is no exception. It can help avoid the surprises caused by hidden costs. For example, negotiations in the Middle Eastern countries or Russia may last three times longer than the average domestic negotiations, dramatically increasing the costs of doing business. Furthermore, without accurate information, a company cannot combat phenomena such as price escalation.

Terms of Sale

Incoterms define the buyer and seller's responsibilities for delivery of goods under an export sales contract. Set by the International Chamber of Commerce (ICC), they have been the internationally accepted standard definitions for terms of sale since 1936.

Incoterms 2000 went into effect on January 1, 2000, with significant revisions to better reflect changing transportation technologies and the increased use of electronic communications. Although the same terms may be used in domestic transactions, they gain new meaning in the international arena. The terms are grouped into four categories:

1. "E" terms: Whereby the seller makes the goods available to the buyer only at the seller's own premises (the "E"-terms).
2. "F" terms: Whereby the seller is called upon to deliver the goods to a carrier appointed by the buyer.
3. "C"-terms: Whereby the seller has to contract for carriage but without assuming the risk of loss or damage to the goods or additional costs after the dispatch.
4. "D"-terms: Whereby the seller has to bear all costs and risks to bring the goods to the destination determined by the buyer.

Incoterms are available in 31 languages. The most common of the Incoterms used in international marketing are summarized in Exhibit 9.5.

It is important that the exporter consult the ICC text with proper Incoterms definitions in order to have legal protection should a dispute arise concerning the particular shipment.

When an Incoterm is specific, there is no dispute as to the delivery terms in the transaction.

Incoterms provide the basis to define the respective responsibilities of the buyer and seller during the transportation of the goods, and identifying the point at which the transfer of title occurs. Under all Incoterms, the seller must supply the goods according to the sale contract for timely delivery. In addition, the seller must prepare and clear the goods for export, that is, provide packaging and checking operations (measuring, weighing, counting) and all necessary documentation, except for the EX term (defined below). The buyer must take delivery of the goods at designated point of delivery and assume all risks and pay all charges from that point on.

EX factory, warehouse, etc. at Named Point of Origin. Prices quoted ex-works (EXW) apply only at the point of origin, and the seller agrees to place the goods at the disposal of the buyer at the specified place on the date or within the fixed period. All other charges are for the account of the buyer.

FCA (Free Carrier) Named Inland Carrier at Named Point of Shipment. One of the new Incoterms is free carrier (FCA), which replaced a variety of FOB terms for all modes of transportation except vessel. FCA (named inland point) applies either to a designated inland point of departure or named point. The seller is responsible for loading goods into the means of transportation; the buyer is

EXHIBIT 9.5. Selected International terms of Sale (Incoterms)

INCOTERMS	RISK (TITLE) TRANSFER FROM SELLER TO BUYER	COSTS INCURRED BY EXPORTER
E TERMS		
EX-Works, Factory, Warehouse	At point of Origin	A. Cost of Goods at Point of Origin
F TERMS		
FCA (Free Carrier), Name Inland Carrier at Named Inland Point of Departure	Loaded on Inland Carrier	B. (A) plus Loading onto Inland carrier
FCA (Free Carrier) Name Inland Carrier at Name Port of Shipment	At Named Port of Shipment	C. (A), (B), plus Transportation to named Port of Shipment
FAS Named Port of Shipment	Alongside Vessel, Port of Shipment	D. (A) to (C) plus transportation to dock
FOB Named Vessel at Named Port of Shipment	Goods pass ship's rail Named Port of Shipment	E. (A) to (D) plus Loading onto Vessel
C TERMS		
CFR Named Port of Importation	Goods pass ship's rail Named Port of Shipment	F. (A) to (E) plus Ocean Freight Charges
CIF Named Port of Importation	Goods pass ship's rail Named Port of Shipment	G. ((A) to (F) plus Insurance
D TERMS		
DDU Named Port of Destination	Unloaded on Dock Post of Destination	H. ((A) to (G) plus Unloading at Port of Destination
DDP Named Port of Destination	Delivered at Buyer's Warehouse	I. (A) to (H) plus Import Duties and Inland Transportation charges

SOURCE: www.icc.wbo.org/incoterms, accessed September 12, 2003.

responsible for all subsequent expenses. If a port of exportation is named, the costs of transporting the goods to the named port are included in the price.

FAS (Free Along Side) Named Port of Shipment. Free alongside ship (FAS) at a named U.S. port of export means that the exporter quotes a price for the goods, including charges for delivery of the goods alongside a vessel at the port. The seller handles the cost of unloading and wharfage; loading, ocean transportation, and insurance are left to the buyer.

FOB (Free on Board) Named Vessel at Named Port of Shipment. Free on board (FOB) applies only to vessel shipments. The seller quotes a price covering all expenses up to, and including, delivery when goods pass ship's rail. The seller pays for the loading of the goods unto the vessel; ocean transportation is left to the buyer.

CFR (Cost and Freight) Named Port of Importation. Under cost and freight (CFR) to a named overseas port of import, the seller quotes a price for the goods, including the cost of transportation to the named port of debarkation. However, delivery occurs when goods pass ship's rail. The cost of insurance and the choice of insurer are left to the buyer.

CIF (Cost, Insurance, Freight) Named Port of Importation. With cost, insurance, and freight (CIF) to a named overseas port of import, the seller quotes a price including insurance, all transportation, and miscellaneous charges to the point of debarkation from the vessel. However, delivery of the goods occurs when goods pass ship's rail. If other than waterway transport is used, the terms are CPT (carriage paid to) or CIP (carriage and insurance paid to).

DDU (Delivered Duty Unpaid) to Named Port of Destination. With delivery duty unpaid (DDU), the seller delivers the goods when goods are placed at disposal of buyer, not including import duties. Buyer must pay all custom costs at destination as well as import duties.

DDP (Delivered Duty Paid) to Named Port of Importation. With delivered duty paid (DDP), the seller delivers the goods, with import duties paid including inland transportation from import point to the buyer's premises.

Under terms of sales, Ex-works signifies the maximum obligation for the buyer; delivered duty paid (DDU) puts the maximum burden on the seller. Careful determination and clear understanding of terms used, and their acceptance by the parties involved, are vital if subsequent misunderstandings and disputes are to be avoided not only between the parties but also within the exporter's own organization. These terms are also powerful competitive tools. The exporter should therefore learn what importers usually prefer in the particular market and what the specific transaction may require. An inexperienced importer may be discouraged from further action by a quote such as ex-plant Jessup, Maryland, whereas CIF Helsinki will enable the Finnish importer to handle the remaining costs because they are incurred in a familiar environment, thus making it a more competitive term.

Increasingly, exporters are quoting more inclusive terms. The benefits of taking charge of the transportation on either a CIF or DDP basis include the following:

1. Exporters can offer foreign buyers an easy-to-understand "delivered cost" for the deal.
2. By getting discounts on volume purchases for transportation services, exporters cut shipping costs and can offer lower overall prices to prospective buyers.
3. Control of product quality and service is extended to transport, enabling the exporter to ensure that goods arrive to the buyer in good condition
4. Administrative procedures are cut for both the exporter and the buyer.

These are the fundamental reasons why John Deere & Co., for example, carries out transactions on a DDP basis. Transportation costs are cut by 10 percent on the average due to its control of shipments.

When taking control of transportation costs, however, the exporter must know well in advance what impact the additional costs will have on the bottom line. If the approach is implemented incorrectly, exporters can be faced with volatile shipping rates, unexpected import duties, and restive customers. Most exporters do not want to go beyond the CIF quotation because of uncontrollable and unknown factors in the destination country. Whatever terms are chosen, the program should be agreed to by the exporter and the buyer(s) rather than imposed solely by the exporter.

Freight forwarders are useful in determining costs, preparing quotations, and making sure that unexpected changes do not cause the exporter to lose money. Freight forwarders are useful to the exporter not only as facilitators and advisors but also in keeping down some of the export-related costs. Rates for freight and insurance provided to freight forwarders may be far more economical than to an individual exporter because of large-volume purchases, especially if export sales are infrequent. Some freight forwarders can also provide additional value-added services, such as taking care of the exporter's duty-drawback receivables.

Terms of Payment

Of course payment is always key, but even more so in exporting. Because delivery of the goods can occur prior to payment, at about the same time as delivery, or after delivery to the shipping company, and because greater distances (both physical and cultural) between buyer and seller are usually involved than in domestic transactions, arrangement for payment is an essential component of the sales contract. The exporter has in all likelihood already formulated a credit policy that determines the degree of risk the firm is willing to assume and the preferred selling terms. The main objective is to meet the importer's requirements without jeopardizing the firm's financial well-being. The following factors are central in negotiating terms of payment:

1. Amount of payment and the need for protection.
2. Terms offered by competitors.
3. Practices in the industry.
4. Capacity for financing international transactions.
5. Relative strength of the parties involved. If the exporter is well established in the market with a unique product and accompanying service, price, and terms of trade can be set to fit the exporter's desires. If, on the other hand, the exporter is breaking into a new market or if competitive pressures call for action, pricing and selling terms should be used as major competitive tools. Both parties have their own concerns and sensitivities; therefore, this very basic issue should be put on the negotiating table at the very beginning of the relationship.

The basic methods of payment for exports vary in terms of their attractiveness to the buyer and the seller, from cash in advance to open account or consignment selling. Neither of the extremes will be feasible for longer-term relationships, but they do have their use in certain situations. For example, in the 1999–2000 period very few companies were exporting into Russia except on a cash-in-advance basis, due to the country's financial turmoil. An exporter may use multiple methods of payment with the same buyer. For example, in a distributor relationship, the distributor may purchase samples on open account, but orders have to be paid for with a letter of credit. These methods are depicted in the risk triangle presented in Exhibit 9.6. As can be seen, the most attractive payment term for the exporter is the least attractive to the importer and vice versa:

- Cash in Advance: The most favorable term to the exporter is cash in advance because it relieves the exporter of all risk and allows for immediate use of the money. For the buyer, this is not an attractive alternative as it ties

EXHIBIT 9.6. Methods of Payment for Exports

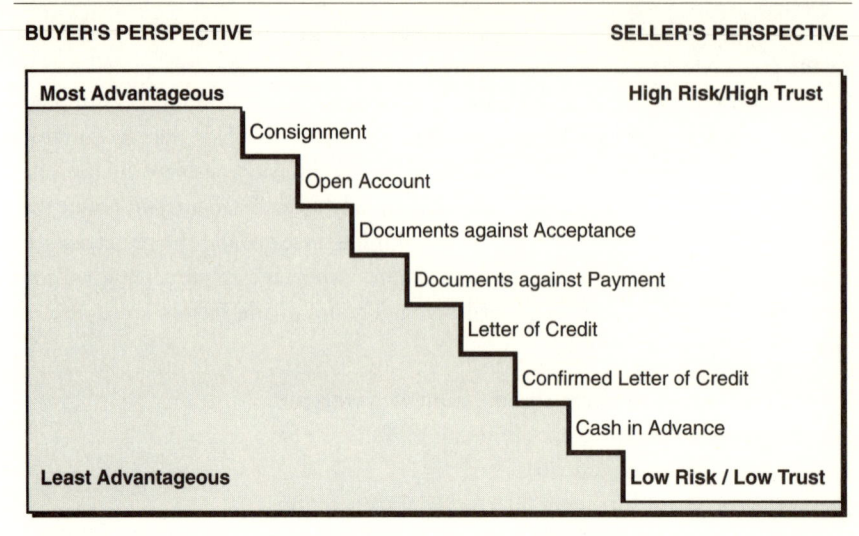

BUYER'S PERSPECTIVE	SELLER'S PERSPECTIVE
Most Advantageous	High Risk/High Trust
Consignment	
Open Account	
Documents against Acceptance	
Documents against Payment	
Letter of Credit	
Confirmed Letter of Credit	
Cash in Advance	
Least Advantageous	Low Risk / Low Trust

SOURCE: Adapted from Chase Manhattan Bank, *Dynamics of Trade Finance* (New York: Chase Mahattan Bank, 1984), 5.

up his capital. It is not widely used, however, except for smaller, first-time transactions or situations in which the exporter has reason to doubt the importer's ability to pay. Cash-in-advance terms are also found when orders are for custom-made products, because the risk to the exporter is beyond that of a normal transaction. In some instances, the importer may not be able to buy on a cash-in-advance basis because of insufficient funds or government restrictions.

- Open Account: While this form of payment is a normal manner of doing business in one's domestic market, it is different for exports due to the relatively high level of risk incurred. An open account is simply an unsecured debt. The exporter is putting full faith in the buyer's creditworthiness and credit references. And then there is the extra expense: it is tying up its own capital to extend credit. Not only is there no guarantee of payment, but if the debt turns bad, the problems of overseas litigation and collection are considerable.

    In less-developed countries, importers usually need proof of debt in their application to the central bank for hard currency, which will not allow them to deal on an open-account basis. On the other hand, open account is sometimes used by multinationals in their internal transactions and with special, trusted partners.

- Consignment Sales: The most favorable term to the importer is consignment selling, but it represents very high risk and exposure for the exporter. Under this term, goods are made available to the buyer on a deferred payment basis, and allow the importer to pay after the goods are actually sold. This approach places the entire burden on the exporter, and its use should be carefully weighed against the objectives of the transaction.

If the exporter wants entry into a specific market through specific intermediaries, consignment selling may be the only method of gaining acceptance by intermediaries. The arrangement will require clear understanding as to the parties' responsibilities—for example, which party is responsible for insurance until the goods have actually been sold. If the goods are not sold, returning them will be costly and time-consuming; for example, there is getting through customs or paying, avoiding paying, or trying to get refunds on duties. Due to its burdensome characteristics, consignment is not a very common way to do business, even though it is relatively common in certain type of goods such as agricultural and manufacturing inputs.

- Documentary Collections: Under these terms, the seller ships the goods, and the shipping documents and the draft demanding payment are presented to the importer through banks acting as the seller's agent. The draft, also known as the bill of exchange, may be either a sight draft or a time draft (Exhibit 9.7).

  A *sight draft* document against payment is payable on presentation to the drawee, that is, the party to whom the draft is addressed. A *time draft* document against acceptance allows for a delay of 30, 60, 90, 120, or 180 days. This enables the buyer to take possession of the goods, and by accepting the draft, obtain the stipulated payment delay from date of acceptance. A *date draft* is similar to a time draft, only payment must be made on a specified date, regardless of the date the goods arrive in importing country and the draft presented and accepted by the foreign buyer.

  When a time draft is drawn on and accepted by a bank, it becomes a banker's acceptance, which is sold in the short-term money market. Time drafts drawn on and accepted by a business firm become trader's acceptances, which are normally not marketable. A draft is presented to the drawee, which accepts it by writing or stamping a notice of acceptance on it. With both sight and time drafts, the buyer can effectively extend the period of credit by avoiding receipt of the goods. A date draft requires payment on a specified date, regardless of the date on which the buyer accepts the goods and the draft.

- A Letter of Credit: This offers a unique alternative to credit extension. It allows buyer and seller to achieve an acceptable compromise by protecting

EXHIBIT 9.7. Documentary Collection

(1) U.S. $ 500,000.00	(2) Anywhere, Japan	(3) December 17, 20 00
AT (4) Sight DAYS AFTER		(5)
(6) PAY TO THE ORDER OF ABC Exporters, Ltd.		
Five Hundred Thousand and 00/100 U.S. (7) ---------- DOLLARS		
VALUE RECEIVED AND CHARGE THE SAME TO THE ACCOUNT OF: (9) TO: First Union National Bank Charlotte, N.C.	(8)	"Drawn under First Union National Bank Irrevocable L/C No. L000000 dated December 4, 2000"
		(10) ABC Exporters, Ltd.
NO. (11) ABC35		(12) _____ (AUTHORIZES SIGNATURE)

(1) U.S. $ 100,000.00	(2) Anywhere, Japan	(3) December 17, 20 00
AT (4) 90 Days of B/L Date DAYS AFTER		(5)
(6) PAY TO THE ORDER OF ABC Exporters, Ltd.		
One Hundred Thousand and 00/100 U.S. (7) ---------- DOLLARS		
VALUE RECEIVED AND CHARGE THE SAME TO THE ACCOUNT OF: (9) TO: First Union National Bank Charlotte, N.C.	(8)	"Drawn under First Union National Bank Irrevocable L/C No. L000000 dated December 5, 2000"
		(10) ABC Exporters, Ltd.
NO. (11) ABC18		(12) _____ (AUTHORIZES SIGNATURE)

SOURCE: http://www.firstunion.com.

the interest of both parties involved. It allows the exporter to obtain assurance of payment as soon as the goods are shipped, shipping documents are presented to the bank, and other conditions of the letter of credit are met. The importer is prepared to pay in advance to eliminate the risk of paying without assurances that the goods will be shipped on time, as is the case of cash in advance.

The letter of credit is an instrument issued by a bank at the request of a buyer. The bank promises to pay a specified amount of money on presentation of documents stipulated in the letter of credit, usually the bill of lading, consular invoice, and a description of the goods. Letters of credit are

EXHIBIT 9.8. Letter of Credit: Process and Parties

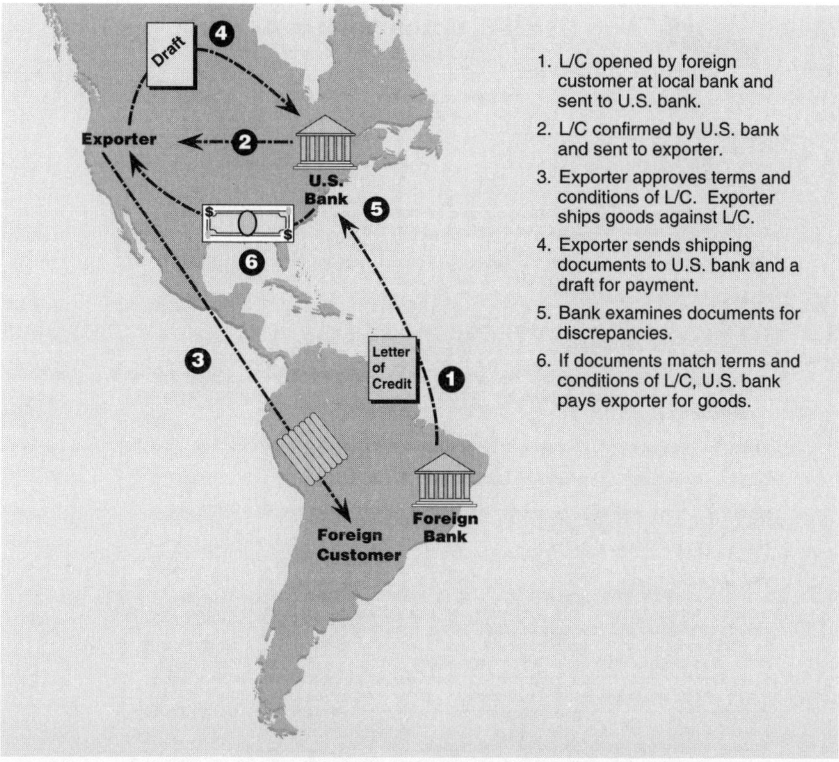
Draft
4
Exporter
2
U.S. Bank
5
6
3
Letter of Credit
1
Foreign Customer
Foreign Bank
1. L/C opened by foreign customer at local bank and sent to U.S. bank.
2. L/C confirmed by U.S. bank and sent to exporter.
3. Exporter approves terms and conditions of L/C. Exporter ships goods against L/C.
4. Exporter sends shipping documents to U.S. bank and a draft for payment.
5. Bank examines documents for discrepancies.
6. If documents match terms and conditions of L/C, U.S. bank pays exporter for goods.

SOURCE: Based on Faren L. Foster and Lynn S. Hutchins, "Six Steps to Quicker Collection of Export Letters of Credit," *Export Today* 9 (November–December 1993): 26–30.

one of the most frequently used methods of payment in international transactions. Exhibit 9.8 summarizes the process of obtaining a letter of credit and the relationship between the parties involved.

Letters of credit can be classified along three dimensions:

1. Irrevocable versus revocable: An irrevocable letter of credit can neither be canceled nor modified without the consent of the beneficiary (exporter), thus guaranteeing payment. According to the new rules drawn by the International Chamber of Commerce, all letters of credit are considered irrevocable unless otherwise stated.
2. Confirmed versus unconfirmed: In the case of a U.S. exporter, a U.S. bank might confirm the letter of credit and thus assume the risk, including the transaction (exchange) risk. The single best method of payment for the exporter in most cases is a confirmed, irrevocable letter of credit. Banks

EXHIBIT 9.9. Letter of Credit

```
                    First Union National Bank
   FIRST              International Division
   UNION
                  IRREVOCABLE LETTER OF CREDIT      SAMPLE COPY
                        DECEMBER 05, 20___

    ABC EXPORTERS, LTD.                    LETTER OF CREDIT NO.
    9876 FIRST STREET                      L000000
    ANYWHERE, JAPAN

    WE HEREBY OPEN OUR IRREVOCABLE LETTER OF CREDIT IN YOUR FAVOR, FOR THE ACCOUNT
    OF XYZ IMPORTERS, INC 1234 MAIN STREET, ANYWHERE, U.S.A. 54321 IN THE
    AGGREGATE AMOUNT OF: USD100,000.00 (UNITED STATES DOLLARS ONE HUNDRED THOUSAND
    AND 00/100) AVAILABLE WITH ANY BANK BY NEGOTIATION OF YOUR DRAFTS AT 90 DAYS
    OF BILL OF LADING DATE ON FIRST UNION NATIONAL BANK WHEN ACCOMPANIED BY THE
    FOLLOWING DOCUMENTS:

    1. COMMERCIAL INVOICE IN TRIPLICATE
    2. CERTIFICATE OF ORIGIN
    3. PACKING LIST IN DUPLICATE
    4. FULL SET CLEAN "ON BOARD" OCEAN BILL OF LADING ISSUED TO ORDER OF FIRST
       UNION NATIONAL BANK MARKED NOTIFY XYZ IMPORTERS, INC AND MARKED FREIGHT
       "COLLECT"

    COVERING MERCHANDISE AS PER P.O. NUMBER 10205 DATED NOVEMBER 25, 20___

    PARTIAL SHIPMENTS ALLOWED / TRANSHIPMENTS PROHIBITED

    SHIPMENT FROM: FOB ANY JAPANESE PORT    FOR TRANSPORTATION TO: USA PORT
    LATEST SHIPMENT DATE: JANUARY 15, 20___
    EXPIRY DATE: JANUARY 31, 20___

    SPECIAL CONDITIONS:
    1. IF DOCUMENTS PRESENTED DO NOT COMPLY WITH THE TERMS AND CONDITIONS OF THIS
    CREDIT, A DISCREPANCY FEE FOR EACH SET OF DOCUMENTS WILL BE DEDUCTED FROM ANY
    REMITTANCE MADE TO THE BENEFICIARY UNDER THE CREDIT.
    2. DOCUMENTS MUST BE PRESENTED FOR NEGOTIATION WITHIN 15 DAYS OF SHIPMENT
    DATE, BUT WITHIN THE VALIDITY OF THE CREDIT.
    3. DRAFT(S) DRAWN UNDER THIS CREDIT MUST STATE ON THEIR FACE "DRAWN UNDER
    FIRST UNION NATIONAL BANK IRREVOCABLE LETTER CREDIT NUMBER L000000 DATED
    DECEMBER 05, 20___" AND DATED SAME DATE AS ON BOARD DATE OF BILL OF LADING.

    WE HEREBY ENGAGE WITH DRAWERS, ENDORSERS, AND BONA FIDE HOLDERS OF DRAFTS
    DRAWN UNDER AND IN COMPLIANCE WITH THE TERMS AND CONDITIONS OF THIS CREDIT,
    THAT THE SAME SHALL BE HONORED ON DUE PRESENTATION AND DELIVERY OF DOCUMENTS
    TO THE DRAWEE. THE AMOUNT OF ANY DRAFT(S) DRAWN UNDER THIS CREDIT MUST,
    CONCURRENTLY WITH NEGOTIATION, BE ENDORSED BY THE NEGOTIATING BANK ON THE
    REVERSE HEREOF.

    UNLESS EXPRESSLY STATED HEREIN, THIS CREDIT IS SUBJECT TO UNIFORM CUSTOMS AND
    PRACTICES FOR DOCUMENTARY CREDITS PUBLICATION NO. 500.

    DIRECT ALL INQUIRIES TO FIRST UNION NATIONAL BANK, INTERNATIONAL DIVISION,
    301 SOUTH TRYON STREET/T-7, CHARLOTTE, NC 28288-0742.

        SINCERELY,  SAMPLE COPY
        _____
        AUTHORIZED SIGNATURE
        FIRST UNION NATIONAL BANK
        CHARLOTTE, NORTH CAROLINA
```

SOURCE: http://www.firstunion.com.

may also assume an advisory role but not assume the risk; the underlying assumption is that the bank and its correspondents are better able to judge the credibility of the bank issuing the letter of credit than is the exporter.

3. Revolving versus nonrevolving: Most letters of credit are nonrevolving; that is, they are valid for the one transaction only. In case of established

relationships, a revolving letter of credit may be issued. Exhibit 9.9 provides an example of a letter of credit.

The letter of credit provides advantages to both the exporter and the importer, which explains its wide use. The approach substitutes the credit of the bank for the credit of the buyer and is as good as the issuing bank's access to dollars. In custom-made orders, an irrevocable letter of credit may help the exporter secure pre-export financing. The importer will not need to pay until the documents have arrived and been accepted by the bank, thus giving an additional float. The major caveat is that the exporter has to comply with all the terms of the letter of credit.

For example, if the documents state that shipment is made in crates measuring 4×4×4 and the goods are shipped in crates measuring 4×3×4, the bank will not honor the letter of credit. If there are changes, the letter of credit can be amended to ensure payment. Importers have occasionally been accused of creating discrepancies to slow down the payment process or to drive down the agreed-upon price. In some cases, the exporter must watch out for fraudulent letters of credit, especially in the case of less-developed countries. In these cases, exporters are advised to ship only on the basis of an irrevocable letter of credit, confirmed by their bank, even after the credentials of the foreign contact have been established.

With the increasing amount of e-commerce, things will have to change. Solutions include online issuance and status reporting on letters of credit, creating a worldwide network of electronic trade hubs, and offering a smart card that will allow participating companies to transact financial business online. For example, TradeCard is an online service for B2B exchanges. Once an exporter and importer have agreed on the terms, the buyer creates an electronic purchase order, which specifies the terms and conditions. Once it is in electronic format, the seller formally agrees to the contract. The purchase order is stored in TradeCard's database. The system then creates both a commercial invoice and a packing list, and a promise of payment is included with the invoice for the seller. A third-party logistics provider sends proof of delivery electronically to TradeCard, which then debits the buyer's account and credits the seller's account.

The letter of credit is a promise to pay but not a means of payment. Actual payment is accomplished by means of a draft, which is similar to a personal check. Like a check, it is an order by one party to pay another. Most drafts are documentary, which means that the buyer must obtain possession of various shipping documents before obtaining possession of the goods involved in the transaction. Multinational corporations in their dealings with their own subsidiaries and in well-established business relationships mainly use clean drafts—orders to pay without any other documents.

Getting Paid for Exports

The term *commercial risk* refers primarily to the insolvency of, or protracted payment default by, an overseas buyer. The usual reasons for domestic commercial defaults—deterioration of conditions in the buyer's market, fluctuations in demand, unanticipated competition, or technological changes—are magnified in the export arena by the geographic and cultural distances in international markets.

In addition, noncommercial or political risk that is completely beyond the control of either the buyer or the seller also factors in to international markets. For example, the foreign buyer may be willing to pay, but the local government may use every trick in the book to delay payment as far into the future as possible.

These challenges must be addressed through actions by either the company itself or support systems. The decision must be an informed one, based on detailed and up-to-date information in international credit and country conditions. In many respects, the assessment of a buyer's creditworthiness requires the same attention to credit checking and financial analysis as for domestic buyers; however, the assessment of a foreign private buyer is complicated by some of the following factors:

1. Credit reports may not be reliable.
2. Audited reports may not be available.
3. Financial reports may have been prepared according to a different format.
4. Many governments require that assets be annually reevaluated upward, which can distort results.
5. Statements are in local currency.
6. The buyer may have the financial resources in local currency but may be precluded from converting to dollars because of exchange controls and other government actions.

More than one credit report should be obtained (from sources such as the two in Exhibit 9.10), and it should be determined how each credit agency obtains its reports. They may use the same correspondent agency, in which case it does the exporter no good to obtain the same information from two sources and to pay for it twice. Where private-sector companies (such as Dun & Bradstreet or Veritas) are able to provide the needed credit information, the services of the U.S. Department of Commerce's International Company Profiles (ICP) are not avail-

EXHIBIT 9.10. Providers of International Credit Information

SOURCE: Courtesy of the U.S. Commercial Service (http://www.usatrade.gov); copyright © Dun & Bradstreet and The Guild Group.

able. However, currently 50 countries are still served by the ICP. Local credit reporting agencies, such as Profancresa in Mexico, may also provide regional services (in this case, throughout Latin America). With the growth of e-commerce, a company may want to demonstrate its creditworthiness to customers and suppliers in a rapid and secure fashion. The Coface Group (of which Veritas is the information arm in the Americas) introduced the "©rating" system, available on the World Wide Web and designed to assess a company's performance in paying its commercial obligations.

Beyond protecting oneself by establishing creditworthiness, an exporter can match payment terms to the customer. In the short term, an exporter may require payment terms that guarantee payment. In the long term, the best approach is to establish a relationship of mutual trust, which will ensure payment even if complications arise during a transaction. Payment terms need to be stated clearly and followed up effectively. If prompt payment is not stressed and enforced, some customers will assume they can procrastinate. The average time to collect on bills is summarized in Exhibit 9.11.

Should a default situation occur in spite of the preparatory measures discussed above, the exporter's first recourse is the customer. Communication with the customer may reveal a misunderstanding or error regarding the shipment. If the customer has financial or other concerns or objections, rescheduling

EXHIBIT 9.11. Average Collection Times Abroad

COUNTRY	NUMBER OF DAYS
Argentina	173
Brazil	113
Kenya	102
Italy	89
Taiwan	78
Mexico	77
Japan	65
United Kingdom	59
Finland	56
Switzerland	51
Germany	47
Canada	31

SOURCE: Foreign Credit Interchange Bureau.

the payment terms may be considered. Third-party intervention through a collection agency may be needed if the customer disputes the charges. For example, the Total Credit Management Group, a cooperative of leading credit and collection companies in 46 countries, can be employed. Only when further amicable demands are unwarranted should an attorney be used.

Pricing Under Varying Currency Conditions

For the past decade of more, U.S. exporters have had to deal with the extremes of currency fluctuations: low values in the early to mid-1990s, high values since then until early 2002, and then a substantial depreciation vis-à-vis other major currencies. When the exporter's domestic currency is weak, strategies should include stressing the price advantage to customers and expanding the scale and scope of the export operation. Sourcing can be shifted to domestic markets and the export price can be subjected to full costing. However, under the opposite scenario, the exporter needs to engage in nonprice competition, minimizing the price dimension as much as possible. Costs should be reduced by every means, including enhancing productivity. At this time the exporter should prioritize efforts to markets that show the greatest returns and may also attempt to protect itself by manipulating leads and lags in export and import payments or receivables in anticipation of either currency revaluations and devaluations. This, however, requires thorough market knowledge and leverage over overseas partners. Alternatives available to exporters under differing currency conditions are summarized in Exhibit 9.12.

Whatever the currency movements are, the exporter needs to decide how to

EXHIBIT 9.12. Exporter Strategies under Varying Currency Conditions

WEAK	STRONG
1. Stress price benefits	1. Nonprice competition
2. Expand product line	2. Improve productivity/cost reduction
3. Shift sourcing to domestic market	3. Sourcing overseas
4. Exploit all possible export opportunities	4. Prioritize exports
5. Case-for-goods trade	5. Countertrade with weak currency
6. Full-costing	6. Marginal-cost pricing
7. Speed repatriation	7. Slow collections
8. Minimize expenditure in local currency	8. Buy needed services abroad

SOURCE: Adapted from S. Tamer Cavusgil, "Unraveling the Mystique of Export Pricing," *Business Horizons* 31 (May–June 1988): 3.

adjust pricing accordingly. An exporter with a strong home currency has three alternatives. First, making no change in the home currency price will result in a less favorable (i.e., higher) price in foreign currencies. This is called a pass-through and, most likely, will produce lower sales revenue, especially without additional marketing. Second, the export price can be decreased in conjunction with increases in the value of the home currency to maintain stable export prices in foreign currencies. This second alternative is a sample of the absorption approach; i.e., the increase in the price is absorbed into the margin of the product, possibly even resulting in a loss.

For pass-through to work, customers have to have a high level of preference for the exporter's product. In some cases, exporters may have no choice but to pass most of the increase to the customer due to the cost structure of the firm. Exporters using the absorption approach have as their goal long-term market-share maintenance, especially in a highly competitive environment.

The third alternative is to pass through only a share of the increase, maintaining sales if possible while at the same time preserving profitability. According to a study on exporter responses to foreign-exchange rate changes over a period of 1973 to 1997, Japanese exporters have the highest tendency to dampen the effects of exchange-rate fluctuations in foreign-currency export prices in both directions by adjusting their home-currency prices. Furthermore, Japanese exporters put a larger emphasis on stabilizing the foreign currency prices of their exports during a weak yen than when the yen is strong. German exporters display completely the opposite behavior.

The strategic response depends on market conditions and may result in different strategies for each market or product. Destination-specific adjustment of mark-ups in response to exchange rate changes has been referred to as pricing-to-market. For example, a mark-up change will be more substantial in a price-sensitive market and/or product category.

In addition, the exporter needs to consider the reactions of local competitors, who may either keep prices stable (hoping that price increases in imports will improve their position) or increase prices along with those of imports in search of more profits. U.S. automakers were criticized for raising their domestic prices at a time when the prices of Japanese imports were forced up by the higher value of the yen during the mid-1990s. Instead of trying to capture more market share, the automakers went for more profits. If the exporter faces a favorable domestic currency rate, pass-through means providing international customers with a more favorable price, while absorption means that the exporter keeps the export price stable and pocket a higher level of profits.

Some exporters prefer price stability to the greatest possible degree and allow mark-ups to vary in maintaining stable local currency prices. Harley-Davidson, for example, maintains its price to distributors as long as the spot exchange rate does not move more than plus or minus 5 percent from the rate in effect when the quote was made. If the movement is an additional 5 percentage points in either direction, Harley and its distributors will share the costs or benefits. Beyond that the price will have to be renegotiated to bring it more in line with current exchange rates and the economic and competitive realities of the market. During times of exchange-rate gains, rather than lower the price, some exporters use other support tools (such as training and trade deals) with their distributors or customers, on the premise that increasing prices after a future currency swing in the opposite direction may be difficult.

Beyond price manipulation, other adjustment strategies exist. They include the following:

1. Market refocus: If lower values of the target market currencies make exporting more difficult by, for example, making collections times longer, exporters may start looking at other markets for growth. For example, U.S. construction industry sales to Mexico grew by nearly 150 percent in 1998 after markets in Thailand and Indonesia dried up. In some cases, the emphasis may switch to the domestic market, where market share gain at the expense of imports may be the most efficient way to grow.

    Currency appreciation does not always lead to a dire situation for the exporter. Domestic competitors may depend very heavily on imported components and may not able to take advantage of the currency-related price pressure on the exporter. The manufacturing sectors of Indonesia, Malaysia, Philippines, and Thailand use over 30 percent imported parts and raw materials in the production process.

2. Streamlined operations: The exporter may start using more aggressive methods of collection, insisting on letters of credit and insurance to guarantee payments. Some have tightened control of their distribution networks by cutting layers or taking over the responsibility from independent intermediaries. On the product side, exporters may focus on offerings that are less sensitive to exchange-rate changes.
3. Shift in production: Especially when currency shifts are seen as long-term, exporters will increase direct investment. With the high value of the yen, Japanese companies shifted production bases to lower-cost locations or closer to final customers. Matsushita Electric, for example, moved a substantial share of its production to Southeast Asian countries, while earth-moving-equipment maker Komatsu launched a $1 billion joint venture with Texas-based Dresser Industries to build equipment in the United States. Remaining units in Japan will focus on research and development, design, software, and high-precision manufactured goods.

In some cases, even adverse developments in the currency market have not had an effect on international markets or exporters. During the currency crisis in Asia, U.S. oil toolmakers and oil-field service companies were never hurt by the high value of the dollar because their expertise was in demand. Similarly, many U.S. firms such as IBM did not suffer because their exported products are both built and sold in other countries. In some cases, imported goods may be in demand because no domestic production exists, which is the case in the United States with consumer goods such as electronics and cameras.

Price Negotiations

The final export price is negotiated in person or electronically. Since pricing is the most sensitive issue in business negotiations, the exporter should be ready to discuss price as part of a comprehensive package and should avoid price concessions early on in the negotiations.

An importer may reject an exporter's price at the outset in the hopes of gaining an upper hand or obtaining concessions later on. These concessions include discounts, an improved product, better terms of sales/payment, and other possibly costly demands. The exporter should prepare for this by obtaining relevant information on the target market and the customer, as well as by developing counter-proposals for possible objections. For example, if the importer states that better offers are available, the exporter should ask for more details on such offers and try to convince the buyer that the exporter's total package is indeed superior. In the rare case that the importer accepts the initial bid without comment, the exporter should make sure the extended bid was correct by checking the price calculations and the Incoterm used. Furthermore, competitive prices should be revisited to ascertain that the price reflects market conditions accurately.

During the actual negotiations, pricing decisions should be postponed until all of the major substantive issues have been agreed upon. Since quality and reliability of delivery are critical dimensions of supplier choice (in addition to price), especially when long-term export contracts are in question, the exporter must want to reduce pressure on price by emphasizing these two areas and how they fit with the importer's needs.

Leasing

Organizational customers frequently prefer to lease major equipment, making it a $200+ billion industry. About 30 percent of all capital goods (50 percent of commercial aircraft) are leased in the United States, with eight out of ten companies involved in leasing. Although a major force in the United States, Japan, and Germany, leasing has grown significantly elsewhere as well; for example, one of the major international trade activities of Russia, in addition to shipping and oil, is equipment leasing. The Russians view leasing not only as a potential source of hard currency but also as a way of attracting customers who would be reluctant to buy an unfamiliar product.

Trade liberalization around the world is expected to benefit lessors both through expected growth in target economies and through the eradication of country laws and regulations hampering outside lessors. For example, the NAFTA agreement and the pent-up demand for machinery, aircraft, and heavy equipment for road building provide a promising opportunity for U.S. leasing companies in Mexico.

For the marketing manager who sells products such as printing presses, computers, forklift trucks, and machine tools, leasing may allow penetration of markets that otherwise might not exist for the firm's products if the firm had to sell them outright. Balance-of-payment problems have forced some countries to prohibit or hinder the purchase and importation of equipment into their markets; an exception has been made if the import is to be leased. In developing countries, the fact that leased products are serviced by the lessor may be a major benefit because of the shortage of trained personnel and scarcity of spare parts. At present, leasing finances over $40 billion in new vehicles and equipment each year in developing countries. The main benefit for the lessor is that total net income, after charging off pertinent repair and maintenance expenses, is often higher than it would be if the unit was sold.

In today's competitive business climate, traditional financial considerations are often only part of the asset-financing formula. Many leasing companies have become more than a source of capital, developing new value-added services that have taken them from asset financiers to asset managers or forming relationships with others who can provide these services. In some cases, lessors have even evolved into partners in business activities. El Camino Resources International, which has leased assets of $836 million (half of it outside the United States), targets high-growth, technology-dependent companies, such as Internet providers and software developers for their hardware, software, and technical services needs, including e-commerce as well as Internet and intranet development.

Summary

The status of price has changed to that of a dynamic element of the marketing mix. This has resulted from both internal and external pressures on business firms. Management must analyze the interactive effect that pricing has on the other elements of the mix and how pricing can assist in meeting the overall goals of the marketing strategy. The process of setting an export price must start with the determination of an appropriate cost baseline and should include variables such as export-related costs to avoid compromising the desired profit margin. The quotation needs to spell out the respective responsibilities of the buyer and the seller in getting the goods to the intended destination. The terms of sale indicate these responsibilities but may also be used as a competitive tool. The terms of payment have to be clarified to ensure that the exporter will indeed get paid for the products and services rendered. Facilitating agents such as freight forwarders and banks are often used to absorb some of the risk and uncertainty in preparing price quotations and establishing terms of payment.

CHAPTER 10

Export Channel Management

Channel decisions are always crucial, never more so than in exporting. The choice is the most long-term of the marketing mix decisions in that, once established, it cannot easily be changed. Each firm confronts a number of alternatives that can be successfully used to cover an export market. The most important channels decisions include identification of the best channels for transfer title or ownership of goods, necessary coverage of the market, degree of integration desired, and type and number of intermediaries needed to reach marketing goals.

Channel Systems

In general, companies use one or more of the following distribution systems:

1. The firm sells directly to customers through its own field sales force or through electronic commerce.
2. The company operates through independent intermediaries, usually at the local level.
3. The business depends on an outside distribution system that may have regional or global coverage.

Optimal distribution systems are flexible and are able to adjust to market conditions and the firm's needs.

A channel of distribution should be seen as more than a sequence of marketing institutions connecting producers and consumers; it should be a team working toward a common goal. Too often intermediaries are mistakenly perceived as temporary market-entry vehicles and not the partners with whom marketing efforts are planned and implemented. In today's marketing environment, being close to customers, whether they are the final buyer or an intermediary, and solving their problems are vital to bringing about success.

Channel Structure

Since most exporters cannot or do not want to control the distribution function completely, structuring channel relationships becomes a crucial task. In export marketing, a new dimension is added to the task: the export channel decision in addition to making market-specific decisions. An experienced exporter may decide that control is of utmost importance and choose to perform tasks itself and incur the information collection and adaptation costs.

An infrequent exporter, on the other hand, may be quite dependent on experienced intermediaries to get its product to markets. Whether export tasks are self-performed or assigned to export intermediaries, the distribution function should be planned so that the channel will function as one rather than as a collection of different or independent units.

A generalization of channel configurations for consumer and industrial products as well as services is provided in Exhibit 10.1. Channels can vary from direct, producer-to-consumer types to elaborate, multilevel channels employing many types of intermediaries, each serving a particular type of distributor. Channel configurations for the same product will vary within industries, even within the same firm, because national markets quite often have unique features. This may mean dramatic departures from accepted policy for a company. Others are entered indirectly by using domestically based intermediaries: either by using the services of trading companies or through selling to larger companies, which then market the products alongside their own.

The connections made by marketing institutions are not solely for the physical movement of goods. They also serve as transactional title flows and informational communications flows. Rather than unidirectional, downward from the producer, the flows are usually multidirectional, both vertical and horizontal. As

EXHIBIT 10.1. Channel Configurations

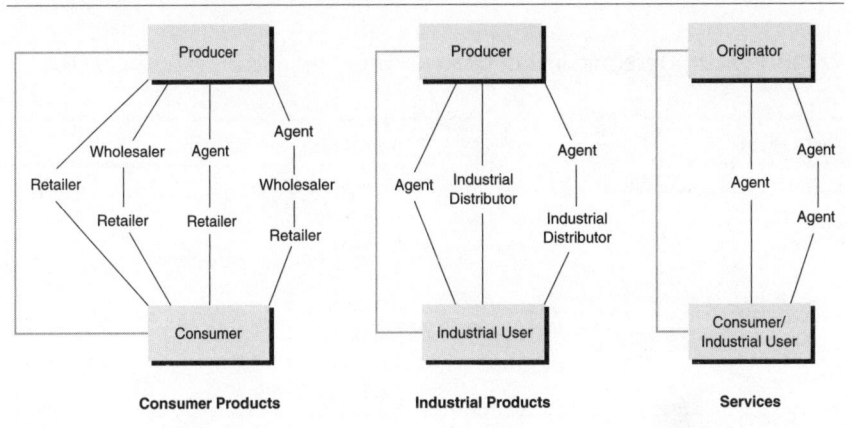

an example, the manufacturer relies heavily on the retailer population for data on possible changes in demand. Communications from retailers may be needed to coordinate a cooperative advertising campaign instituted by a manufacturer. The three flows—physical, transactional, and informational—do not necessarily take place simultaneously or occur at every level of the channel. Agent intermediaries, for example, act only to facilitate the information flow; they do not take title and often do not physically handle the goods. Similarly, electronic intermediaries, such as amazon.com, have to rely on facilitating agents to perform the logistics function of their operation.

Because only a few products are sold directly to ultimate users, an exporter has to decide on alternative ways to move products to chosen markets. The basic marketing functions of exchange, physical movement, and various facilitating activities must be performed, but the exporter may not be equipped to handle them. Intermediaries can therefore be used to gain quick, easy, and relatively low-cost entry to a targeted market.

Channel Design

The term *channel design* refers to the length and the width of the channel employed. The number of levels, or different types, of intermediaries, determines length. In the case of consumer products, the most traditional is the producer-wholesaler-retailer-customer configuration. The number of institutions of each type in the channel determines channel width. An industrial goods exporter may grant exclusive distribution rights to a foreign entity, whereas a consumer goods exporter may want to use as many intermediaries as possible to ensure intensive distribution.

Channel design is determined by factors that can be summarized as the 11 Cs, listed in Exhibit 10.2. These factors are integral to both the development of new marketing channels and the modification and management of existing ones.

EXHIBIT 10.2. Determinants of Channel Structure and Relationships (The 11 Cs)

EXTERNAL	INTERNAL
Customer characteristics	Company objectives
Culture	Character
Competition	Capital
	Cost
	Coverage
	Control
	Continuity
	Communication

Their individual influences will vary from one market to another and seldom, if ever, can one factor be considered without the interactive effects of the others. The exporter should use the 11 Cs checklist to determine the proper approach to reach intended target audiences before selecting channel members to fill the roles. The first three factors are givens, since the firm must adjust to the existing structures. The other eight are controllable to a certain extent by the exporter.

Customer Characteristics

The demographic and psychographics characteristics of targeted customers will form the basis for channel design decisions. Answers to questions such as what customers need—as well as why, when, and how they buy—are used to determine ways in which the products should be made available to generate a competitive advantage.

In the early stages of product introduction, the exporter may concentrate efforts on only the most attractive markets and later, having attained a foothold, expand distribution. Customer characteristics may cause the same product to be distributed through two different types of channels. Many industrial goods exporters' sales, such as those of Caterpillar, are handled by individual dealers, except when the customer might be the central government or one of its entities, in which case sales are direct from the company itself. Furthermore, primary target audiences may change from one market to another.

In business-to-business marketing, the adoption of e-commerce provides new opportunities for exporters. Expanding network and customer bases can access new export markets. Six sectors are forecast to leading the way in business-to-business online transactions: retail, motor vehicles shipping, industrial equipment, technological products, and government. At the same time, the explosive growth of the Internet poses a direct threat and challenge to traditional intermediaries, leading possibly to elimination, or disinters mediation.

Culture

In planning a distribution system, the exporter must analyze existing channel structures, or what might be called distribution culture. For example, the manner in which Japanese channels of distribution are structured and managed presents one of the major reasons for the apparent failure of foreign firms to establish major market penetration in Japan. In any case, and in every country, exporters must study distribution systems in general and the types of linkages between channel members for their specific type of product in particular. Usually the exporter has to adjust to existing structures to gain distribution.

In addition to structure, functions performed by the various types of intermediaries have to be outlined. Retailers in Japan demand more from manufacturers and wholesalers than do U.S. retailers; for example, they expect to be able to return merchandise for full credit even if there is no reason other than lack of sales. Retailers also expect significant amounts of financing and frequent delivery of products. Retailers, on their part, offer substantial services to their clientele and take great pains to build close relationships with their customers.

Additionally, an analysis is needed of the relationships between channel members—for example, the extent of vertical integration. The linkage can be based on ownership, contract, or the use of expert or referent power by one of the channel members. The Japanese distribution system often financially links producers, importers, distributors, and retailers, either directly or through a bank or a trading company. Interdependence in a number of southern European markets is forged through family relationships or is understood as an obligation.

Foreign legislation affecting distributors and agents is an essential part of the distribution culture of a market. For example, legislation may require that only firms that are 100 percent locally owned represent foreign firms. Before China's entry into the WTO in late 2001, foreign companies were barred from importing their own products, distributing them, or providing after-sales service. These functions were to be performed by Chinese companies or Sino-foreign joint ventures. Now, these restrictions will all be phased out within three years. This means that General Motors China Group will regain control over its marketing. Up to now, Chinese companies have handled the importing, distributing, and selling, and GM's cars have often passed through four different entities before customers see them. In the future, GM wants to build a consistent network of dealers and start providing financing, which also becomes allowed.

While distribution decisions have been mostly tactical and made on a market-by-market basis, marketing managers have to be cognizant of globalization in the distribution function as well. This is taking place in two significant ways. Distribution formats are crossing borders, especially to newly emerging markets. While supermarkets accounted only for 8 percent of consumer nondurable sales in urban areas in Thailand in 1990, the figure today is over 50 percent. Other such formats include department stores, minimarts, and super centers.

The second globalization trend is the globalization of intermediaries themselves either independently or through strategic alliances. Entities, such as Toys"R"Us® from the United States, Galleries Lafayette from France, Marks & Spencer from the United Kingdom, and Takashimaya and Isetan from Japan have expanded to both well-developed and newly emerging markets. Within the European Union, a growing number of EU-based retailers are merging and establishing a presence in other EU markets. In many cases, exporters are providing new technologies to these intermediaries and helping to train them with the hope of

EXHIBIT 10.3. Internationalization of Retailers

APPROACH	OBJECTIVE	EXAMPLE
Business exporter	Reconfigure retailing approach across markets with consistent core and focus on scale	Carrefour, IKEA, Makro, Wal-Mart
Concept exporter	Export concept but let local partners execute	Benetton
Skills exporter	Export unique skills	Price/Costco
Superior operator	Focus on operating capability; implemented through acquisition	Ahold, Tengelmann

SOURCES: Jody Evans, Alan Treadgold, and Felix T. Mavondo, "Psychic Distance and the Performance of International Retailers," *International Marketing Review* 17 (nos. 4 and 5, 2000): 373–391; and Denise Incandela, Kathleen McLaughlin, and Christiana Smith, "Retailers to the World," *The McKinsey Quarterly* 35 (no. 3, 1999): 84–97.

establishing solid relationships that will withstand competition, especially from local entities that typically start beefing up their own operations. The strategic options chosen by retailers are presented in Exhibit 10.3.

Competition

Channels used by competitors may be the only product distribution system that is accepted by both the trade and consumers. In this case, the exporter's task is to use the structure effectively and efficiently, or even innovatively. This may mean, for example, that the exporter chooses a partner capable of developing markets rather than one who has existing contacts. The most obvious distributors may be content with the status quo in the market and be ready to push products that are the most profitable for them regardless of who made them.

Two approaches may be applicable if those serving major customer prospects with similar product lines are not satisfactory. First, the exporter may form jointly owned sales companies with distributors (or with other exporters) to exercise more control. Second, the approach may be to seek a good company fit in terms of goals and objectives. Should a new approach be chosen, it must be carefully analyzed and tested against the cultural, political, and legal environments in which is to be introduced. In some cases, the exporter cannot manipulate the distribution variable. In other cases, domestic competitors either through contractual agreements or through other means may block all feasible channels.

No channel of distribution can be properly selected unless it meets the requirements set by overall company objectives for market share and profitability. In distribution, this often calls for a compromise between cost and control objectives. While integrated channels (exporter owned and operated) may be

EXHIBIT 10.4. Distribution Expansion through Partnerships

	Where/what	Partners	Key success factors
New channels (exclusive supply arrangements)	• Airlines • Airports • Bookstores • Cruise lines • Department stores • Hotels • Supermarkets	• United, Canadian • Host International • Barnes & Noble • Holland America • Nordstrom • Starwood Hotels • Kraft Foods	• Starbucks invests very little capital in international expansion (< 5% of revenue) • Local partners bear all business risk • Licensing allows stricter control over all operations than does franchising—e.g., parent-company consultants visit each store once a month • Local partners contribute regulatory and cultural expertise—e.g., on product adaptations
New markets (through licenses with retailers) — Starbucks Coffee	• Japan • Malaysia • Philippines • Singapore • South Korea • Taiwan • Thailand	• Sazaby (joint venture) • Berjaya Coffee (licensee) • Restaurant Brands (licensee) • Rustan Coffee (licensee) • Bonvest Holdings (licensee) • ESCO (licensee) • President Group (joint venture) • Coffee Partners (licensee)	
New products	• Ice cream • Bottled frappuccino • Coffee-enhanced dark beer • Online catalog	• Dreyer's • PepsiCo • Red Hook Brewery • America Online	

SOURCES: Adapted from Ranjay Gulati, Sarah Huffman, and Gary Nelson, "The Barista Principle—Starbucks and the Rise of Relational Capital," *Strategy and Business 7* (third quarter, 2002): 58–69; and Denise Incandela, kathleen ML. McLaughlin, and Christiana Smith, "Retailers to the World," *The McKinsey Quarterly* 35 (no. 3, 1999): 84–97. See also http://www.starbucks.com

preferred because they facilitate the protection of knowledge-based assets and provide needed high levels of customer service, the cost may be 15 to 35 percent of sales, whereas using distributors may drop the expense to 10 to 15 percent.

Often the use of multiple channels arises with the need to increase sales volume. Rapid expansion can also be achieved through partnerships as shown by the Starbucks example in Exhibit 10.4. Partnerships can be undertaken if appropriate controls are in place to secure expansion with relatively little investment. If expansion is too rapid and the adjustments made to local market conditions too extensive, a major asset—standardization and economies of scale and scope—can be lost.

Character

The nature of the product, its character, will have an impact on the design of the channel. The channel must "fit" the product, just as the product must "fit" the market. Generally, the more specialized, expensive, bulky, or perishable the product and the more after-sale service it may require, the more likely the channel is to be relatively short. Staple items, such as soap, tend to have longer channels. The type of channel chosen must match the overall positioning of the product in the market. Changes in overall market conditions, such as currency fluctuations, may require changes in distribution as well. An increase in the value of the billing currency may cause a repositioning of the marketed product as a luxury item, necessitating an appropriate channel (such as an upper-grade department store) for its distribution.

Rules of thumb aside, particular products may be distributed in a number of ways even to the same target audience. A dual channel may be used in which both intermediaries and a direct contact with customers are used. In some cases, a channel may extend beyond having one tier of distributors and resellers to include importers or agents. Another alternative, hybrid channels, features sharing of marketing functions, with the manufacturer handling promotion and customer generation, and the intermediaries, sales and distribution. The hybrid strategy is based more on cooperation and partnership, while the dual channel may result in conflict if disagreements arise as to who is to handle a specific customer.

Capital

The term *capital* is used to describe the financial requirements in setting up a channel system. The exporter's financial strength will determine the type of channel and the basis on which channel relationships will be built. The stronger the exporter's finances, the more able the firm is to establish channels it either owns or controls. Intermediaries' requirements for beginning inventories, selling on a consignment basis, preferential loans, and need for training all will have an impact on the type of approach chosen by the exporter. For example, an industrial goods manufacturer may find that potential distributors in a particular country lack the capability of servicing the product. The exporter then has two options: (1) set up an elaborate training program at headquarters or regionally or (2) institute company-owned service centers to help distributors. Either approach will require a significant investment, but is necessary to ensure customer trust through superior execution of marketing programs.

Cost

Closely related to the capital dimension is cost—that is, the expenditure incurred in maintaining a channel once it is established. Costs will naturally vary over the life cycle of a relationship with a particular channel member as well as over the life cycle of the products marketed. Cost incurred varies directly with the level of control desired. An example of the costs involved is promotional money spent by a distributor for the exporter's product. A cooperative advertising deal between the exporter and the intermediary would typically split the costs of the promotional campaign executed in the local market.

Costs will vary in terms of the relative power of the manufacturer vis-à-vis its intermediaries. Concentrated distribution systems tend to erode the marketing strength of manufacturers, which lay in their networks of distribution depots that delivered direct to stores. Now, retailers want delivery to their central distribution centers. In addition, they are pushing stockholding costs to manufacturers by demanding more frequent deliveries, in smaller, mixed loads, with shorter delivery time.

Costs may also be incurred in protecting the company's distributors against adverse market conditions. A number of U.S. manufacturers helped their distributors maintain competitive prices through subsidies when the exchange rate for the U.S. dollar caused pricing problems. Extra financing aid has been extended to distributors that have been hit with competitive adversity. Such support, although often high in monetary cost, will pay back manyfold through a faultless manufacturer-distributor relationship.

Coverage

The term *coverage* is used to describe both the number of areas in which the exporter's products are represented and the quality of that representation. In other words, coverage represents the number of outlets needed to effectively cover the target market. Coverage is therefore two-dimensional in that horizontal coverage and vertical coverage need to be considered in channel design. The number of areas to be covered depends on the dispersion of demand in the market and also on the time elapsed since the product's introduction to the market. Three different approaches are available:

1. Intensive coverage, which calls for distributing the product through the largest number of different types of intermediaries and the largest number of individual intermediaries of each type.
2. Selective coverage, which entails choosing a number of intermediaries for each area to be penetrated.
3. Exclusive coverage, which involves only one entity in a market.

Generally, intensive and selective coverage calls for longer channels using different types of intermediaries, usually wholesalers and agents. Exclusive distribution is conducive to more direct sales. For some products, such as ethnic or industrial products, customers are concentrated geographically and allow for more intensive distribution with a more direct channel. A company typically enters a market with one local distributor, but as volume expands, the distribution base often has to be adjusted. The advantages of a single distributor are listed in Exhibit 10.5.

EXHIBIT 10.5. Advantages of a Single Distributor

1. One corporate presence eliminates confusion among buyers and local officials.
2. The volume of business that results when exports are consolidated will attract a larger/more qualified distributor. The distributor will thus have greater influence in its local business community.
3. Communication is less plagued by noise. This will have a positive effect in many areas, from daily information flows to supervising and training.
4. More effective coordination of the sales and promotional effort can be achieved through mutual learning.
5. Logistics flows are more economical.
6. A stronger presence can be maintained in smaller markets or markets in which resources may dictate a holding mode, until more effective penetration can be undertaken.
7. Distributor morale and the overall principal-intermediary relationship are better through elimination of intrabrand competition.

SOURCE: Adapted from Business International Corporation, *201 Checklists: Decision Making in International Operations* (New York: Business International Corporation, 1980), 26–27.

Control

The design of the channel structure is directly related to the extent of control wanted and needed by the exporter. Generally speaking, the more control wanted, the more likely that a direct channel of distribution is developed. The use of indirect channels through independent intermediaries will automatically lead to loss of some control over the marketing of the firm's products. The looser the relationship is between the exporter and intermediaries, the less control the exporter can exert. The longer the channel, the more difficult it becomes for the exporter to have a final say in pricing, promotion, and the types of outlets in which the product will be made available.

In the initial stages of internationalization or specific market entry, an intermediary's specialized knowledge and working relationships are needed, but as exporters' experience base and sales in the market increase, many opt to establish their own sales offices. Use of intermediaries provides quick entry using an existing system in which complementary products provide synergistic benefits. Furthermore, payments are received from one entity rather than from multiple customers.

The issue of control correlates heavily with the type of product or service being marketed. In the case of industrial and high technology products, control will be easier to institute because intermediaries are dependent on the exporter for new products and service. Where the firm's marketing strategy calls for a high level of service, integrated channels are used to ensure that the service does get performed. Later on, an exporter may want to coordinate programs across markets on a regional basis, which is much easier if the channel is controlled.

The exporter's ability and willingness to exercise any type of power—whether reward, coercive, legitimate, referent, or expert—determines the extent of control. The exercise of control causes more incidents of conflict in channels of distribution than any other activity in the relationship. This points to the need for careful communication with foreign intermediaries about the exporter's intentions and also the need for certain control measures. These might include the exporter's need to be the sole source of advertising copy or to be in charge of all product-modification activities. Generally, the more control the exporter wishes to have, the more cost is involved in securing that control.

Continuity

Channel design decisions are the most long-term of the marketing mix decisions. Utmost care must therefore be taken in choosing the right type of channel, given the types of intermediaries available and any environmental threats that may affect the channel design. Product positioning will influence the type of intermediaries chosen to ensure continuity. Nurturing continuity rests heavily on the exporter because foreign distributors may have a more short-term view of the relationship. For example, Japanese wholesalers believe that it is important for manufacturers to follow up initial success with continuous improvement of the product. If such improvements are not forthcoming, competitors are likely to enter the market with similar, lower-priced products, and the wholesalers of the imported product will turn to the Japanese suppliers.

Continuity is also expressed through visible market commitment. Industries abroad may be quite conservative; distributors will not generally support an outsider until they are sure it is in the market to stay. Such commitments include sending in technical or sales personnel or offering training, and setting up wholly-owned sales subsidiaries from the start—and staffing them with locals to help communicate that the company is there for the long term. Investment in distributors may be literal (resulting in co-ownership in the future) or abstract (resulting in more solid commitment in the relationship).

Communication

Communication provides the exchange of information essential to the functioning of the channel. Communication is an important consideration in channel design, and it gains more emphasis in international distribution because of various types of distances that may cause problems. In the buyer-seller relationships in international markets, the distance that is perceived to exist between a buyer and a seller has five aspects, all of which are amplified in the international setting:

1. Social distance: the extent to which each of the two entities in a relationship is familiar with the other's ways of operating.
2. Cultural distance: the degree to which the norms, values, or working methods between the two entities differ because of their separate national characteristics.
3. Technological distance: the differences between the product and process technologies of the two entities.
4. Time distance: the time that must elapse between establishing contact or placing an order and the actual transfer of the product or service involved.
5. Geographical distance: the physical distance between the locations of the two entities.

All these dimensions must be considered when determining whether to use intermediaries and, if they are to be used, what types to use.

Communication, if properly utilized, will assist the exporter in conveying the firm's goals to the distributors, in solving conflict situations, and in marketing the product overall. Communication is a two-way process that does not permit the exporter to dictate to intermediaries. Cases are well known in which the exporter has not been able to make the firm's domestic marketing program functional in a new setting. Prices may not be competitive; promotional materials may be obsolete or inaccurate and not well received overall. This may be compounded if the exporter tries to transplant domestic procedures and programs in foreign markets. Solving these types of problems is important to the welfare of both parties.

Channels of distribution, because of their sequential positioning of the entities involved, are not conducive to noiseless communication. The exporter must design a channel and choose intermediaries that guarantee good information flow. Proper communication involves not only the passage of information between channel members but also a better understanding of each party's needs and goals. This can be achieved through personal visits, exchange of personnel, or distribution advisory councils. Consisting of members from all channel participants, advisory councils meet regularly to discuss opportunities and problems that may have arisen

Selection of Intermediaries

Once the basic design of the channel has been determined, the exporter must begin a search to fill the defined roles with the best available candidates and must secure their cooperation. Two basic decisions are involved in choosing the type of intermediaries to serve a particular market. First, the exporter must determine the type of relationship to have with intermediaries.

The alternatives are distributorship and agency relationship. A *distributor* will purchase the product and will therefore exercise more independence than agencies. Distributors are typically organized along product lines and provide the exporter with complete marketing services. *Agents* have less freedom of movement than distributors because they operate on a commission basis and do not usually physically handle the goods. This, in turn, allows the exporter control to make sure, for example, that the customer gets the most recent and appropriate product version. In addition to the business implications, the choice of type will have legal implications in terms of what the intermediary can commit its principal to and the ease of termination of the agreement.

Second, the exporter must decide whether to utilize indirect exporting, direct exporting, or integrated distribution in penetrating a foreign market. *Indirect exporting* requires dealing with independent intermediaries, both domestic and international, as sales intermediary for the exporter. The benefits, especially in the short term, are that the exporter can use someone else's international channels without having to pay to set them up. But there may be long-term concerns in using this strategy if the exporter wants to actively and aggressively get into the market itself. Firms very early on in their internationalization process only practice indirect exporting. With *direct exporting*, the exporter takes direct responsibility for its products abroad by either selling directly to the foreign customer or finding a local representative to sell its products exclusively in the export market.

The third category of export marketing strategy, *integrated distribution*, the exporter serves the market with many different channel structures depending on the needs of the different markets. It requires, for example, to make an investment in the foreign market for the purpose of distributing its products in that market or more broadly. This could mean a sales office, a distribution hub, or even an assembly operation or manufacturing facility. The last two strategies require longer-term commitment to a market; however, it is riskier because the exporter is making a major financial investment.

Sources for Finding Intermediaries

Firms that have successful international distribution attest to the importance of finding top representatives. This undertaking should be held in the same regard as recruiting and hiring within the company because an ineffective foreign distributor can set an exporter back years; it is almost better to have no distributor than a bad one in a major market.

The approach can be either passive or active. Foreign operations for a number of smaller firms usually start with a passive approach. Distributors, wherever they are, are always on the lookout for product representation that can be profitable and status enhancing. The initial contact may result from an advertisement or from a trade show the exporter has participated in, resulting in an unsolicited order from abroad and the established distribution through the distributor making the inquiry.

The exporter's best interest lies in taking an active role. The exporter should not simply use the first intermediary to show an interest in the firm. The choice should be a result of a careful planning process. The exporter should start by gaining an understanding of market conditions in order to define what is expected of an intermediary and what the exporter can offer in the relationship. At the same time, procedures need to be set for intermediary identification and evaluation. The exporter does not have to do all of this independently; both governmental and private agencies can assist the exporter in locating intermediary candidates.

Governmental Agencies

The U.S. Commercial Service is the "global solutions unit of the U.S. Department of Commerce."[1] One element of its mission is to promote U.S. export services particularly to small and medium-sized firms that wish to enter into exporting. Through its Web site, www.export.gov, it is the U.S. government portal for all export-related assistance offered to the export community as well as a variety of low cost services that allows exporters to search for suitable agents and distributors abroad. Among its important services are the Trade Opportunities Program (TOP), a program an exporter can subscribe to which matches product interests of over 70,000 foreign buyers with those indicated by the U.S. subscribers; The Country Directories of International Contacts (CDIC), which provides names and contact information for directories of importers, agents, trade associations, and government agencies on a country-by-country basis; and The U.S. Exporters Yellow Pages, a directory that includes information and display advertisements on more than 11,000 U.S. companies interested in exporting. Commercial News USA is a catalog magazine featuring advertisements by U.S. producers distributed worldwide 12 times each year. Some very useful programs that allow the exporter to locate the most qualified representatives are included.

Other important programs offered by the U.S. Commercial Service through its export portal to identify potential intermediaries are:

- **BuyUSA Online**

    This service allows U.S. exporters to search for thousands of pre-screened export leads, international business contacts, and personalized counseling. It provides online tools and assistance by trade specialists to complete

---

[1] www.export.gov/comm_suc/about_us, accessed September22, 2003.

export transactions online. A valuable Web site can be used by the exporter to contact potential intermediaries online.

- **Gold Key Services**
  The U.S. Commercial Service, with 150 offices in 85 countries, can arrange appointments between an exporter and carefully selected potential overseas agents and distributors.
- **Platinum Services**
  Provides U.S. companies with intense export consulting for six months to one year through the offices of the U.S. Commercial Service in 85 countries.
- **International Partner Search**
  At the request of the exporter (who provides background information and criteria), this program delivers detailed company information of up to five foreign companies who express interest in the company's products and services.
- **Agriculture-Specific Services**
  This program offers a biweekly newsletter distributed overseas by the USDA of U.S. products offered for sale, e-mail alerts on agricultural export opportunities, a list of U.S. suppliers distributed overseas to prospective buyers of U.S. agricultural goods, and a searchable list for foreign representatives of industry associations to assist the exporter in developing channels of distribution.
- **Video Services**
  The video services offer a variety of video tools designed to help U.S. companies meet pre-qualified overseas buyers, distributors, and agents, and hold business meetings right from an Export Assistance Center.
- **International Company Profile**
  Provides an affordable, fast credit check and background information of one potential business partner as requested by the exporter. An example of an ICP is provided in Figure 11.3. Furthermore, individual state agencies provide similar services. These are all available on an online basis.
- **Trade Missions**
  The U.S. government-sponsored trade missions escort groups of U.S. companies to foreign countries and arrange for meetings with potential buyers, foreign agents and distributors, as well as meetings with foreign government officials and regulatory offices such as customs. A calendar of such trade missions is published on the export portal.

EXHIBIT 10.6. Sample Report from the International Company Profile

I. FOREIGN COMPANY CONTACT AND SIZE INFORMATION:
China Power
Rm. 2301, Saxson road
Beijing 1000301, China
Mr. Sam, President
Tel: 86-10-6606-3072
Fa: 86-10-6606-3071
1992
Sales: RMB 1000,000,000
Employees: 80 including 15 at the headquarters

II. BACKGROUND AND PRODUCT INFORMATION
Operation:
The firm is mainly engaged in selling industrial automation products. It is also engaged in contracting factory automation system projects which consist of system design, programming, installation, and presales service. The firm started to provide services for machine tools refitting in the United States in 1996.
Company Background/History:
The firm is a wholly foreign owned enterprise registered in June of 1992 with the Municipal Administration for Industry & Commerce. The registered capital was USD 1,250,000. The firm is a subsidiary of Can International Ltd., who owns 100 percent of the firm.
Business Size: small
Major Subsidiaries:
Name: China Power
Add: Rm. 22, Saxon Road, Beijing
Tel: 86-10-6606-3072
Ownership: 80 percent owned by the firm
Parent Company:
Name: ABZ Ltd., Hong Kong
Line of Business: Investment
Public Record:
According to management, an introduction to the firm and its products was included in editions of the following publications: The People's Daily Overseas Edition, the Science & Technology Daily, the Industrial & Commercial Times, the Worker's Daily, and the Computer World.
Location:
A site visit was made on September 19, 1996. The firm is located in a prime commercial area. It rents office space of 130 square meters at the address shown above. It occupies one floor in a ten-story building, the condition of which is good.
Key Company Officials:
Mr. Sam, President, born on October 24, 1958, was a graduate of Oxford University in 1982. He is now active in the firm's day-to-day operation in charge of the overall management. Prior to joining the firm, he was employed by the Ministry of Communications from 1982–1989 and China Harbor Engineering Co. 1989–1992.
Mr. Taylor, Vice President, was born in 1948. He joined the firm in 1995 and is currently active in the day-to-day operations responsible for marketing and sales. Prior to joining the firm, he was employed as Chief Representative from 1984–1995 by CROWE, a foreign plastic company merged by Miller Automation.
Ms. Young, Vice President, is currently active in the firm's day-to-day operations in charge of finance.

III. REFERENCES
Foreign Firms Represented:
MILLER AUTOMATION for industrial automation products.
WILDWOOD WARE for Ministry of Machinery's industrial software.
ZXC for low voltage electrical components.
CONTON for industrial computer.
TBP for analyzing instruments.
TINNER for power station meter & instruments.
Bank References: The firm maintains

(Continued)

EXHIBIT 10.6. (Continued.)

banking relationships with the Industrial & Commercial Bank of China Beijing Branch. However, Mr. Sam declined to provide the account number.

Local Chamber/Trade Association:
Under current investigation, the firm is not known to be a member of any local chambers or trade associations. However, President Sam is a member of China Harbor Association and China Material Handling Association.

Trade References:
PURCHASE TERRITORY:
International: 100 percent
Import from 90 percent from the U.S.A., 10 percent from Germany, Sweden and other countries
SALES TERRITORY: Local and International Local: 95 percent; International: 5 percent
Exporting to South Africa
CUSTOMER TYPE:
Manufacturers: 100 percent
Major customers include Glass Bulb Co., Ltd.
Other customers include Iron & Steel Corporation
PURCHASING AND SELLING ITEM TERMS:
Purchasing Terms: L/C at sight
Selling Terms: T/T
IMPORT & EXPORT: YES

IV. FINANCIAL DATA/CREDIT WORTHINESS INFORMATION
Financial Highlights of the firm for the period January 1 to December 31 as shown below:
AMOUNT IN RMB
Sales   100,000,000
Total Assets   30,000,000

The firm declined to provide its financial statement due to "tax concerns."

V. MARKET INFORMATION OUTLOOK
According to Mr. Sam, the firm is the sole "Gold Partner" of Miller Automation. "Note: To be a "Gold Partner," the sales volume should be more than 50 percent in the China market.

VI. SPECIAL REQUEST INFORMATION: N/A

VII. REPUTATION: Unknown

VIII. POST COMMENTS/EVALUATION
As far as can be seen from the information supplied, the firm seems to be a satisfactory contact, EAJ Inc., however, wish to contact USFCS Hong Kong to obtain more information of China Powe's parent Company, Can International Ltd.

IX. SOURCES OF INFORMATION
Dun & Bradstreet Report

NOTE: The information in this report has been supplied to the United States Government by commercial and government sources in the countries covered and is intended for the sole use of the purchaser. You are requested to honor the trust of these sources making secondary distribution of the data. While every effort is made to supply current and accurate information, the U.S. Government assumes no responsibility or liability for any decision based on the content of the ICP.

SOURCE: Example provided by Export Promotion Services, International Trade Administration, U.S. Department of Commerce.

Private Sources

The easiest approach for the firm seeking intermediaries is to consult trade directories. Country and regional business directories such as Kompass (Europe), Bottin International (worldwide), Nordisk Handelskalendar (Northern Europe), and the Japan Trade Directory are good places to start. Company lists by country and line of business can be ordered from Dun & Bradstreet, Rueben H. Donnelly, Kelly's Directory, and Johnston Publishing. Telephone directories, especially the yellow page sections or editions, can provide distributor lists. The Jaeger and Waldmann International Telex Directory can also be consulted. Although not detailed, these listings will give addresses and an indication of the products sold.

The firm can solicit the support of some of its facilitating agencies, such as banks, advertising agencies, shipping lines, and airlines. All these have substantial international information networks and can put them to work for their clients. The services available will vary by agency, depending on the size of its foreign operations. Some of the major U.S. flagship carriers—for example, Northwest Airlines—have special staffs for this purpose within their cargo operations. Banks usually have the most extensive networks through their affiliates and correspondent banks. Similarly, the exporter may solicit the help of associations or chambers of commerce.

The exporter can take an even more direct approach by buying space to solicit representation. Advertisements typically indicate the type of support the exporter will be able to give to its distributor. For example, Medtech International, an exporter of surgical gloves, advertises for intermediaries in magazines such as *International Hospital Supplies*. Trade fairs are an important form to meet potential distributors and to get data on intermediaries in the industry. Increasingly, exporters are using their Web sites to attract international distributors and agents. For example, P&D Creative, Inc. uses its Web page to solicit distribution for its line of environmentally safe cleaning products It promotes its site in search engines and internationally oriented newsgroups and provides pricing and product information of interest to intermediaries.

The exporter may also deal directly with contacts from previous applications, launch new mail solicitations, use its own sales organization for the search, or communicate with existing customers to find prospective distributors. The latter may happen after a number of initial (unsolicited) sales to a market, causing the firm to want to enter the market on a more formal basis. If resources permit, the exporter can use outside service agencies or consultants to generate a list of prospective representatives.

Sources other than the U.S. government for locating foreign intermediaries are summarized in Exhibit 10.7. The purpose of going through such a list is to generate as many prospective representatives as possible for the next step,

EXHIBIT 10.7. Nongovernment Sources for Locating Foreign Intermediaries

1. Distributor Inquiries
2. Host Government
   - Representative Offices
   - Import Promotion Efforts
3. Trade Sources
   - Magazines, Journals
   - Directories
   - Associations and Chambers of Commerce
   - Banks, advertising agencies, carriers
4. Field Organizations
5. Customers
6. Direct-mail solicitations/contact of previous applicants
7. Trade missions, trade fairs
8. Web sites
9. Independent Consultants

screening. In most firms, the evaluation of candidates involves both what to look for and where to go for the information. At this stage, the exporter knows the type of distributor that is needed. The potential candidates must now be compared and contrasted against determining criteria. Although the criteria to be used vary by industry and by product, a good summary list is provided in Exhibit 10.8. Especially when various criteria are being weighed, these lists must be updated to reflect changes in the environment and the exporter's own situation. Some criteria can be characterized as determinant, in that they form the core dimensions along which candidates must perform well, whereas some criteria, although important, may be used only in preliminary screening. This list should correspond closely to the exporter's own determinants of success—all the things that have to be done better to beat out competition.

Before signing a contract with a particular agent or a distributor, exporters should satisfy themselves on certain key criteria. A number of these key criteria can be easily quantified, thereby providing a solid base for comparisons between candidates, whereas others are qualitative and require careful interpretation and confidence in the data sources providing the information.

Performance

The financial standing of the candidate is one of the most important criteria, as well as a good starting point. This figure will show whether the distributor is making money and is able to perform some of the necessary marketing functions such as extension of credit to customers and risk absorption. Financial reports

EXHIBIT. 10.8. Selection Criteria for Choosing an International Distributor

CHARACTERISTICS	WEIGHT	RATING
Goals and strategies	—	—
Size of the firm	—	—
Financial strength	—	—
Reputation	—	—
Trading areas covered	—	—
Compatibility	—	—
Experience in products/with competitors	—	—
Sales organization	—	—
Physical facilities	—	—
Willingness to carry inventories	—	—
After-sales service capability	—	—
Use of promotion	—	—
Sales performance	—	—
Relations with local government	—	—
Communications	—	—
Overall attitude/commitment	—	—

are not always complete or reliable, or they may lend themselves to interpretation differences, pointing to a need for third-party opinion. Many Latin American intermediaries lack adequate capital, a situation that can lead to more time spent managing credit than managing marketing strategy.

Sales are another excellent indicator. What the distributor is presently doing gives an indication of how he or she could perform if chosen to handle the exporter's product. The distributor's sales strength can be determined by analyzing management ability and the adequacy and quality of the sales team. If the intermediary is an importer or wholesaler, its ability to provide customer service to the next channel level is a critical determinant of future sales.

The distributor's existing product lines should be analyzed along four dimensions: competitiveness, compatibility, complementary nature, and quality. Quite often, exporters find that the most desirable distributors in a given market are already handling competitive products and are therefore unavailable. In that case, the exporter can look for an equally qualified distributor handling related products. The complementary nature of products may be of interest to both parties, especially in industrial markets, where ultimate customers may be in the market for complete systems or one-stop shopping. The quality match for products is important for product positioning reasons; a high-quality product may suffer unduly from a questionable distributor reputation.

The number of product lines handled gives the exporter an indication of the level of effort to expect from the distributor. Some distributors are interested in carrying as many products and product lines as possible to enhance their own standing, but they have the time and the willingness to actively sell only those that bring the best compensation. At this time, it is also important to check the candidate's physical facilities for handling the product. This is essential particularly for products that may be subject to quality changes, such as food products. The assessment should also include the candidate's marketing materials, including a possible Web site, for adequacy and appropriateness.

The distributor's market coverage must be determined. The analysis of coverage will include not only how much territory, or how many segments of the market, are covered, but also how well the markets are served. Again, the characteristics of the sales force and the number of sales offices are good quantitative indicators. To study the quality of the distributor's market coverage, the exporter can check whether the sales force visits executives, engineers, and operating people or concentrates mainly on purchasing agents. In some areas of the world, the exporter has to make sure that two distributors will not end up having territorial overlaps, which can lead to unnecessary conflict.

Professionalism

The distributor's reputation must be checked. The distributor's customers, suppliers, facilitating agencies, competitors, and other members of the local business community should be contacted for information on the business conduct of the distributor in such areas as buyer-seller relations and ethical behavior. This effort will shed light on variables that may be important only in certain parts of the world; for example, variables such as political clout, which is essential in certain developing countries.

The exporter must acknowledge the distributor as an independent entity with its own goals. The distributor's business strategy must therefore be determined, particularly what the distributor expects to get from the relationship and where the exporter fits into those plans. Because a channel relationship is long term, the distributor's views on future expansion of the product line or its distribution should be clarified. This phase will also require a determination of the degree of help the distributor would need in terms of price, credit, delivery, sales training, communication, personal visits, product modification, warranty, advertising, warehousing, technical support, and after-sales service. Leaving uncertainties in these areas will cause major problems later. Finally, the exporter should determine the distributor's overall attitude in terms of cooperation and commitment to the exporter. An effective way of testing this, and weeding out the less interested candidates, is to ask the distributor to assist in developing a local marketing plan or to develop one. This endeavor will bring out potential problem areas and will spell out which party is to perform the various marketing functions. It is important that both parties commit to two-way communication to ensure long-term success, especially in cases of considerable distances.

A criteria list is valuable only when good data are available on each and every criterion. Although the initial screening can take place at the firm's offices, the three to five finalists should be visited. No better method of assessing distributors exists than visiting them, inspecting their facilities, and interviewing their various constituents in the market. A number of other critical data sources are important for firms without the resources for on-site inspection. The distributor's suppliers or firms not in direct competition can provide in-depth information. A bona fide candidate will also provide information through a local bank. Credit reports are available through the National Association of Credit Management, Dun & Bradstreet, and local credit-reporting agencies.

The Distributor Agreement

When the exporter has found a suitable intermediary, a foreign sales agreement is drawn up. The agreement can be relatively simple, but given the numerous differences in the market environments, certain elements are essential. The checklist presented in Exhibit 10.9 is the most comprehensive in stipulating the nature of the contract and the respective rights and responsibilities of the exporter and the distributor.

Contract duration is important, especially when an agreement is signed with a new distributor. In general, distribution agreements should be for a specified, relatively short period (one or two years). The initial contract with a new distributor should stipulate a trial period of either three or six months, possibly with minimum purchase requirements. Duration should be determined with an eye on the local laws and their stipulations on distributor agreements. These will be discussed later in conjunction with distributor termination.

Geographic boundaries for the distributor should be determined with care, especially by smaller firms. Future expansion of the product market might be complicated if a distributor claims rights to certain territories. The exporter should retain the right to distribute products independently, reserving the right to certain customers. For example, many exporters maintain a dual distribution system, dealing directly with certain large accounts. This type of arrangement should be explicitly stated in the agreement. Transshipments, sales to customers outside the agreed-upon territory or customer type, have to be explicitly prohibited to prevent the occurrence of parallel importation.

The payment section of the contract should stipulate the methods of payment as well as how the distributor or agent is to draw compensation.

EXHIBIT 10.9. Elements of a Distributor Agreement

A. Basic Components
   1. Parties to the agreement
   2. Statement that the contract supersedes all previous agreements
   3. Duration of the agreement (perhaps a three- or six-month trial period)
   4. Territory:
      a. Exclusive, nonexclusive, sold
      b. Manufacturer's right to sell direct at reduced or no commission to local government and old customers
   5. Products covered
   6. Expression of intent to comply with government regulations
   7. Clauses limiting sales forbidden by U.S. Export Controls or practices forbidden by the Foreign Corrupt Practices Act
B. Manufacturer's Rights
   1. Arbitration:
      a. If possible, in the manufacturer's country
      b. If not, before International Chamber of Commerce or American Arbitration Association, or using the London Court of Arbitration rules
      c. Definition of rules to be applied (e.g., in selecting the arbitration panel)
      d. Assurance that award will be binding in the distributor's country
   2. Jurisdiction that of the manufacturer's country (the signing completed at home); if not possible, a neutral site such as Sweden or Switzerland
   3. Termination conditions (e.g., no indemnification if due notice given)
   4. Clarification of tax liabilities
   5. Payment and discount terms
   6. Conditions for delivery of goods
   7. Nonliability for late delivery beyond manufacturer's reasonable control
   8. Limitation on manufacturer's responsibility to provide information
   9. Waiver of manufacturer's responsibility to keep lines manufactured outside the United States (e.g., licensees) outside of covered territory
   10. Right to change prices, terms, and conditions at any time
   11. Right of manufacturer or agent to visit territory and inspect books
   12. Right to repurchase stock
   13. Option to refuse or alter distributor's orders
   14. Training of distributor personnel in the United States subject to:
       a. Practicality
       b. Costs to be paid by the distributor
       c. Waiver of manufacturer's responsibility for U.S. immigration approval
C. Distributor's Limitations and Duties
   1. No disclosure of confidential information
   2. Limitation of distributor's right to assign contract
   3. Limitation of distributor's position as legal agent of manufacturer
   4. Penalty clause for late payment

EXHIBIT 10.9. Elements of a Distributor Agreement (Continued)

5. Limitation of right to handle competing lines
6. Placement of responsibility for obtaining customs clearance
7. Distributor to publicize designation as authorized representative in defined area
8. Requirement to move all signs or evidence identifying distributor with manufacturer if relationship ends
9. Acknowledgment by distributor of manufacturer's ownership of trademark, trade names, patents
10. Information to be supplied by the distributor:
    a. Sales reports
    b. Names of active prospects
    c. Government regulations dealing with imports
    d. Competitive products and competitors' activities
    e. Price at which goods are sold
    f. Complete data on other lines carried (on request)
11. Information to be supplied by distributor on purchasers
12. Accounting methods to be used by distributor
13. Requirement to display products appropriately
14. Duties concerning promotional efforts
15. Limitation of distributor's right to grant unapproved warranties, make excessive claims
16. Clarification of responsibility arising from claims and warranties
17. Responsibility of distributor to provide repair and other services
18. Responsibility to maintain suitable place of business
19. Responsibility to supply all prospective customers
20. Understanding that certain sales approaches and sales literature must be approved by manufacturer
21. Prohibition of manufacture or alteration of products
22. Requirement to maintain adequate stock, spare parts
23. Requirement that inventory be surrendered in event of a dispute that is pending in court
24. Prohibition of transshipments

SOURCE: Adapted from "Elements of a Distributor Agreement," *Business International*, March 29, 1963, 23–24. Some of the sections have been changed to reflect the present situation.

Distributors derive compensation from various discounts, such as the functional discount, whereas agents earn a specific commission percentage of net sales (such as 15 percent). Given the volatility of currency markets, the agreement should also state the currency to be used. The exporter also needs to make sure that none of the compensation forwarded to the distributor is in violation of the Foreign Corrupt Practices Act or the OECD guidelines. A violation occurs if a payment is made to influence a foreign official in exchange for business favors, depending on the nature of the action sought. So-called grease or facilitating payments, such as a small fee to expedite paperwork through customs, are not considered violations.

Product and conditions of sale need to be agreed on. The products or product lines included should be stipulated, as well as the functions and responsibilities of the intermediary in terms of carrying the goods in inventory, providing service in conjunction with them, and promoting them. Conditions of sale determine which party is to be responsible for some of the expenses involved, which will in turn have an effect on the price to the distributor. These conditions include credit and shipment terms.

Effective means of communication between the parties must be stipulated in the agreement if an exporter-distributor relationship is to succeed. The exporter should have access to all information concerning the marketing of his or her products in the distributor's territory, including past records, present situation assessments, and marketing research concerning the future. Communication channels should be formal for the distributor to voice formal grievances. The contract should state the confidentiality of the information provided by either party and protect the intellectual property rights (such as patents) involved.

Managing Channel Relationships

A channel relationship can be likened to a marriage: It brings together two independent entities that have shared goals. For the relationship to work, each party must be open about its expectations and openly communicate changes perceived in the other's behavior that might be contrary to the agreement. The closer the relationship is to a distribution partnership, the more likely marketing success will materialize. Conflict will arise, ranging from small grievances (such as billing errors) to major ones (rivalry over channel duties), but it can be managed to enhance the overall channel relationship. In some cases, conflict may be caused by an outside entity, such as gray markets, in which unauthorized intermediaries compete for market share with legitimate importers and exclusive distributors. Nevertheless, the exporter must solve the problem.

The relationship has to be managed for the long term. An exporter may in some countries have a seller's market situation that allows it to exert pressure on its intermediaries for concessions, for example. However, if environmental conditions change, the exporter may find that the channel support it needs to succeed is not there because of the manner in which it managed channel relationships in the past. Firms with harmonious relationships are typically those with more experience abroad and those that are proactive in managing the channel relationship. Harmonious relationships are also characterized by more trust,

EXHIBIT 10.10. Performance Problems and Remedies When Using Overseas Distributors

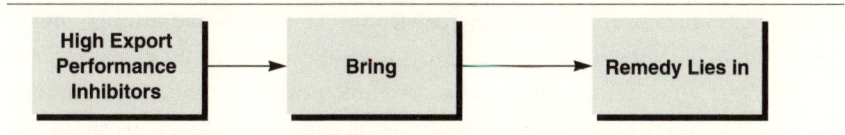

High Export Performance Inhibitors → Bring → Remedy Lies in

Separate Ownership	• Divided Loyalties • Seller–Buyer Atmosphere • Unclear Future Intentions	Offering good incentives, helpful support schemes, discussing plan frankly, and interacting in a mutually beneficial way
Geographic, Economic, and Cultural Separation	• Communication Blocks • Negative Attitudes toward Foreigners • Physical Distribution Strains	Making judicious use of two-way visits, establishing a well-managed communication program, including distributor advisory council
Different Rules of Law	• Vertical Trading Restrictions • Dismissal Difficulties	Full compliance with the law, drafting a strong distributor agreement

SOURCE: Adapted from Philip J. Rosson, "Success Factors in Manufacturer-Overseas Distributor Relationships in International Marketing," in *International Marketing Management*, ed. Erdener Kaynak (New York: Praeger, 1984): 91–107.

communication and cooperation between the entities and, as a result, by less conflict and perceived uncertainty.

As an exporter's operations expand, the need for coordination across markets may grow. Therefore, the exporter may want to establish distributor advisory councils to help in reactive measures (e.g., how to combat parallel importation) or proactive measures (e.g., how to transfer best practices from one distributor to another). Naturally, such councils are instrumental in building esprit de corps for the long-term success of the distribution system.

Factors in Channel Management

An excellent framework for managing channel relationships is shown in Exhibit 10.10. The complicating factors that separate the two parties fall into three categories: ownership, geographic, cultural, and economic distance, and different rules of law. Rather than lament their existence, both parties need to take strong action to remedy them. Often, the major step is acknowledgment that differences do indeed exist.

In exporting, manufacturers and distributors are usually independent entities. Distributors typically carry the products of more than one manufacturer and judge products by their ability to generate revenue without added expense. This may produce strains and conflict, which need to be resolved through monetary and psychological awards.

Distance, whether it is geographic, psychological, economic, or a combination, can be bridged through effective two-way communication. This should go beyond normal routine business communication to include innovative ways of sharing pertinent information. The exporter may place one person in charge of distributor-related communications or put into effect an interpenetration strategy—that is, an exchange of personnel so that both organizations gain further insight into the workings of the other.

The existence of cross-cultural differences in people's belief systems and behavior patterns has to be acknowledged and acted on for effective channel management. For example, in markets where individualism is stressed, local channel partners may seek arrangements that foster their own self-interest and may expect their counterparts to watch out for themselves. Conflict is seen as a natural phenomenon. In societies of low individualism, however, a common purpose is fostered between the partners.

Economic distance manifests itself in exchange rates, for example. Instability of exchange rates can create serious difficulties for distributors in their trading activities, not only with their suppliers but also with their domestic customers. Manufacturers and distributors should develop and deploy mutually acceptable mechanisms that allow for some flexibility in interactions when unforeseen rate fluctuations occur.

Laws and regulations in many markets may restrict the manufacturer in terms of control. For example, in the European Union, the exporter cannot prevent a distributor from reexporting products to customers in another member country, even though the exporter has another distributor in that market. EU law insists on a single market where goods and services can be sold throughout the area without restriction.

Most of the criteria used in selecting intermediaries can be used to evaluate existing intermediaries as well. If not conducted properly and fairly, however, evaluation can be a source of conflict. In addition to being given the evaluation results in order to take appropriate action, the distributor should be informed of the evaluative criteria and should be a part of the overall assessment process. Again, the approach should be focused on serving mutual benefits. For example, it is important that the exporter receive detailed market and financial performance data from the distributor. Most distributors identify these data as the key sources of power in distribution and may, therefore, be inherently reluctant to provide them in full detail. The exchange of such data is often the best indicator of a successful relationship.

A part of the management process is channel adjustment. This can take the form of channel shift (eliminating a particular type of channel), channel modification (changing individual members while leaving channel structure intact), or role or relationship modification (changing functions performed or the reward structure) as a result of channel evaluation. The need for channel change should be well established and not executed hastily because it will cause a major distraction in the operations of the firm. Some companies have instituted procedures that require executives to consider carefully all of the aspects and potential results of change before execution.

Gray Markets

Gray markets, or parallel importation, refer to authentic and legitimately manufactured trademark items that are produced and purchased abroad but imported or diverted to the United States by bypassing designated channels. The value of gray markets in the United States has been estimated at $20 billion at retail. Gray-marketed products vary from inexpensive consumer goods (such as chewing gum) to expensive capital goods (such as excavation equipment). The phenomenon is not restricted to the United States; Japan, for example, has witnessed gray markets because of the high value of the yen and the subsidization of cheaper exports through high taxes. Japanese exporters thus often found it cheaper to go to Los Angeles to buy export versions of Japanese-made products.

Various conditions allow unauthorized resellers to exist. The most important are price segmentation and exchange rate fluctuations. Competitive conditions may require the exporter to sell essentially the same product at different prices in different markets or to different customers. Because many products are priced higher in, for example, the United States, a gray exporter can purchase them in Europe or the Far East and offer discounts between 10 and 40 percent below list price when reselling them in the U.S. market. Exchange rate fluctuations can cause price differentials and thus opportunities for gray exporters. In these cases, the gray market goods typically cost more than those usually available through authorized suppliers. In other cases, if there are multiple production sites for the same product, gray markets can emerge due to negative perceptions about the country of origin, as seen in the case highlighted in Exhibit 11.12.

Gray market flows have increased as current barriers to trade are being eliminated. The European Union has significant parallel importation due to significant price differentials in ethical drugs, which are in turn the result of differences in regulation, insurance coverage, medical practice, and exchange rates. Of the 15 member countries, only Denmark grants manufacturers the freedom to price their ethical drugs. The share of parallel trade is estimated at 15 percent and is expected to grow since the European Commission is supporting the practice. A similar controversy has emerged in the United States, where prescription drugs are priced at 34 percent higher than in Canada and where some are advocating the reimportation of these drugs from Canada to the United States.

Opponents and supporters of the practice disagree on whether the central issue is price or trade rights. Detractors typically cite the following arguments:

1. The gray market unduly hurts the legitimate owners of trademarks.
2. Without protection, trademark owners will have little incentive to invest in product development.
3. Gray exporters will "free ride" or take unfair advantage of the trademark owners' marketing and promotional activities.
4. Parallel imports can deceive consumers by not meeting product standards or their normal expectations of after-sale service.

The bottom line is that gray market goods can severely undercut local marketing plans, erode long-term brand images, eat up costly promotion funds, and sour manufacturer-intermediary relations. The opponents scored a major victory when the European Court of Justice ruled in 2001 against Tesco, which imported cheap Levi jeans from the United States and sold them at prices well below those of other retailers. The decision backed Levi's claim that its image could be harmed if it lost control of import distribution. Tesco can continue sourcing Levi's products within the EU from the cheapest provider, but not from outside the EU.

Proponents of parallel importation approach the issue from an altogether different point of view. They argue for their right to "free trade" by pointing to manufacturers that are both overproducing and overpricing in some markets. The main beneficiaries are consumers, who benefit from lower prices and discount distributors, with whom some of the manufacturers do not want to deal and who have now, because of gray markets, found a profitable market niche. In response to the challenge, manufacturers have chosen various approaches. Despite the Supreme Court ruling in May 1988 to legitimize gray markets in the United States, foreign manufacturers, U.S. companies manufacturing abroad, and authorized retailers have continued to fight the practice. In January 1991, the U.S. Customs Service enacted a new rule whereby trademarked goods that have been authorized for manufacture and sale abroad by U.S. trademark holders will no longer be allowed into the United States through parallel channels. Those parallel importing goods of overseas manufacturers will not be affected.

The solution for the most part lies with the contractual relationships that tie businesses together. In almost all cases of gray marketing, someone in the authorized channel commits a diversion, thus violating the agreements signed. One of the standard responses is therefore disenfranchisement of such violators. This approach is a clear response to complaints from the authorized dealers who are being hurt by transshipments. Tracking down offenders is quite expensive and time-consuming; however, some of the gray exporters can be added to the authorized dealer network if mutually acceptable terms can be reached, thereby increasing control of the channel of distribution.

Finally, a one-price policy can eliminate one of the main reasons for gray markets. This means choosing the most efficient of the distribution channels through which to market the product, but it may also mean selling at the lowest price to all customers regardless of location and size. Other strategies include producing different versions of products for different markets and promoting the benefits of dealing with authorized dealers (and, thereby, the dangers of dealing with gray market dealers).

Termination of the Channel Relationship

Many reasons exist for the termination of a channel relationship, but the most typical are changes in the exporter's distribution approach (for example, establishing a sales office) or a (perceived) lack of performance by the intermediary. On occasion, termination may result from either party not honoring agreements; for example, by selling outside assigned territories and initiating price wars.

Channel relationships go through a life cycle. The concept of an international distribution life cycle is presented in Exhibit 10.11. Over time, the

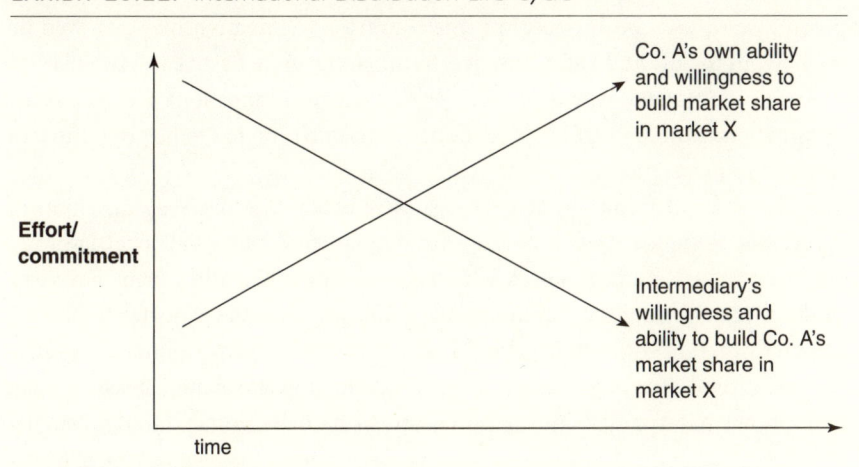

EXHIBIT 10.11. International Distribution Life Cycle

SOURCE: Framework courtesy of Professor David Arnold, Harvard Business School, and Professor John Quelch, London Business School.

exporter's capabilities increase while a distributor's ability and willingness to grow the exporter's business in that market decreases. When a producer expands its market presence, it may expect more of a distributor's effort than the distributor is willing to make available. Furthermore, with expansion, the exporter may want to expand its product line to items that the distributor is neither interested in nor able to support. In some cases, intermediaries may not be interested in growing the business beyond a certain point (e.g., due to progressive taxation in the country) or as aggressively as the principal may expect (i.e., being more of an order-taker than an order-getter). As a exporter's operations expand, it may want to start to coordinate operations across markets for efficiency and customer-service reasons or to cater to global accounts—thereby needing to control distribution to a degree that independent intermediaries are not willing to accept, or requiring a level of service that they may not be able to deliver. If termination is a result of such a structural change, the situation has to be handled carefully. The effect of termination on the intermediary has to be understood, and open communication is needed to make the transition smooth. For example, the intermediary can be compensated for investments made, and major customers can be visited jointly to assure them that service will be uninterrupted.

Termination conditions are one of the most important considerations in the distributor agreement, because the just causes for termination vary and the penalties for the exporter may be substantial. Just causes include fraud or deceit, damage to the other party's interest, or failure to comply with contract obligations concerning minimum inventory requirements or minimum sales levels. These must be spelled out carefully because local courts are often favorably disposed toward local businesses. In some countries, termination may not even be possible. In the EU and Latin America, terminating an ineffective intermediary is time-consuming and expensive. One year's average commissions are typical for termination without justification. A notice of termination has to be given three to six months in advance.

The time to think about such issues is before the overseas distribution agreement is signed. It is especially prudent to find out what local laws say about termination and to check what type of experience other firms have had in the particular country. Careful preparation can allow the exporter to negotiate a termination without litigation. If the distributor's performance is unsatisfactory, careful documentation and clearly defined performance measures may help show that the distributor has more to gain by going quietly than by fighting.

Summary

Channels of distribution consist of the marketing efforts and intermediaries that facilitate the movement of goods and services. Decisions that must be made to establish an international channel of distribution focus on channel design and the selection of intermediaries for the roles that the exporter will not perform. The channel must be designed to meet the requirements of the intended customer base, coverage, long-term continuity of the channel once it is established, and the quality of coverage to be achieved.

Having determined the basic design of the channel, the exporter will then decide on the number of different types of intermediaries to use and how many of each type, or whether to use intermediaries at all, which would be the case in direct distribution using, for example, sales offices or e-commerce. The process is important because the majority of international sales involve distributors, and channel decisions are the most long-term of all marketing decisions. The more the channel operation resembles a team, rather than a collection of independent businesses, the more effective the overall marketing effort will be.

CHAPTER 11

International Transportation and Logistics

International transportation is of major concern to the exporter because transportation determines how and when goods will be received. The transportation issue can be divided into three components: infrastructure, the availability of modes, and the choice of modes.

Transportation Infrastructure

In industrialized nations, firms can count on an established transportation network. Internationally, however, major variations in infrastructure may be encountered.

Some countries may have excellent inbound and outbound transportation systems but weak transportation links within the country. This is particularly true in former colonies, where the original transportation systems were designed to maximize the extractive potential of the countries. In such instances, shipping to the market may be easy, but distribution within the market may represent a very difficult and time-consuming task.

The exporter must therefore learn about existing and planned infrastructures abroad. In some countries, for example, railroads may be an excellent transportation mode, far surpassing the performance of trucking, whereas in others, the use of railroads for freight distribution may be a gamble at best.

The transportation methods used to carry cargo to seaports or airports must also be investigated. Mistakes in the evaluation of transportation options can prove to be very costly. Extreme variations also exist in the frequency of transportation services. For example, a ship may not visit a particular port for weeks or even months. Sometimes, only carriers with particular characteristics, such as small size, will serve a given location. All of these infrastructure concerns must be taken into account in the initial planning of the firm's transportation service.

Availability of Modes

Even though goods are shipped abroad by rail or truck, international transportation frequently requires ocean or air freight, which many corporations only rarely use domestically. In addition, combinations such as land bridges or sea bridges frequently permit the transfer of freight among various modes of transportation, resulting in intermodal movements. The exporter must understand the specific properties of the different modes in order to use them intelligently.

Ocean Shipping

Water transportation is a key mode for international freight. Three types of vessels operating in ocean shipping can be distinguished by their service: liner service, bulk service, and tramp or charter service. *Liner service* offers regularly scheduled passage on established routes. *Bulk service* mainly provides contractual services for individual voyages or for prolonged periods of time. *Tramp service* is available for irregular routes and is scheduled only on demand.

In addition to the services offered by ocean carriers, the type of cargo a vessel can carry is also important. Most common are conventional (break bulk) cargo vessels, container ships, and roll-on-roll-off (RO-RO) vessels. Conventional cargo vessels are useful for oversized and unusual cargoes but may be less efficient in their port operations. It is a reflection of the premium assigned to speed and ease of handling that has caused a decline in the use of general cargo vessels and a sharp increase in the growth of container ships, which carry standardized containers that greatly facilitate the loading and unloading of cargo and intermodal transfers.

As a result, the time the ship has to spend in port is reduced. Roll-on-roll-off vessels are essentially oceangoing ferries. Trucks can drive onto built-in ramps and roll off at the destination. Another vessel similar to the RO-RO vessel is the LASH (lighter aboard ship) vessel. LASH vessels consist of barges stored on the ship and lowered at the point of destination. These individual barges operate on inland waterways, a feature that is particularly useful in shallow water.

The availability of a certain type of vessel, however, does not automatically mean that it can be used. The greatest constraint in international ocean shipping is the lack of ports and port services. For example, modern container ships cannot serve some ports because the local equipment is unable to handle the resulting traffic. This problem is often found in developing countries, where local authorities lack the funds to develop facilities. In some instances, governments purposely limit the development of ports to impede the inflow of imports.

Increasingly, however, nations recognize the importance of appropriate port structures and are developing such facilities in spite of the heavy investments necessary. If such investments are accompanied by concurrent changes in the overall infrastructure, transportation efficiency should, in the long run, more than recoup the original investment.

Large investments in infrastructure are usually necessary to produce results. Selective allocation of funds to transportation tends to only shift bottlenecks to some other point in the infrastructure. If these bottlenecks are not removed, the consequences may be felt in the overall economic performance of the nation. A good example is provided by the Caribbean. Even though geographically close to the United States, ocean carriers serve many Caribbean nations poorly. As a result, products that could be exported from the region to the United States are at a disadvantage because they take a long time to reach the U.S. market.

For many products, quick delivery is essential because of required high levels of industry responsiveness to orders. From a regional perspective, maintaining adequate facilities is therefore imperative in order to remain on the list of areas and ports served by international carriers. Investment in leading-edge port technology can also provide an instrumental competitive edge and cause entire distribution systems to be reconfigured to take advantage of possible savings.

Air Shipping

Air freight is available to and from most countries, including the developing world, where it is often a matter of national prestige to operate a national airline. The total volume of air freight in relation to the total volume of shipping in international business remains quite small. Yet 40 percent of the world's manufactured exports by value travel by air. Clearly, high-value items are more likely to be shipped by air, particularly if they have a high density, that is, a high weight-to-volume ratio.

Over the years, airlines have made major efforts to increase the volume of air freight. Many of these activities have concentrated on developing better, more efficient ground facilities, introducing air freight containers, and providing and marketing a wide variety of special services to shippers. In addition, some air freight companies have specialized and become partners in the international logistics effort.

Changes have also taken place within the aircraft. Forty years ago, the holds of large propeller aircraft could take only about 10 tons of cargo. Today's jumbo jets can load up to 105 metric tons of cargo with an available space of 636 cubic meters and can therefore transport bulky products. In addition, aircraft manufacturers have responded to industry demands by developing both jumbo cargo planes and combination passenger and cargo aircraft. The latter carry passengers in one section of the main deck and freight in another. Carriers on routes that would be uneconomical for passengers or freight alone use these hybrids.

From the shipper's perspective, the products involved must be amenable to air shipment in terms of their size. In addition, the market situation for any given product must be evaluated. For example, air freight may be needed if a product is perishable or if, for other reasons, it requires a short transit time. The level of customer service needs and expectations can also play a decisive role. For example, the shipment of an industrial product that is vital to the ongoing operations of a customer may be much more urgent than the shipment of packaged consumer products.

Choice of Modes

The exporter must make the appropriate selection from the available modes of transportation. This decision, of course, will be heavily influenced by the needs of the firm and its customers. The manager must consider the performance of each mode on four dimensions: transit time, predictability, cost, and noneconomic factors.

Transit Time

The period between departure and arrival of the carrier varies significantly between ocean freight and air freight. For example, the 45-day transit time of an ocean shipment can be reduced to 24 hours if the firm chooses air freight. The length of transit time will have a major impact on the overall operations of the firm. As an example, a short transit time may reduce or even eliminate the need for an overseas depot. Also, inventories can be significantly reduced if they are replenished frequently. As a result, capital can be freed up and used to finance other corporate opportunities.

Transit time can also play a major role in emergency situations. Perishable products require shorter transit times. Rapid transportation prolongs the shelf life in the foreign market. For products with a short life span, air delivery may be the only way to enter foreign markets successfully. For example, international sales of cut flowers have reached their current volume only as a result of air freight. At all times, the international marketing manager must understand the interactions between different components of the logistics process and their effect on transit times. Unless a smooth flow can be assured throughout the entire supply chain, bottlenecks will deny any timing benefits from specific improvements.

Predictability

Providers of both ocean and air freight service wrestle with the issue of reliability. Both modes are subject to the vagaries of nature, which may impose delays. Yet because reliability is a relative measure, the delay of one day for air freight tends to be seen as much more severe and "unreliable" than the same delay for ocean freight. But delays tend to be shorter in absolute time for air shipments. As a result, arrival time via air is more predictable.

This attribute has a major influence on corporate strategy. For example, because of the higher predictability of air freight, inventory safety stock can be kept at lower levels. Greater predictability can also serve as a useful sales tool for foreign distributors, who are able to make more precise delivery promises to their customers. If inadequate port facilities exist, air freight may again be the better alternative. Unloading operations from oceangoing vessels are more cumbersome and time-consuming than for planes. Finally, merchandise shipped via air is likely to suffer less loss and damage from exposure of the cargo to movement. Therefore, once the merchandise arrives, it is more likely to be ready for immediate delivery—a fact that also enhances predictability.

Cost

International transportation services are usually priced on the basis of both cost of the service provided and value of the service to the shipper. Because of the high value of the products shipped by air, air freight is often priced according to the value of the service. In this instance, of course, price becomes a function of market demand and the monopolistic power of the carrier.

The exporter must decide whether the clearly higher cost of air freight can be justified. In part, this will depend on the cargo's properties. For example, the physical density and value of the cargo will affect the decision. Bulky products may be too expensive to ship by air, whereas very compact products may be more amenable to air freight transportation. High-priced items can absorb transportation cost more easily than low-priced goods because the cost of transportation as a percentage of total product cost is lower. As a result, sending diamonds by air freight is easier to justify than sending coal by air. To keep costs down, a shipper can join groups such as shippers associations, which give the shipper more leverage in negotiations. Alternatively, a shipper can decide to mix modes of transportation in order to reduce overall cost and time delays. For example, part of the shipment route can be covered by air, while another portion can be covered by truck or ship. Most important, however, are the overall logistical considerations of the firm. The manager must determine how important it is for merchandise to arrive on time, which will be different for regular garments than for high-fashion dresses.

Although costs are the major consideration in modal choice, an overall perspective must be employed. Simply comparing transportation modes on the basis of price alone is insufficient. The manager must factor in all corporate activities

EXHIBIT 11.1. Evaluating Transportation Choices

	MODE OF TRANSPORTATION				
CHARACTERISTIC OF MODE	AIR	PIPELINE	HIGHWAY	RAIL	WATER
Speed (1 = fastest)	1	4	2	3	5
Cost (1 = highest)	1	4	2	3	5
Loss and Damage (1 = least)	3	1	4	5	2
Frequency* (1 = best)	3	1	2	4	5
Dependability (1 = best)	5	1	2	3	4
Capacity† (1 = best)	4	5	3	2	1
Availability (1 = best)	3	5	1	2	4

* Frequency: number of times mode is available during a given time period.
† Capacity: ability of mode to handle large or heavy goods.

SOURCE: Ronald H. Ballou, *Business Logistics Management,* 4th ed. © 1998. Reprinted by permission of Pearson Education, Inc., Upper Saddle River, NJ.

that are affected by modal choice and explore the total cost effects of each alternative. The final selection of a mode will depend on the importance of different modal dimensions to the markets under consideration. A useful overall comparison between different modes of transportation is provided in Exhibit 11.1.

Noneconomic Factors

Often, noneconomic dimensions will enter into the selection process for a proper form of transportation. The transportation sector, nationally and internationally, both benefits and suffers from heavy government involvement. Governmental pressure is exerted on shippers to use national carriers, even if more economical alternatives exist.

Such preferential policies are most often enforced for government cargo. Restrictions are not limited to developing countries. For example, in the United States, all government cargo and all official government travelers must use national carriers.

The International Shipment: Decision Paths

In an era of new trade opportunities, competent transport management is more important than ever before. In domestic operations, export decisions are guided by the experience of the manager, possible industry comparison, an intimate knowledge of trends, and the development of heuristics—or rules of thumb. In exporting, demand for transportation services derives from the export order. The exporter frequently has to respond to the importer's needs and, consequently, may not have a complete understanding of all the variables involved in international transportation. The exporter, however, cannot lose sight of the fact that transportation management becomes an integral part of the export order. From the exporter's point of view, the delivery of the goods to the importing country involves considerations concerning storage and inventory management, packaging and handling, time frame, and the landed cost of the product, since these issues have a direct impact on the export price quoted to the buyer:

1. Storage and inventory management: The export order cycle involves the placement of an order, processing and shipping it, and receipt of goods by the importer. The decisions to use particular modes of transportation and the costs associated with each transportation alternative available affects storage and inventory management. Both exporter and importer evaluate the need to replace inventory and obtain adequate storage space in order to maintain targeted inventory levels. This involves a careful balancing between available stocks, inventory turnover, storage space, location, and the financial capabilities of the firm. The time and cost associated with transporting the goods from the seller's country into the importing country has a significant impact on these decision areas, as the choice of transportation mode involves, among other factors, a trade-off between time involved and transportation costs.

2. Packaging and handling: Adequate packaging and handling are important elements of traffic management. These activities involve delivering the goods to their final destination undamaged and in good condition, given the normal handling of the package in a particular transportation mode. The package must protect the contents from damage, pilferage, loss, and other hazards of shipment such as climate, unsheltered storage, moving, shifting, and so on. Because freight charges are levied on total gross weight, that is, the total weight of the goods plus packaging, the exporter may be tempted to under pack in order to economize. Care should be exercised to avoid this, as the packages may be damaged in transit to the pier. The receiving document (dock receipt) will show the condition of the packages as received by the shipping company. If the terms of sale call for a "clean" shipping document, that is, a document indicating that the goods have been received in apparent good condition, such a document will not be issued and significant problems can arise in expediting payment, especially if a letter of credit is involved.

Proper packaging involves protection as well as the particular requirements of the mode or transportation. For example, hazardous, fragile, or perishable materials are also subject to specific packaging requirements that must be conformed to. With availability of a wide variety of packaging materials today, the exporter can greatly minimize the total gross weight and provide for light and protective packaging. With some effort to research different types of containers, and packaging materials, the exporter can significantly reduce costs and still conform to accepted packaging practices.

3. Time frame: Consideration of the time it takes to transport a shipment from point-of-export to final destination is an extremely important factor that affects the decision to use a particular mode of transportation. Modes of transportation vary in the speed with which they transport the goods, ranging from a low 30 miles to high 600 miles-per-hour. Consideration must be given to the time involved and costs associated with a particular transportation mode.
4. Landed cost of the product: Transportation costs must be added to product costs, thus influencing the landed cost of the product. Considering the distance that separates the exporting and importing markets and the escalating-price factor in export pricing, the landed cost can be many times greater than the cost of the product. Consequently the landed cost affects the importer's finances and demand. This, in turn, affects the exporter's export sales volume and export potential.

The International Shipment: Alternative Modes

International shipments usually involve not just one carrier but also multiple types of carriers. The shipment must be routed to the port of export, where it is transferred to another mode of transportation—for example, from truck or rail to vessel. Documentation requirements arise as there is a need to comply with both exporting and importing document generation and to document the movement of the goods. Documentation represents the "paper trail" of a shipment in question. Recognizing the impact both in terms of time and money that documentation can have, most countries have greatly simplified required documentation for shipments. The savings on the elimination of red tape is significant.

Few exporters, especially small or medium-sized firms and those new to exporting, are familiar with the many and varied details involved in transportation. These may include arranging for shipment from the factory, transfer from train to vessel, securing of rates and space on vessels, clearing customs, stowing, delivery at the port of destination to docks, clearance through local customs, and finally, delivery to the buyer. Larger exporters have a separate department or staff to secure transportation services and proper documentation, whereas smaller firms rely on support agencies for this work.

EXHIBIT 11.2. Documentation for an International Shipment

A. Documents Required by the U.S. Government
   1. Shipper's export declaration
   2. Export license
B. Commercial Documents
   1. Commercial invoice
   2. Packing list
   3. Inland bill of lading
   4. Dock receipt
   5. Bill of lading or airway bill
   6. Insurance policies or certificates
   7. Shipper's declaration for dangerous goods
C. Import Documents
   1. Import license
   2. Foreign exchange license
   3. Certificate of origin
   4. Consular invoice
   5. Customs invoice

SOURCES: Dun & Bradstreet, *Exporter's Encyclopedia* (New York: Dun & Bradstreet, 1985). Ortiz-Buonafina, *Profitable Export Marketing* (Englewood Cliffs, NJ: Prentice-Hall, 1984), http://www.gov/marketingandtrade/

Documentation

The documentation that will be generated by a particular export shipment varies according country of destination and product type. According to terms of sale, the exporter must clear the goods for export, i.e., ensure proper packaging and routing, as well as obtaining the necessary documentation for the goods to clear customs. Exhibit 11.2. provides a summary of the main documents used in international shipments.

Documents Required by the U.S. Government. These documents must be presented at point of departure and must be completed before the shipment leaves the U.S port.

- **Shipper's Export Declaration (SED):**
  The Shipper's Export Declaration, commonly referred to as the SED, is a general requirement for all shippers exporting to the rest of the world, except to Canada. It has two purposes. First, it serves as a statistical tool to gather U.S. foreign trade statistics. The data gathered is summarized periodically in U.S. foreign trade reports and published annually by the Bureau of the Census. Second, it also serves to identify the proper authorization to

export. For such purposes, the shipper completing the SED must provide a) the Schedule B or HTS (Harmonized Trade Classification) number for the product being exported, and b) a validated license number (Export Control Classification Number) or a General License symbol. Shippers can be exempt from submitting an SED at time of shipment if the shipper files electronically on a monthly basis and if the value of any individual Schedule B number commodity is less than $2,500.[1]

- **Export License:**
Most commodities exported from the United States move under a General License. The general license is permission granted that requires no specific requirement and as such is a "self-licensing" procedure. However, there are certain commodities that require a special license called a validated license. This license applies for commodities listed in the Commodity Control List. Exporters need to be aware of the U.S. export control system and need to check if any of the product lines or countries comes under U.S. export controls.

Commercial Documents. These documents represent the documentation of the commercial transaction. The terms of sale indicate at which point the transfer of title occurred. The importer must obtain these documents in order to present evidence of title and clear the goods through importing country customs.

- **Packing List:**
The packing list is a detailed summary of the contents of each unit, package, crate, container, etc. that comprise one shipment. It is a valuable document because it represents a validation by the exporter of the contents of the shipment. The packing list is particularly valuable to process claims due to partial loss and duty valuation at import point.
- **Inland Bill of Lading:**
This represents the contract between the shipper and the inland carrier that takes goods to the point of export. An Inland Bill of Lading serves as evidence of inland transportation charges.
- **Dock Receipt:**
This is a document issued at the pier by the ocean shipping company. It is a receipt of the goods for shipment and either for shipment or on board. This document is evidence of delivery of the goods to the shipping company and the condition of the goods at the time of delivery. It contains all the necessary information in order to issue the final Bill of Lading.

---

[1] www.export.gov, accessed September 26, 2003.

The Shipping Documents. The shipping document is the single most important document in the export transaction. The importer must have this document in order to establish title conditions and authority to take possession of the goods once customs is cleared. The shipping documents represent (a) a contract of carriage from one point to another, (b) evidence of title and (c) evidence of the condition of the goods received by shipping company.

There are two shipping documents:

- *Ocean Bill of Lading* is a contract of carriage between ocean carrier and shipper or shipper's agent. This bill of lading may be either negotiable or straight. A negotiable bill of lading is a contract made out "to order," meaning that the holder of the documents is the owner of the goods. The purpose of this type of document is to allow the shipper to maintain control of the shipment until the document is endorsed to a third party. It allows the shipper to transfer title after shipment. A transfer represents an unrestricted transfer to title, and the importer needs to present the original document to customs in order to clear goods and take possession of them.

    A straight bill of lading is a contract between the shipper and a specific consignee. (It can be a banking institution or a specific firm or individual.) A straight bill of lading is a restrictive transfer of title; that is, possession does not relieve the holder from legal claims by the shipper or seller of the goods. A copy of the bill of lading is enough to claim goods from customs.

    If goods are received by shipping company, the bill of lading is said to be "clean." If goods appear to be damaged or if there is a discrepancy in weight declared and weight measured, the bill of lading is said to be "foul." It is important to point out that collections under a letter of credit cannot be processed unless a clean bill of lading is presented to the bank holding the letter of credit. A foul bill of lading can still be processed but only if the buyer or owner of the letter of credit agrees. In the case of a confirmed letter of credit, the bank issuing the confirmation must also agree. This causes significant delays that can be costly to the importer.

- *Airwaybill* is a contract between air carrier and shipper or shipper's agent. An airwaybill is a contract of air carriage between shipper and consignee. Commonly called an AWB, this document is a straight document, meaning that the transfer is restrictive, as noted above. However, the document can be consigned to a bank for payment under documentary collection and letters of credit, and must be duly endorsed for the importer to be able to clear goods from customs.

Other Commercial Documents: **Commercial Invoice.** The commercial invoice is the accounting document that represents the bill of sale from seller to buyer. It should contain a detailed description of the goods and the transaction between the two parties. The commercial invoice includes all the information, which may have been presented to the buyer through the *pro-forma* invoice, which is the offer to sell.

Other Commercial Documents: **Insurance Policies or Certificates.** A large variety of problems may arise due to damage of an export shipment. Consequently, the exporter needs to be fully insured to cover all possible losses arising during the movement of the goods from exporting to importing country. For example, shipment by sea or cargo can be subject to total loss due to rolling, pitching, or water damage. The ocean bill of lading does not have insurance coverage. Due to the large number of possible hazards, the exporter needs to obtain full marine insurance. By air, cargo can be subject to temperature extremes, pressure, and turbulence. While airlines offer insurance on the airwaybill, this does not create an insurance certificate, which may be necessary if a letter of credit is involved.

The exporter needs to know the exact route of the shipment in order to obtain the necessary insurance and documents needed to complete the transaction.

Other Special Purpose Documents. Some shipments may require specific purpose documents for shipment of dangerous, toxic, or flammable goods. Similarly, live animals must be cleared for transportation across national borders. It is the exporter's responsibility to obtain all necessary documentation for special exports that need this type of documentation.

Documents Required by Importing Country. Importing countries may impose some specific requirements that are needed in order for the importer to clear customs in the foreign country. It is the exporter's responsibility to obtain the documents that are issued in the U.S.

- **Import License and/or Foreign Exchange License:**
  Special permits that a foreign country may require in order to import the goods into a country. An import license may be required to import a specific commodity or product and the foreign exchange license may be required to obtain the necessary foreign exchange to pay for the goods. These restrictions are less common today than ever before; however, countries have the right from time to time to impose restrictions when economically necessary.

- **Certificate of Origin:**
  A signed statement providing evidence of the origin of the goods. This document, when required, must be prepared by the exporter and taken to the Chamber of Commerce in the locale where the exporter operates for validation. This document details the shipment and states the origin of the goods. This is a very common document as it is usually necessary to establish the type of duties that a product is subject to the importing country.
- **Consular and/or Customs Invoice:**
  Consular and/or customs invoices may be necessary to clear customs in the importing country (notably Latin America). This document is similar to the SED in that it allows foreign countries to maintain statistical data on imports. The exporter must obtain this certificate from the county's consulate (if a special form is required), or present a commercial invoice for certification. Consulates usually charge for certification.

The need to prepare the proper set of documents needed to process the shipment from exporting to importing country cannot be overemphasized. Export documentation should be completed according to customs requirements and the requirement of the transaction itself. In many cases, the country requires the documentation to be *legalized*. This means that the shipper or shipper's agent must swear to and present the full set of documents to the foreign consulate in the U.S. port of exit. Errors incurred in generating the necessary documentation usually result in fines assessed to the foreign buyer and this can hurt the relationship between exporter and importer if these errors are recurrent.

Assistance with International Shipments

Several intermediaries provide services in the physical movement of goods. One very important distribution decision an exporter makes is the selection of an international freight forwarder. Such an international freight forwarder acts as an agent for the exporter in moving cargo to the overseas destination. Independent freight forwarders are regulated and, in the United States, should be certified by the Federal Maritime Commission. The forwarder advises the exporter on shipping documentation and packing costs and will prepare and review the documents to ensure that they are in order. Forwarders will also book the necessary space aboard a carrier. They will make necessary arrangements to clear outbound goods with customs and, after clearance, forward the documents either to the customer or to the paying bank. A customs broker serves as an agent for an importer with authority to clear inbound goods through customs and ship them on to their destination. These functions are performed for a fee. Customs brokers are often regulated by their national customs service.

Summary

International transportation differs from domestic activities in that it deals with greater distances, new variables, and greater complexity because of country-specific differences. The exporter needs to understand transportation infrastructures in other countries and modes of transportation such as ocean shipping and air freight. The choice among these modes will depend on the customer's demands and the firm's consideration of the mode's transit time, predictability, and cost requirements. In addition, noneconomic factors such as government regulations weigh heavily in this decision. Finally, the exporter needs to ensure that proper documentation is generated in order to complete the export order.

CHAPTER 12

Export Communication and Promotional Strategy

Ideal marketing communication is a dialogue that allows sellers and buyers to achieve mutually satisfying exchange agreements. As a two-way process of listening and responsiveness, it forms the basis of a relationship between buyer and seller that should be established as early as possible in that relationship and deepened over time. Marketing communications include verbal as well as nonverbal communication reflected in the concept of "silent languages."

Promotional strategy, for the purposes of our discussion here, is the process of establishing "communication" between exporters and their constituents in the foreign market. This process allows exporters to communicate all the elements of the marketing strategy to their target market and obtain feedback to control the entire process. It extends beyond the conveying of ideas to include persuasion and thus enables the marketing process to function more effectively and efficiently.

The Marketing Communications Process

As shown in the communications model presented in Exhibit 12.1, effective communication requires three elements—the sender, the message, and the receiver—connected by a message channel. The process may begin with an unsolicited inquiry from a potential customer or as a planned effort by the exporter. Whatever the goal of the communications process, the sender needs to study receiver characteristics before encoding the message in order to achieve maximum impact. Encoding the message simply means converting it into forms (both literal and symbolic) that are properly understood by the receiver. This is not a simple task, however. For example, if a Web site's order form asks only for typical U.S.-

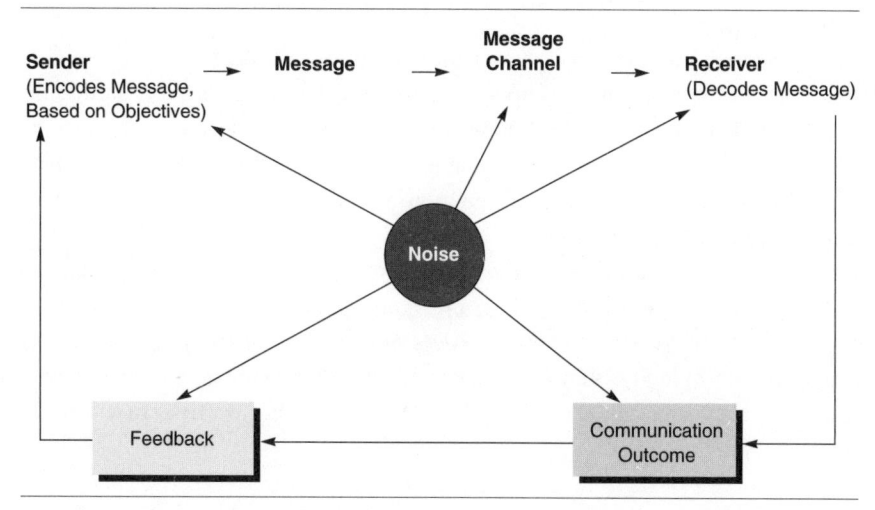

EXHIBIT 12.1. The Marketing Communications Process

```
Sender                  Message
(Encodes Message,  →  Message  →  Channel  →  Receiver
Based on Objectives)                              (Decodes Message)

                          Noise

        Feedback  ←                    Communication Outcome
```

SOURCE: Adapted from Terence A. Shimp, *Advertising, Promotion, and Supplemental Aspects of Integrated Marketing Communications*, 82 © 2003. Reprinted by permission of South-Western, Mason, OH.

type address information, such as a zip code, and does not include anything for other countries, the would-be buyer from abroad will think the company doesn't want to do business outside the United States.

The message channel is the path that the message travels from sender (source) to receiver. This channel links the receiver to the sender, and it can range from sound waves conveying the human voice in personal selling to transceivers or intermediaries such as print and broadcast media. Although technological advances (for example, fax, video conferencing, and the Internet) may have made buyer-seller negotiations more efficient, the fundamental process and its purpose have remained unchanged. Face-to-face contact is still necessary for two basic reasons. The first is the need for detailed discussion and explanation, and the second is the need to establish the rapport that forms the basis of lasting business relationships. Technology will then support in the maintenance of the relationship.

The message channel also exists in mass communications. Complications in exporting may arise if a particular medium does not reach the targeted audience. This may be the case for Internet communications due to varying online penetration rates around the world. Once a sender has placed a message into a channel or a set of channels and directed it to the intended destination, the completion of the process is dependent on the receiver's decoding—that is, transforming the message symbols back into thought. If there is an adequate amount of overlap between sender characteristics and needs reflected in the encoded message and receiver characteristics and needs reflected in the decoded message, the communications process has worked.

A message moving through a channel is subject to outside influences, distractions, and various kinds of noise that interfere with its accurate reception. In exporting, this noise might be literal—a bad telephone connection, failure to express a quotation in the inquirer's system of currency and measurement, or lack of understanding of the recipient's environment due to, for example, having an English-language only Web site.

The exporter also should be most alert to cultural noise. The lack of language skills may hinder successful negotiations, whereas translation errors may render a promotional campaign or brochure useless. Similarly, nonverbal language and its improper interpretation may cause problems. While eye contact in North America and Europe may be direct, the cultural style of the Japanese may involve markedly less eye contact.

The success of the outcome is determined by how well objectives have been met in generating more awareness, a more positive attitude, or increased purchases. For example, sales literature developed in the local language and culture of the product line offered may result in increased inquiries or even more sales. Regardless of whether the situation calls for interpersonal or mass communications, the collection and observation of feedback is necessary to analyze the success of the communications effort. The initial sender-receiver relationship is transposed, and interpretative skills similar to those needed in developing messages are needed. To make effective and efficient use of communications requires considerable strategic planning. Examples of concrete ways in which feedback can be collected are inquiry cards and toll-free numbers distributed at trade shows to gather additional information. Similarly, the Internet allows exporters to track traffic flows and to install registration procedures that identify individuals and track their purchases over time.

A Promotional Strategy for Exports

A comprehensive export marketing strategy requires the consideration, implementation, and coordination of a promotional strategy to establish flows of communication and information between the exporter and the identified target market.

The basic steps of a comprehensive export marketing strategy are outlined in Exhibit 12.2. Few, if any, firms can afford expenditures for promotion that is done as "art for art's sake" or only because major competitors do it. The first step in developing the strategy is to assess what company or product characteristics and benefits should be communicated to the export market. This requires constant

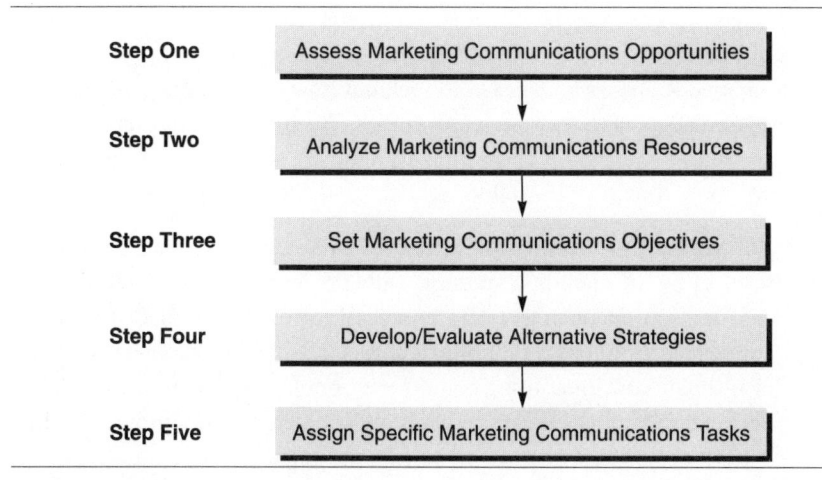

EXHIBIT 12.2. Steps in Formulating Marketing Communications Strategy

Step One	Assess Marketing Communications Opportunities
Step Two	Analyze Marketing Communications Resources
Step Three	Set Marketing Communications Objectives
Step Four	Develop/Evaluate Alternative Strategies
Step Five	Assign Specific Marketing Communications Tasks

SOURCE: Framework adapted from Wayne DeLozier, *The Marketing Communication Process* (New York: McGraw-Hill, 1976), 272.

monitoring of the various environments and understanding target audience characteristics.

Certain rules of thumb can be followed in evaluating promotion resources. A sufficient commitment is necessary, which may mean a relatively large amount of money. The exporter has to operate in any market according to the rules of the particular marketplace. In the United States, for example, this means high promotional costs—perhaps 30 percent of exports or even more during the early stage of entry. In heavily contested markets, the level of spending may even have to increase.

Financial constraints often force exporters to concentrate their promotional efforts on key markets. A specific objective might be to spend more than the closest competitors do in the market. An exporter may have to limit this effort to one country, even one area, at a time to achieve set goals with the available budget. International campaigns require patient investment; the market has to progress through awareness, knowledge, liking, preference, and favorable purchase intentions before payback begins. Payback periods of less than two years are often not realistic.

For many exporters, a critical factor is the support of the intermediary. Whether a distributor is willing to contribute a $3 million media budget or a few thousand dollars makes a big difference. In some cases, intermediaries take a leading role in the promotion of the product in a market. In most cases, however, the exporter should strive to retain some control of the campaign rather than allow intermediaries or sales offices a free hand in the various markets operated in. Although markets may be dissimilar, common themes and common objectives need to be incorporated into the individual campaigns.

Alternative strategies are needed to spell out how the firm's resources can be combined and adapted to market opportunities. The tools the exporter has available to formulate the export promotion strategy are referred to as the promotional mix. They consist of the following:

1. Advertising: Any form of nonpersonal presentation of ideas, goods, or services by an identified sponsor, with predominant use made of mass communication, such as print, broadcast, or electronic media, or direct communication that is pinpointed at each business-to-business customer or ultimate consumer using computer technology and databases.
2. Personal selling: The process of assisting and persuading a prospect to buy a good or service or to act on an idea through use of person-to-person communication with intermediaries and/or final customers.
3. Publicity: Any form of nonpaid, commercially significant news or editorial comment about ideas, products, or institutions.
4. Sales promotion: Direct inducements that provide extra product value or incentive to the sales force, intermediaries, or ultimate consumers and are intended to accelerate the purchase decision.
5. Sponsorship: The practice of promoting the interests of the company by associating it with a specific event (typically sports or culture) or a cause (typically a charity or a social interest).

The choice of tools leads to either a *push* or a *pull* emphasis in marketing communications. Push strategies focus on the use of personal selling. Despite its higher cost per contact, personal selling is appropriate for the exporting of industrial goods, which have shorter channels of distribution and smaller target populations than do consumer goods. Governmental clients are typically serviced through personal selling efforts. Some industries, such as pharmaceuticals, traditionally rely on personal selling to service the clientele.

On the other hand, pull strategies depend on mass communications tools, mainly advertising. Advertising is appropriate for consumer-oriented products with large target audiences and long channels of distribution.

No promotional tool should be used in isolation or without regard to the others; hence, we see a trend toward *integrated marketing communications*. Promotional tools should be coordinated according to target market and product characteristics, the size of the promotional budget, the type and length of international involvement, and control considerations. As an example, industrial purchasing decisions typically involve eight to eleven people. Because a salesperson may not reach all of them, the use of advertising may be necessary to influence the participants in the decision-making process. In addition, steps must be taken to have information readily available to prospects that are interested in the exporter's products. This can be achieved with the development of a Web site and participating in trade shows.

Finally, specific marketing communications tasks must be assigned, which may require deciding on a division of labor with foreign intermediaries or with other exporters for cooperative communications efforts. In cases in which the locally based intermediaries are small and may not have the resources to engage in promotional efforts, the exporter may suggest dealer-participatory programs. In exchange for including the intermediaries' names in promotional material without any expense to them—for example, in announcing a sweepstakes—the exporter may request increased volume purchases from the intermediaries.

Export Promotion Tools

The main export promotion tools used by exporters to communicate with the foreign marketplace from their domestic base are: business and trade journals, directories, direct advertising, the Internet, trade fairs and missions, and personal selling. If the exporter's strategy calls for a major promotional effort in a market, it is advisable either to use a domestic agency with extensive operations in the intended market or to use a local agency and work closely with the company's local representatives in media and message choices.

Business/Trade Journals and Directories

Many varied business and trade publications, as well as directories, are available to the exporter. Some, such as *Business Week, Fortune, The Economist, The Wall Street Journal*, and *Financial Times*, are standard information sources worldwide. Extensions of these are their regional editions; for example, *The Asian Wall Street Journal* or *Business Week—Europe*. Trade publications can be classified as (1) *horizontal*, which cater to a particular job function cutting across industry lines, such as Purchasing World or Industrial Distribution, and (2) *vertical*, which deal with a specific industry, such as Chemical Engineering or International Hospital Supplies. These journals are global, regional, or country-specific in their approaches. Many U.S.-based publications are available in national language editions, with some offering regional buys for specific export markets.

The exporter should also be aware of the potential of government-sponsored publications. For example, *Commercial News USA*, published by the U.S. Department of Commerce, is an effective medium for the exporter interested in making itself and its products known worldwide for a modest sum. For less than $500, an

EXHIBIT 12.3. Examples of International Trade Publications and Directories

Feed Management — Serving the United States & Canada	
Feed International — Serving Europe, Asia, Pacific, Middle East & Africa	
Alimentos Balanceados Para Animales — Serving Latin America in Spanish	
Feed International China Edition — Serving the People's Republic of China in Chinese	

SOURCES: http://www.wattmm.com; and http://www.guiaexport.bellsouth.com.

exporter can reach 140,000 potential buyers in 152 countries through the publication, distributed to recipients free of charge 12 times a year.

Directories provide a similar tool for advertising efforts. Many markets feature exporter yellow pages, some of which offer online versions in addition to the traditional print ones. For example, MyExports.com (formerly the *U.S. Exporters' Yellow Pages*) offers U.S. firms a means to promote their businesses worldwide at no cost (if they just want to be listed), and at low cost for an advertisement or link to their e-mail or homepage. Some of the directories are country-specific. For example, BellSouth's *Guia Internacional* allows exporters to showcase their products to 425,000 Latin American and Caribbean importers. A number of online directories, such as *Internet International Business Exchange* (http://www.imex.com), provide the exporter the opportunity to have banner ads for $150 to $1,000 a month. Examples of international trade publications and directories are provided in Exhibit 12.3.

The two main concerns when selecting media are effectiveness in reaching the appropriate target audience(s) and efficiency in minimizing the cost of doing so, measured in terms of cost per thousand. If the exporter is in a position to define the target audience clearly (for example, in terms of demographics or product-related variables), the choice of media will be easier. In addition, consideration should be given to how well a given medium will work with the other tools. For example, advertisements in publications and directories may have the function of driving customers and prospects to the exporter's Web site.

In deciding which publications to use, the exporter must apply the general principles of the marketing promotional strategy. Coverage and circulation information is available from Standard Rate & Data Service (http://www.srds.com). SRDS provides a complete list of international publications in the International Section of the Business Publication, and audit information similar to that on the U.S. market is provided for the United Kingdom, Italy, France, Austria, Switzerland, Germany, Mexico, and Canada.

Outside of these areas, the exporter has to rely on the assistance of publishers or local representatives. Actual choices are usually complicated by lack of sufficient funds and concern over the information gap. The simplest approach may be to use U.S. publishers, in which the exporter may have more confidence in terms of rates and circulation data. If a more localized approach is needed, a regional edition or national publication can be considered. Before advertising is placed in an unfamiliar journal, the exporter should analyze its content and overall quality of presentation.

Direct Marketing

The purpose of direct marketing is to establish a relationship with a customer in order to initiate immediate and measurable responses. This is accomplished through direct-response advertising, telemarketing, and direct selling.

Direct mail is by far the dominant direct-response medium, but some advertising is also placed in mass media, such as television, magazines, and newspapers. Direct mail can be a highly personalized tool of communication if the target audience can be identified and defined narrowly. Ranging from notices to actual samples, it allows for flexibility in the amount of information conveyed and in its format. Direct mail is directly related in its effectiveness to the availability and quality of the mailing lists. Mailing lists may not be available around the world in the same degree that they are in, say, the United States. However, more and better lists are surfacing in Asia, Latin America, and the Middle East. In addition, reliable, economical, global postal and delivery services have become available.

Catalogs are typically distributed to overseas customers through direct mail, although many catalogs have online versions as well. Their function is to make the exporter's name known, generate requests for further information, stimulate orders, and serve as a reminder between transactions. Catalogs are particularly useful if a firm's products are in a highly specialized field of technology and if only the most highly qualified specialists are to be contacted. In many markets, especially the developing ones, people may be starving for technology information and will share any mailings they receive. Due to this unsatisfied demand, a very small investment can reach many potential end users.

The growing mail-order segment is attracting an increasing number of foreign entrants to markets previously dominated by local firms. However, because consumers are wary of sending orders and money to unknown companies overseas, the key to market penetration is a local address. Despite the economic promise of emerging markets such as China, India, and Russia, the development of direct marketing is constrained by negative attitudes toward Western business practices and problems with distribution networks and marketing support systems, as well as bureaucratic obstacles. Traditional direct mail is undergoing major change. New types of mail services (e.g., the Mexican Post Office's Buzon Espresso) will enable companies to deal with their customers more efficiently when customers buy through catalogs or electronic means. New electronic media will assume an increasing share in the direct-response area. However, direct marketing will continue to grow as a function of its target ability, its measurability, and the responsiveness of consumers to direct marketing efforts.

In the past, U.S. exporters thought that country-specific offices were almost essential to bringing their companies closer to overseas customers. Now with functioning telecommunication systems and deregulation in the industry, telemarketing (including sales, customer service, and help-desk-related support) is flourishing throughout the world. A growing number of countries in Latin America, Asia, and Europe are experiencing growth in this area as consumers are becoming more accustomed to calling toll-free numbers and more willing to receive calls from exporters.

Internet

The Internet is rapidly becoming a potent tool in the export promotion strategy. One of the most important considerations in the use of the Internet is the use of a Web site, which is seen as necessary if for no other reason than image; lack of a Web presence may convey a negative image to the various constituents of the exporter. This means having a well-designed and well-marketed site.

Having a Web presence will support the exporter's marketing communications effort in a number of ways. First, it allows the company to increase its presence in the marketplace and to communicate its overall mission and information about its marketing mix. Second, the Internet allows 24-hour access to customers and prospects. Providing important information during decision-making can help the customer clarify the search. The potential interactivity of the Web site (e.g., in providing tailor-made solutions to the customer's concerns) may provide a competitive advantage as the customer compares alternative sites. Third, the Internet can improve customer service by allowing customers to serve themselves when and where they choose. Fourth, the Internet allows the exporter to gather information, which has its uses not only in research but also in database development for subsequent marketing efforts. While the data collected may be biased, they are also very inexpensive to collect. If the data are used to better cater to existing customers, then data collected through Internet interaction are the best possible. Fifth, the Internet offers the opportunity to actually close sales. This function is within the realm of e-commerce. It will require a significant commitment on the part of the exporter in terms of investment in infrastructure to deliver not only information but also the product to the customer. E-commerce is discussed in more detail in Chapter 5.

Trade Shows and Missions

Marketing goods and services through trade shows is a European tradition that dates back to A.D 1240. After sales force costs, trade shows are one of the most significant cost items in marketing budgets. Although they are usually associated with industrial firms, some consumer-products firms are represented as well. Typically, a trade show is an event at which manufacturers, distributors, and other vendors display their products or describe their services to current and prospective customers, suppliers, other business associates, and the press. The International Automotive Services Industries Show and the International Coal Show, for example, run eight hours for three days, plus one or two preview days, and register 25,000 attendees. In the consumer goods area, expositions are the most common type of show. Tickets are usually sold; typical expositions include home/garden, boat, auto, stereo, and antiques. Although a typical trade show or typical participant does not exist, U.S. firms allocate, on average, $73,000 for each show and attend nine or ten shows annually.

Whether an exporter should participate in a trade show depends largely on the type of business relationship it wants to develop with a particular country. More than 16,000 trade shows create an annual $50 billion in business worldwide. A company looking only for one-time or short-term sales might find the expense prohibitive, but a firm looking for long-term involvement may find the investment worthwhile. Arguments in favor of participation include the following:

1. Some products, by their very nature, are difficult to market without providing the potential customer a chance to examine them or see them in action. Trade fairs provide an excellent opportunity to introduce, promote, and demonstrate new products. Auto shows, such as the ones in Detroit, Geneva, and Tokyo, feature "concept" cars to gauge industry and public opinion.

2. An appearance at a show produces goodwill and allows for periodic cultivation of contacts. Beyond the impact of displaying specific products, many firms place strong emphasis on "waving the company flag" against competition.
3. The opportunity to find an intermediary may be one of the best reasons to attend a trade show. A show is a cost-effective way to solicit and screen candidates to represent the firm, especially in a new market.
4. Attendance is one of the best ways to contact government officials and decision-makers.
5. Trade fairs provide an excellent chance for market research and collecting competitive intelligence. The exporter is able to view most rivals at the same time and to test comparative buyer reactions. Trade fairs provide one of the most inexpensive ways of obtaining evaluative data on the effectiveness of a promotional campaign.
6. Exporters are able to reach a sizable number of sales prospects in a brief time period at a reasonable cost per contact. According to research by Hannover Messe, more than 86 percent of all attendees represent buying influences (managers with direct responsibility for purchasing products and services).

On the other hand, the following are among the reasons cited for nonparticipation in trade fairs:

1. High costs. These can be avoided by participating in events sponsored by the U.S. Department of Commerce or exhibiting at U.S. trade centers or export development offices. An exporter can also lower costs by sharing expenses with distributors or representatives. Further, the costs of closing a sale through trade shows are estimated to be much lower than for a sale closed through personal representation.
2. Difficulty in choosing the appropriate trade fairs for participation. This is a critical decision. Because of scarce resources, many firms rely on suggestions from their foreign distributors on which fairs to attend and what specifically to exhibit.
3. For larger exporters with multiple divisions, the problem of coordination. Several divisions may be required to participate in the same fair under the company banner. Similarly, coordination is required with distributors and agents if joint participation is desired, which requires joint planning.

Trade show participation is too expensive to be limited to the exhibit alone. A set of promotional objectives would include targeting accounts and attracting buyers to the show with preshow promotion using mailings, advertisements in the trade journals, or Web site information. Contests and giveaways are effective in attracting participants to the company's exhibition area. Major customers and attractive prospects are invited to a special hospitality suite. Finally, a system is needed to evaluate performance and to track qualified leads. Exporters may participate in general or specialized trade shows. *General trade fairs* offer a variety of products for different types of end users (consumer or B2B). Examples of general trade fairs are Sporting Goods Exhibitions and Apparel and Home Furnishings, textile and supplies shows.

Specialized or *vertical trade fairs* usually exhibit one type of product category or product line. Examples of specialized trade fairs are Machinery, Equipment and Inputs for Agriculture and Agro-Industry, and International Exhibitions on Transportation Technology and Equipment.

Certified Trade Fair Program

For small and medium-sized companies, the benefit of a group pavilion is in the cost and ease of the arrangements. These pavilions are often part of government-sponsored export-promotion programs. The rationale of these programs is that many small and medium-sized firms that are export-capable hesitate to enter export markets due to their lack of experience in international marketing. Trade fairs, on the other hand, are excellent vehicles to allow potential exporters to actually show their products. Trade fairs are like marketplaces where buyers and sellers can meet and interact for their mutual benefit.

The U.S. Department of Commerce has developed the Certified Trade Fair Program to encourage private organizations to recruit new-to-market and new-to-export U.S. firms to exhibit in trade fairs. In order to get certification for an event, the fair has to be a leading international trade event and the organizer must be able to give assistance to recruited U.S. firms in freight forwarding, customs clearance, exhibit designing and setup, public relations and overall show promotion.[1] Certification means that the U.S. Department of Commerce has found the applicable trade fair to be a good market opportunity for U.S. exporters and the organizer is capable of performing the tasks required for certification. The Federation of International Trade Associations offers sites for search of trade show listings through its Web sites www.fita.orga/shows.html, www.go-events.com, and www.expoworld.net.

Other promotional events that the exporter can use are trade missions, seminar, solo exhibitions, video/catalog exhibitions, and virtual trade shows. *Trade missions* can be specialized government or industry-organized, both of which aim at expanding the sale of U.S. goods and services and the establishment of agencies

---

[1] For more information about the certified trade fair program, visit www.stat-usa.gov.

and representative abroad. *Seminar missions* are events in which eight to ten firms are invited to participate in a one- to four-day forum, during which the team members participate in generic discussions on technological issues—that is, following a soft-sell approach. Individual meetings with end users, government, research institutions, and other potentially useful contacts follow this up.

Video/catalog exhibitions allow exporters to publicize their products at low cost. They consist of 20 to 35 product presentations videotapes, each lasting five to ten minutes. They provide the advantage of showing the product in use to potential customers. Virtual trade shows allow exporters to promote their products and services over the Internet and have an electronic presence without actually attending a trade show. Trade leads and international sales interests are collected and forwarded by the sponsor to the companies for follow-up. The information stays online for 365 days for one flat fee. For example, BuyUSA (an online environment sponsored by the U.S. Department of Commerce) offers exporters the opportunity to show their company profile, logo, product listings, Web site link, and catalog in a virtual trade zone. The virtual trade zone is promoted heavily at the trade shows actually attended by the department, giving buyers at the show a chance to review company information for possible contact.

Personal Selling

Personal selling is the most effective of the promotional tools available to the marketer; however, its costs per contact are high. The average cost of sales calls may vary from $200 to $1,100, depending on the industry and the product or service. Personal selling allows for immediate feedback on customer reaction as well as information on markets. The exporter's sales effort is determined by the degree of internationalization in its efforts, as shown in the table in Exhibit 12.4. As the degree of internationalization advances, so will the exporters own role in carrying out or controlling the sales function.

Indirect Exports

When the exporter uses indirect exports to reach international markets, the export process is outsourced; in other words, an intermediary, such as an EMC, takes care of the international sales effort. While there is no investment in international sales by the exporter, there is also no, or very little, learning about sales in the markets that buy the product. The sales effort is basically a domestic one directed by the local intermediary. This may change somewhat if the exporter becomes party to an ETC with other similar producers. Even in that case, the ETC will have its own sales force and exposure to the effort may be limited. Any

EXHIBIT 12.4. Levels of Exporter Involvement in International Sales

TYPE OF INVOLVEMENT	TARGET OF SALES EFFORT	LEVEL OF EXPORTER INVOLVEMENT	ADVANTAGE/ DISADVANTAGE
Indirect exports	Home-country-based intermediary	Low	+No major investment in international sales −Minor learning from/control of effort
Direct exports	Locally based intermediary	Medium	+Direct contact with local market −Possible gatekeeping by intermediary
Integrated exports	Customer	High	+Generation of market-specific assets −Cost/risk

Source: Framework adapted from Reijo Luostarinen and Lawrence Welch, *International Operations of the Firm* (Helsinki, Finland: Helsinki School of Economics, 1990), chapter 1.

learning that takes place is indirect; for example, the intermediary may advise the exporter of product adaptation requirements to enhance sales.

Direct Exports

Over time, the exporter may find it necessary to establish direct contact with the target market(s), although the ultimate customer contact is still handled by locally based intermediaries, such as agents or distributors. The exporter must provide basic selling aid communications, such as product specification and data literature, catalogs, the results of product testing, and demonstrated performance information—everything needed to present products to potential customers. In some cases, the exporter has to provide the intermediaries with incentives to engage in local advertising efforts. These may include special discounts, push money, or cooperative advertising. Cooperative advertising will give the exporter's product local flavor and increase the overall promotional budget for the product. However, the exporter needs to be concerned that the advertising is of sufficient quality and that the funds are spent as agreed. For the exporter-intermediary interaction to work, four general guidelines have to be satisfied:

1. Know the sales scene. Often what works in the exporter's home market will not work somewhere else. This is true especially in terms of compensation schemes. In U.S. firms, incentives and commission play a significant role, while in most other markets salaries are the major shares of compensation. The best way to approach this is to study the salary

structures and incentive plans in other competitive organizations in the market in question.
2. Research the customer. Customer behavior will vary across markets, meaning the sales effort must adjust as well. A clear definition of the target market is a prerequisite for a sound sales force composition.
3. Work with the culture. Realistic objectives have to be set for the salespeople based on their cultural expectations. This is especially true in setting goals and establishing measures such as quotas. If either of these is set unrealistically, the result will be frustration for both parties. Cultural sensitivity also is required in training situations where the exporter has to interact with the intermediary's sales force.
4. Learn from your local representatives. If the sales force perceives a lack of fit between the exporter's product and the market, as well as inability to do anything about it, the result will be suboptimal. A local sales force is an asset to the exporter, given its close contact with customers. Beyond daily feedback, the exporter is wise to undertake two additional approaches to exploit the experience of local salespeople. First, the exporter should have a program by which local salespeople can visit the exporter's operations and interact with the staff. If the exporter is active in multiple markets of the same region, it is advisable to develop ways to put salespeople in charge of the exporter's products in different markets together to exchange ideas and best practices. Naturally, it is in the best interest of the exporter also to make regular periodic visits to markets entered.

Of course the exporter can employ its own sales reps, but this approach requires more commitment of time and resources. It is also important to sell with intermediaries by supporting and augmenting their efforts. Close cooperation with the intermediaries is important at this stage, in that some of them may be concerned about the motives of the exporter in the long term. For example, an intermediary may worry that once the exporter has learned enough about the market, it will no longer need the services of the intermediary. If these suspicions become prevalent, sales information may no longer flow to the exporter in the quantity and quality needed.

Integrated Exports

In the final stage of export-based internationalization, the exporter internalizes the effort through either a sales office in the target market or a direct contact with the buyer from home base. This is part of the exporter's perceived need for increased customer relationship management, where the sales effort is linked to call-center technologies, customer-service departments, and the company's Web site. This may include also automating the sales force. The establishment of a sales office does not have to mean an end to the use of intermediaries; the exporter's salespeople may be dedicated ongoing support of the intermediaries' sales efforts.

At this stage, expatriate sales personnel may be very helpful to manage the effort locally or regionally. The benefits of expatriates are their better understanding of the company and its products, and their ability to transfer best practices to the local operation. With expatriate management, the exporter can exercise a high amount of control over the sales function. Customers may also see the sales office and its expatriate staff as a long-term commitment to the market. The challenges lie mostly in the fit of the chosen individual to the new situation. The cost of having expatriate staff is considerable—approximately 2.5 times the cost at home—and the availability of suitable talent may be a problem, especially if the exporting organization is relatively small. The role of personal selling is greatest when the exporter sells directly to the end user or to governmental agencies, such as foreign trade organizations. Firms selling products with high price tags (such as Boeing commercial aircraft) or companies selling to monopsonies (such as Seagrams liquor to certain Northern European countries, where all liquor sales are through state-controlled outlets) must rely heavily on person-to-person communication, oral presentations, and direct-marketing efforts. Many of these firms can expand their business only if their markets are knowledgeable about what they do. This may require corporate advertising and publicity generation through extensive public relations efforts.

Whatever the sales task, effectiveness is determined by a number of interrelated factors. One of the keys to personal selling is the salesperson's ability to adapt to the customer and the selling situation. This aspect of selling requires cultural knowledge and empathy; for example, in the Middle East, sales presentations may be broken up by long discussions of topics that have little or nothing to do with the transaction at hand. The characteristics of the buying task, whether routine or unique, have a bearing on the sales presentation. The exporter may be faced by a situation in which the idea of buying from a foreign entity is the biggest obstacle in terms of the risks perceived. If the exporter's product does not provide a clear-cut relative advantage over that of competitors, the analytical, interpersonal skills of the salesperson are needed to assist in the differentiation. A salesperson, regardless of the market, must have a thorough knowledge of the product or service. The more the salesperson is able to apply that knowledge to the particular situation, the more likely it is that he or she will obtain a positive result. The salesperson usually has front-line responsibility for the firm's customer relations, having to handle conflict situations such as the parent firm's bias for domestic markets and thus the possibility that shipments of goods to foreign clients receive low priority.

International Negotiations

When exporters travel abroad to do business, they are frequently shocked to discover the extent to which the many variables of foreign behavior and custom complicate their efforts. Given that most negotiations are face to face, they present one of the most obvious and immediate challenges to be overcome. This means that exporters have to adjust their approaches to establishing rapport, information exchange, persuasion, and concession making if they are to be successful in dealing with their clients and partners, such as intermediaries.

The two biggest dangers faced in international negotiations are parochialism and stereotyping. Parochialism refers to the misleading perception that the world of business is becoming ever more American and that everyone will behave accordingly. This approach leads to stereotyping in explaining remaining differences. Stereotypes are generalizations about any given group, both positive and negative. For example, a positive stereotype has a clear influence on decisions to explore business options, whereas a negative stereotype may lead to a request to use a low-risk payment system, such as a letter of credit. In a similar fashion, seemingly familiar surroundings and situations may lull negotiators into a false sense of security. This may be true for a U.S. negotiator in the United Kingdom or Australia thinking that the same language leads to the same behavioral patterns, or even in a far-off market if the meeting takes place in a hotel belonging to a large multinational chain.

The level of adjustment depends on the degree of cultural familiarity the parties have and their ability to use that familiarity effectively. With the increased use of the Internet, the question arises as to how to use it in international negotiations. The Internet allows the exporter to overcome distances, minimize social barriers (e.g., age, gender, status), obtain instant feedback, negotiate from a home base, and do so with a number of parties simultaneously However, it cannot be used in isolation given the critical role of building trust in negotiations. Additionally, its extensive use may restrict much of the interaction to focusing mostly on price. The Internet is effective in the exchange of information and for possible clarification during the course of the process. It should be noted that technology is only gradually making its way to such use.

Stages of the Negotiation Process

The process of international business negotiations can be divided into five stages: the offer, informal meetings, strategy formulation, negotiations, and implementation. Which stage is emphasized and the length of the overall process will vary dramatically by culture. The negotiation process can be a short one, with the stages collapsing into one session, or a prolonged endeavor taking weeks. The differences between northern and southern Europe highlight this. Northern Europe, with its Protestant tradition and indoor culture, tends to emphasize the technical, the numerical, and the tested. Careful pre-negotiation preparations are made. Southern Europe, with its Catholic background and open-air lifestyle, tends to favor personal networks, social contexts, and flair. Meetings in the South are often longer, but the total decision process may be faster.

The offer stage allows the parties to assess each other's needs and degree of commitment. The initiation of the process and its progress are determined to a great extent by background factors of the parties (such as objectives) and the overall atmosphere (for example, a spirit of cooperativeness). As an example, many European buyers may be skittish about dealing with a U.S. exporter, given the perception that a number of U.S. companies focus on short-term gains or leave immediately when the business environment turns sour.

After the buyer has received the offer, the parties meet to discuss the terms and get acquainted. In many parts of the world (Asia, the Middle East, southern Europe, and Latin America), informal meetings may often make or break the deal. Foreign buyers may want to ascertain that they are doing business with someone who is sympathetic and whom they can trust. Both parties have to formulate strategies for formal negotiations. This means not only careful review and assessment of all the factors affecting the deal to be negotiated but also preparation for the actual give-and-take of the negotiations. Exporters should consciously and carefully consider competitive behaviors of clients and partners. Especially in the case of governmental buyers, it is imperative to realize that public-sector needs may not necessarily fit into a mold that the exporter would consider rational. Negotiators may not necessarily behave as expected; for example, the negotiating partner may adjust behavior to the visitor's culture.

The actual face-to-face negotiations and the approach used in them will depend on the cultural background and business traditions prevailing in different countries. The most commonly used are the competitive and collaborative approaches. In a competitive strategy, the negotiator is concerned mainly about a favorable outcome at the expense of the other party, while in the collaborative approach focus is on mutual needs, especially in the long term. For example, an exporter accepting a proposal that goes beyond what can be realistically delivered (in the hopes of market entry or renegotiation later) will lose in the long term. To deliver on the contract, the exporter may be tempted to cut corners in product quality or delivery, eventually leading to conflict with the buyer.

The choice of location for the negotiations plays a role in the outcome as well. Many negotiators prefer a neutral site. This may not always work, for reasons of resources or parties' perceptions of the importance of the deal. The host does enjoy many advantages, such as lower psychological risk due to familiar surroundings. Guests may run the risk of cultural shock and being away from professional and personal support systems. These pressures are multiplied if the host chooses to manipulate the situation with delays or additional demands. Visiting teams are less likely to walk out; as a matter of fact, the pressure is on them to make concessions. However, despite the challenges of being a guest, the visitor has a chance to see firsthand the counterpart's facilities and resources, and to experience the culture of that market.

Negotiator characteristics (e.g., gender, race, or age) may work for or against the exporter in certain cultures. It is challenging to overcome stereotypes, but well-prepared negotiators can overcome these obstacles or even make them work to their advantage. For example, a female negotiator may use her uniqueness in male-dominated societies to gain better access to decision-makers.

How to Negotiate in Other Countries and Cultures

A combination of attitudes, expectations, and habitual behavior influences negotiation style. Although some of the following recommendations may go against the approach used at home, they may allow the negotiator to adjust to the style of the host-country negotiators:

1. Team approach. Using specialists will strengthen the team substantially and allow for all points of view to be given proper attention. Further, observation of negotiations can be valuable training experience for less-experienced participants. Whereas Western teams may average two to four people, a Chinese negotiating team may consist of ten people. A study on how U.S. purchasing professionals conduct negotiations abroad revealed that while the vast majority believed a small team (two to five individuals) was ideal, they also said their teams were often outnumbered by their international counterparts. Even if there are intragroup disagreements during the negotiations, it is critical to show one face to the counterparts and handle issues within the team privately, outside the formal negotiations.
2. Recognition of traditions and customs. For newcomers, status relations and business procedures must be carefully considered with the help of consultants or local representatives. For example, in highly structured societies, such as Korea, great respect is paid to age and position. It is prudent to use informal communication to let counterparts know, or ask

them about, any prestigious degrees, honors, or accomplishments by those who will be facing one another in negotiations. What seem like simple rituals can cause problems. No first encounter in Asia is complete without an exchange of business cards. Both hands should be used to present and receive cards, and respect should be shown by reading them carefully. One side should be translated into the language of the host country.

3. Language capability. Ideally, the export manager should be able to speak the customer's language, but that is not always possible. A qualified individual is needed as part of a marketing team to ensure that nothing gets lost in the translation, literally or figuratively. Whether the negotiator is bilingual or an interpreter is used, it might be a good gesture to deliver the first comments in the local language to break the ice. The use of interpreters allows the negotiator longer response time and a more careful articulation of arguments. If English is being used, a native speaker should avoid both jargon and idiomatic expressions, avoid complex sentences, and speak slowly and enunciate clearly. An ideal interpreter is one who briefs the negotiator on cultural dimensions, such as body language, before any meetings. For example, sitting in what may be perceived as a comfortable position in North America or Europe may be seen by the Chinese as showing a lack of control of one's posture and, therefore, of one's mind.

4. Determination of authority limits. Negotiators from North America and Europe are often expected to have full authority when they negotiate in the Far East, although their local counterparts seldom if ever do. Announcing that the negotiators do not have the final authority to conclude the contract may be perceived negatively; however, if it is used as a tactic to probe the motives of the buyer, it can be quite effective. It is important to verify who does have that authority and what challenges may be faced in getting that decision. In negotiating in Russia, for example, the exporter will have to ascertain who actually has final decision-making authority—the central, provincial, or local government—especially if permits are needed.

5. Patience. In many countries, such as China, Brazil, or Thailand, business negotiations may take three times the amount of time that they do in the United States and Europe. Showing impatience may prolong negotiations rather than speed them up. Also, U.S. executives tend to start relatively close to what they consider a fair price in their negotiations, whereas Chinese negotiators may start with "unreasonable" demands and a rigid posture.

6. Negotiation ethics. Attitudes and values of foreign negotiators may be quite different from those that a U.S. marketing executive is accustomed to. Being tricky can be valued in some parts of the world, whereas it is frowned on elsewhere. For example, Western negotiators may be taken aback by last-minute changes or concession requests by Russian negotiators.
7. Silence. To negotiate effectively abroad, an exporter needs to read correctly all types of communication. U.S. businesspeople often interpret inaction and silence as a negative sign. As a result, Japanese executives tend to expect that they can use silence to get them to lower prices or sweeten the deal. Finns may sit through a meeting expressionless, hands folded and not moving much. There is nothing necessarily negative about this; they show respect to the speaker with their focused, dedicated listening.
8. Persistence. Insisting on answers and an outcome may be seen as a threat by negotiating partners abroad. In some markets, negotiations are seen as a means of establishing long-term commercial relations, not as an event with winners and losers. Confrontations are to be avoided because minds cannot be changed at the negotiation table; this has to be done informally. Saving face or preserving respect is an important concept throughout the Far East.
9. Holistic view. Concessions should be avoided until all issues have been discussed, so as to preclude the possibility of granting unnecessary benefits to the negotiation partners. Concessions traditionally come at the end of bargaining. This is especially true in terms of price negotiations. If price is agreed on too quickly, the counterpart may want to insist on too many inclusions for that price.
10. The meaning of agreements. What constitutes an agreement will vary from one market to another. In many parts of the world, legal contracts are still not needed; as a matter of fact, reference to legal counsel may indicate that the relationship is in trouble. For the Chinese, the written agreement exists mostly for the convenience of their Western partners and represents an agenda on which to base the development of the relationship.

When a verbal agreement is reached, it is critical that both parties leave with a clear understanding of what they have agreed to. This may entail only the relatively straightforward act of signing a distributor agreement, but in the case of large-scale projects, details must be explored and spelled out. In contracts that call for cooperative efforts, the responsibilities of each partner must be clearly specified. Otherwise, obligations that were anticipated to be the duty of one contracting party may result in costs to another. For example, foreign principal contractors may be held responsible for delays that have been caused by the inability of local subcontractors (whose use might be a requisite of the client) to deliver on schedule.

Summary

Effective and efficient communication is needed for the dual purpose of (1) informing prospective customers about the availability of products or services and (2) persuading customers to opt for the exporters offerings over those of competitors. Within the framework of the company's opportunities, resources, and objectives, decisions must be made about whether to direct communications to present customers, potential customers, the general public, or intermediaries. Decisions must be made on how to reach each of the intended target audiences without wasting valuable resources. A decision also has to be made about who will control the communications effort: the exporter, an agency, or local representatives.

The exporter must also choose tools to use in the communications effort. Usually, two basic tools are used: (1) mass selling through business and trade journals, direct mail, the Internet, trade shows and missions, and (2) personal selling, which brings the exporter face-to-face with the targeted customer.

To maximize the outcome of negotiations with clients and partners from other cultural backgrounds, exporters must show adjustment capability to different standards and behaviors. Success depends on being prepared and remaining flexible to accommodate the negotiation style of the host country.

CHAPTER 13

The Export Marketing Plan

The need for thorough planning to ensure successful implementation and execution of programs is obvious. There are all sorts of forms, formulas, and approaches to planning, but all of them have two basic parts: (1) determining specific target markets and (2) determining the type of competitive advantage the firm can develop in the target market.

Determining target market characteristics means identifying the most important demographic and pschychographic characteristics of individual customers as well as logical groupings of customer into segments.

In addition, the marketer must keep in mind other uncontrollable factors in the environment (cultural, political, legal, technological, societal, and economic), and select the most favorable markets for targeting.

Selecting the Target Market and Creating Comparative Advantage

Because every exporter operates in an organizational environment of scarcity and comparative strengths, the selection of a target market is crucial. In some cases, the exporter may select only one segment of the market (e.g., motorcycles of +1,000 cc) or multiple segments (e.g., all types of motorized two-wheeled vehicles); on the other hand, it may opt for an undifferentiated product that is to be mass-marketed (e.g., unbranded commodities or products that satisfy the same need worldwide). With proper knowledge of the characteristics of the target market(s), the exporter is in a position to specify and control the mix of marketing variables (product, price, place, and promotion, discussed in Chapters 9 through 12) that will best serve each target market. Each consists of a submix of variables, and policy decisions must be made on each.

Blending the various elements into a coherent program requires trade-offs based on the type of product or service being offered, the stage of the product's life cycle, and resources available for the marketing effort, as well as the type of customer at whom the marketing efforts are directed.

The second step, creating a competitive advantage, is very important in the success of the export marketing effort. A firm has a competitive advantage when it can provide customers with a benefit that makes the company's products stand above the competition This can be done by identifying what a firm does really well. A distinctive competency is a firm's capability that is better than its competition. In order to develop a competitive advantage, the exporter must turn a distinctive competency into a specific benefit—one that is important to customers. Identifying such a benefit allows the firm to generate a strong preference for its products and services.

Developing and Formulating the Plan

The last step in the strategic planning process is the formulation of the marketing plan. The export marketing plan is a systematic, organized process directing marketing activities in foreign markets to achieve maximum results. The marketing plan is usually prepared on an annual or fiscal-year basis. One master plan is developed to guide all the activities during the typical 12-month cycle. This master plan sets down the parameters and guidelines so that budgets can be developed. The decisions and activities included in a proactive marketing plan must be oriented to the customer, and the marketing plan must address itself to meet the needs of its target market.

The plan is the "cookbook" for the marketing strategy. The ingredients for a successful export marketing strategy are:

- A product oriented to customer needs and wants.
- A marketing organization effective in bringing the product in contact with customers.
- A marketing plan that identifies strategies and responsibilities for implementing action programs to achieve desired results.

The plan should be a working document aimed squarely at specific results and explaining how they will be achieved within the framework of an identified marketing environment. The marketing plan outlined below is a basic template for a logical and effective method for most markets.

EXHIBIT 13.1. The Outline of an Export Marketing Plan

Part I: Situation Analysis
   A. Prepare a Comprehensive Fact Base
      1. Statement of General Business Purpose
      2. Current Situation
         Sales
         Markets
         Trends
         Products
         Competition
   B. List Problems and Opportunities

Part II: Strategy Development and Execution
   A. Objectives and Assumptions
   B. The Export Target Market
   C. The Export Marketing Strategy
      1. Strategic Programs
      2. The Export Transaction

Part I. Situation Analysis
A. Prepare a Comprehensive Fact Base

The formulation of the marketing plan will depend upon a thorough understanding of the export market environment. Every fact that has any significant relevance to the export marketing effort should be evaluated and stated at the beginning of the marketing plan. The effectiveness of the plan flows from a comprehensive fact base, and it may well be the most important part of the entire export marketing plan. It is not enough to have a general understanding of the country. The exporter needs to have a working knowledge of the country's marketing environment and the target market in order to formulate a successful marketing strategy.

1. Statement of General Business Purpose

The export marketing plan begins with a statement of the general business purpose of the firm. The simple statement should briefly describe what business the exporter is in, what products the exporter manufacture or resell, and what customer needs the firm expects to fulfill in the marketplace. This is a positioning statement to identify for all persons that must understand, act upon or approve the plan, exactly how the exporter sees where the company fits into the marketplace.

    The marketing plan needs to specify the scope of the marketing plan. This means designating whether the plan applies to a complete product line, a specific product aimed at a specific country market, a single key country market, and/or a specific geographic or regional area.

2. Current Situation

The foundation of the marketing plan is a statement of the firm's current situation. In this section, the exporter needs to identify the company's strengths and weaknesses objectively, that is, what the firm has to offer in terms of the marketing opportunity that will be pursued by the firm, the markets the firm intends to serve and the market coverage area (scope). It should include a brief description of the export target market and market needs in terms of the company's products.

a) Sales Prospects

The marketing plan needs to specify an estimate of either sales statistics (a firm working on a specific country market) or market potential (for a firm first entering an export market). Export market potential can be derived from:

> *Total imports of the product or product category to the country market*
> *U. S. exports of the product or product category to the country market*
> *U.S. market share in that country import market of the product or product category*

A report showing sales and/or trends over a 3- to 5-year span is necessary and helpful.

b) Markets

The country markets should be described in terms of growth rates for each of the products being offered. It is very important to identify whether the target market is expected to grow, shrink, or remain static over the next year. The country's prospects in terms of economic growth are important, as imports are income elastic, that is, any increase in economic activity results in a growing demand for imports.

c) Trends

Trends such as changes in technology use, demographics, user needs, etc. have an impact on market behavior and therefore, on opportunity and market potential. Therefore, the exporter needs to identify situations in the export marketing environment that may have an impact on market behavior. For example, trends that seem to be forming, such as economic, social, political, and regulatory changes that may influence the export marketing effort, need to be clearly stated.

d) Products

In this section, a list of products and/or product lines being offered in the market must be clearly stated, including the technical description of the product(s). This includes an objective evaluation the quality, features, customer fulfillment factors, exclusive features, benefits, etc. that will help the exporter meet the export market needs and trends.

e) Competition

The competitive environment must be examined if the exporter is to make realistic assumptions concerning the country market. It is important to identify all the facts about the competition, including marketing strategies, products strengths and weaknesses, market capabilities, etc.

B. Problems and Opportunities

If all the relevant facts are clearly stated in the fact base, then a complete listing of *problems and opportunities* will flow from it. Every significant problem should be listed even if it appears unsolvable. By doing so, a problem can be analyzed to determine if it is truly unsolvable. Actually, often where there is a problem an opportunity exists. But the most important opportunities will arise from a keen

(Continued)

perception of the country's export marketing environment, market trends, competitors' weaknesses, and the planner's analytical skills to identify problems and opportunities that become evident from the situation analysis.

PART II Strategy Development and Execution

A. Objectives and Assumptions

The objectives of an export marketing plan will be an outgrowth of the listing of problems and opportunities (and there should be several). Objectives should be *specific and measurable*. An objective should identify an actual end result to be achieved by the plan in a specific time frame. Objectives are the core of the export marketing plan since everything preceding leads up to the objectives and everything that follows aims at achieving them. Objectives establish desired end results. The objectives that the firm seeks to achieve must be very clear and specific and when possible, stated in quantitative measures. Sales and Profitability objectives must be included among stated objectives to provide reasonable guidelines. Objectives will serve as the basis for controlling the export marketing plan, that is, to help the exporter determine if the marketing plan is meeting its goals and objectives. The basic assumptions that guide these objectives must also be clearly stated in order to provide a basis for adjustment as the marketing effort progresses.

B. The Export Target Market

A description of the target market should include a user profile as well as an estimate of market size. This is a crucial aspect of the export marketing strategy, as all the other elements of the marketing strategy will be based on the fulfillment of consumer needs.

C. The Export Marketing Strategy

1. Strategic Programs
   The Export Product Strategy

The most important consideration in formulating the export product strategy is the product/market fit. This section should describe such product decisions concerning product components, quality, design, packaging, branding, and the level of support services (warranties, post-sale services, etc.) that are needed to position the product according to the product/market fit the exporter has identified.

In many instances, the exporter must be prepared to adapt the product to fit the buyer's needs. Without such adaptation the export sale probably will not be completed. When such a case arises, the exporter should carefully weigh the added costs of product adaptation against market potential and opportunity. In some instances, a small variation in the product's features (such as a manual translation) can achieve the purpose of providing the required product for the import market. Being alert to product opportunities can also be an important aspect of the exporter's long term marketing strategy, as product adaptations may range from a simple labeling change to changes in package size, product features, and so on.

Export Channels of Distribution

The design of the channel structure for first entry into export market and maintenance of existing channels is the basic element of the export channel of distribution strategy.

Issues concerning channel support, incentives, and control must be clearly stated to achieve strategic goals.

Export Communication Strategy
The basic elements of the promotional strategy must be identified in terms of each of the tools used to communicate with consumers, such as personal selling effort, advertising and sales promotion activities, and public relations.

Export Pricing Strategy
The specific prices of each product offered in the export market should be detailed, including financing conditions and terms of sales or delivery terms that are standard company policy. The marketing plan should also clearly state the conditions under which different financing or delivery terms would be considered. Prices should not be considered in a vacuum; rather they should reflect the product's positioning in the target market and the buyer's ability to pay and the foreign country financial position (ability to provide foreign currency to importers).

Costs and Profits
All costs related to all and each element of the marketing plan need to be clearly specified, as well as profitability guidelines in order to achieve the objectives stated in the export marketing plan.

2. The Export Transaction
Finally, the export marketing plan needs to identify the steps needed to complete the export transactions that result from the marketing effort. This means identifying the activities needed to complete the financial, physical, and documentary flows of the export transaction.

The Financial Flow

Payment of the goods and payment terms are agreed upon during the negotiation of the export transaction. The exporter should delay any further activity on the export order until such time as the buyer completes the financial arrangements and upon acceptance of financing terms and the transfer of funds has been arranged by the importer.

The Physical Flow

The goods must be prepared for shipment and be delivered to the transporting company. Services of freight forwarders can be very valuable at this point as these organizations specialize in moving goods from warehouse to the point of shipment, seeing to it that the shipment is loaded on to the carrying vessel and obtaining all the necessary documentation. The exporter must make sure that the goods being shipped meet the requirements of the export sale and the instructions and requirements of the transportation company and mode. When packaging the goods, due regard must be given to time of transportation for adequate protection against damage while in transit.

The documentation generated during the preparation of the shipment and loading unto shipping vehicle provides evidence that goods are ready to clear U.S. customs and export regulations. Once the goods arrive at point of destination, the importer must have all the proper documentation in order to process the shipment through customs and take possession of the goods. The terms of sale and financing terms will dictate how the documents are drawn and delivered to the importer.

Document Flow

After the initial steps are taken to start the physical movement of the goods, the exporter needs to identify and prepare the documents that are required to complete the export transaction and allow the importer to process the goods through customs in the importing country. The exporter or freight forwarder must prepare the required documentation to meet requirements of both the exporting and importing countries, financing terms, and mode of transportation. Preparation of these documents can start simultaneously with the physical flow so that the documents can be compiled and dispersed before the goods arrive at their final destination. Generally, ocean and air cargo shipments are subject to similar documentation requirements. However, the procedure of export clearance may be less cumbersome for air cargo shipments, and the importing countries may require less documentation for submission at the import customs point.

Implementing the Market Plan

Once the marketing plan is outlined and completed, it must be implemented, that is, a budget developed and each area of responsibility assigned to the person or personnel in charge of the marketing plan. The *marketing budget* is the financial plan stemming from all the strategic actions required by each program described in the marketing plan. The exporter needs to allocate resources to make the plan a reality. Since all elements of the plan have costs associated with them, the exporter needs to balance available resources between all the strategic activities involved.

The marketing budget usually covers a period of one year, broken into bimonthly or quarterly budgets. Considerations of product adaptation are crucial in the budgeting process as adaptation is intended to obtain the best product/market fit. However, the budget should not be the final word in the planning process. It may be necessary to make adjustments to the budget and the overall plan in order to meet environmental realities.

Controlling the Market Plan

Once the plan in implemented and the budget is complete, the exporter needs to measure actual performance, comparing it to planned performance, and making necessary changes in the plans and the budget. As the plan goes into action, it is necessary to obtain all pertinent information on the actual results in order to compare them to expected results. This comparison allows the exporter to determine whether to continue with the marketing effort, change some of its elements, or redraw the entire export marketing plan. This evaluation should be accompanied with a continued monitoring of the foreign country's environment in order to determine if the plan's assumptions were correct or need adjustments.

Summary

Strategic planning is the cornerstone of a successful export marketing effort. Strategic planning is necessary to understand the task at hand. This involves identifying a target market and developing a competitive advantage. The export Marketing Plan is the final stage of the strategic planning process. This is the strategy that guides the export activities for the next year. Once the plan is developed, it needs to be implemented and controlled in order to achieve expected results.

ABOUT THE AUTHORS

Michael R. Czinkota is one of the foremost experts on international business and marketing in the world. His insights and counsel are frequently sought by the media, global companies, and governments all over the world. He is a dynamic and engaging speaker on issues related to trade, trade policy, and global business strategies. He has served in the U.S. Government as Deputy Assistant Secretary of Commerce, where he was responsible for trade analysis, support of trade negotiations and retaliatory actions, and policy coordination for international finance, investment, and monetary affairs. He currently serves on the faculty of The McDonough School of Business at Georgetown University.

Ilkka Ronkainen is a leading expert in the areas of international business and marketing. He has served on the faculty of The McDonough School of Business at Georgetown University for the past 20 years. In addition, he is the Director of the "School of Business" program in Hong Kong. He is the author of multiple texts, two of which, *International Business* and *International Marketing*, are the leading ones in schools in the Americas, Asia, and Europe. He has an appointment as docent of international marketing at the Helsinki School of Economics. He frequently teaches executive classes in Finland, Germany, Korea, Mexico, Panama, Poland, Trinidad, the United Kingdom, and the United States.

Maria Ortiz-Buonofina, a Fulbright Teaching Scholar, was a member of the Marketing faculty at Florida International University until her retirement at the end of 2003. She is the author of many articles on the export behavior of the firm. She is author of *Profitable Export Marketing: A Strategy for U.S. Business* and co-author (with Dr. Jerry Haar) of *Import Marketing*, which was translated into Spanish. She developed and taught the Export Marketing course at FIU for 23 years.

INDEX

A
Agency for International Development (AID) 72
Amazon.com 47
American Arbitration Association 100
American Hospital Supply 128
Andean Common Market (ANCOM) 82
Ansoff Product-Market Growth Matrix 110
Antitrust law 92
Arab Maghreb Union 83
Arbitration 100
Asian Development Bank 73
Asia Pacific Economic Cooperation (APEC) 83
Association of Southeast Asian Nations (ASEAN) 83

B
Bank of America Commercial Finance/Factoring 69
BellSouth 222
Berne Convention for the Protection of Literary and Artistic Works 137
Bit-tax 48
Boston Consulting Group 6
Boycotts 91, 92
Branding 129–131
Bribery 92
Business-to-business (B2B) research techniques 25–26
BuyUSA 228

C
Campbell Soup Company 127
Capital 177
Capitol Bank 67

Catalog exhibitions 228
Census Bureau *See* U.S. Census Bureau
Certified trade fair program 227–228
Change agents 8–11, 12
Channel design 172–181 *See also* Distribution systems
Channel management 170–201
Channel relationships 194–200
Channel structure 171–172
Character 176–177
Chase Manhattan 69
CIF (cost, insurance, freight) 147
CIT Group 69
Citibank 68
Climate 128
Code law 95–96
Coface Group 163
Commerce Control List (CCL) 89, 90
Commercial banks 67–68
Commercial Finance Association 69
Commercial News USA 221
Commercial risk 65
Commercial Service 86–87, 183–187 *See also* U.S. Department of Commerce
Commerzbank 68
Commodity Credit Corporation (CCC) 72
Common law 95–96
Common Market for Eastern and Southern Africa (COMESA) 83
Communication 180–181
Communication strategy 216–237
Community Patent Convention 99
Competition 175–176
Competitive pricing policy 145
Computer Land 51

Concentration 112–113
Continuity 180
Control 179–180
Corruption 92
Cost 177–178
Cost-plus method 145–146
Counterfeit Intelligence and Investigating Bureau 138
Country commercial guide, examples 40–42
Country Directories of International Contact (CDIC) 183
Country-market selection 109–110, 113
Country-of-origins effects 134–135
Coverage 178–179
Credit policy 64–65
Credit report 162
Credit reporting agencies 163
Culture 173–175
Currency conditions, pricing and 164–167
Currency futures market 75
Currency options 74–75
Customer characteristics 173
Customs brokers 214

D

Dai-Ichi Kangyo Bank of Japan 69
Data analysis 20–21
Data evaluation 20
Data interpretation 20–21
Data sources 17–20
Deere & Co. 75
Delphi techniques 27–28
DHL 47
Direct exporting 182
Direct exports 44, 45, 229–230
Direct marketing 223–224
Directories 221–223
Diversification 112–113
Distribution systems 170 *See also* Channel design
Distributor agreement 191–194
Documentary collections 157–158
Doha round 79
Domino's Pizza 52
Dow Chemical 51

Dresser Industries 167
Dual pricing 145–146
Dual use products 89, 90
Dunkin' Donuts 125, 127

E

East African Community (ECA) 83
Economic Community of Central African States (CEEAC) 83
Economic Community of the Great Lakes Countries 83
Economic Community of West African States (ECOWAS) 83
Economic integration 80–85
Economics and Statistical Administration 20
E-exporting 46–48
El Camino Resources International 169
11 Cs 172–181
Embargoes 88, 91
Encryption 48
Environmental scanning 27
Environmental Superfund 88
E-taxes 47–48
European Commission 198
European Court of Justice 123, 198
European Patent Convention 99
European Union (EU) 89, 98, 99, 124, 132, 136, 196
  economic integration 80
  gray markets 197–198
  intermediaries 174
  privacy rights 21
  regulatory activities 92
Exchange rate 74
Expansion strategies 110–115
Export adaptation 3
Export Control Classification Number (ECCN) 90
Export controls 88–91
Export credit agency (ECA) 69, 70–71
Export credit insurance 72
Export-Import Bank of the United States (Ex-Im Bank) 71, 72, 87
Export intermediaries 54–63
Export management companies (EMCs) 45, 55–58

Export manager, economic integration and 85
Export marketing information system 26–27
Export marketing plan 238–245
Export market research *See* Research
Export market screening 22–25
Export modes 43–53
Export pricing policies 144–145
Export pricing strategies 145–147
Export promotion 86–88
Export promotion tools 221–228
Export-related costs 147–150
Export Trade Certificate of Review 61
Exports, approaches to 43–46
Export trading companies (ETCs) 45, 59–61
Export Trade Act of 1918. *See* Webb-Pomerene Act
Export Trading Company Act 59, 60, 61, 87
Express fee 93
Exterritorial Income (ETI) Tax Exclusion 5

F
Factoring 68–69
Federal Maritime Commission 214
Federal Trade Commission 58
Federation of International Trade Associations (FITA) 55, 58
Financial crises 75–76
Financial risk 65–66
Financing 64–77
Financing sources 66–67
Flick Pen Corporation 130
Foreign accounts receivable financing 67
Foreign Corrupt Practices Act 92, 193
Foreign exchange market 73–74
Foreign exchange risk 66, 73–75
Forfaiting 68–69
Forward market 74, 75
Franchising 50–53 *See also* Licensing
Free Trade Area of the Americas (FTAA) 82
Freight forwarders 61–63, 154–155, 214

G
General Agreement on Tariffs and Trade (GATT) 78–79
General Agreement on Trade in Services (GATS) 79
General Motors 174
Geochron 147
Geography 128
Gillette 127, 130
Gray markets 197–199
Grey Goose 132
Government, international trade and 78–103
Government regulations 123–125
Guinness Brewery 49
Gulf Cooperation Council (GCC) 83

H
Hannover Messe 226
Harley-Davidson 166
Helms-Burton Act 98
High-margin pricing policy *See* Skimming pricing policy
Home country policies 88–90
Host country policies 93–95

I
IBM 121
Igloo Corp. 73
IKEA 108–109, 121
Import controls 88
Incoterms 150–154
Indirect exporting 182
Indirect exports 44, 45, 228–229
Information sources 29–39
Integrated distribution 182
Integrated exports 45–46, 230–232
Intellectual property 48–49
Intellectual Property Rights Improvement Act 138
Intellectual property violation 136–139
Inter-American Convention for Trademark Protection 99
Inter-American Development Bank 73
Intermediaries 181–191, 219, 221
  government assistance 183–186
  private sources 187–188
Internal Revenue Service 150

International Anti-Counterfeiting
   Coalition   138
International Bank for Reconstruction and
   Development   *See* World Bank
International business behavior, regulation
   of   88, 91–93
International Chamber of Commerce
   136, 138, 150, 159
International Company Profile (ICP)   163
International Convention for the
   Protection of Industrial Property   99
International Harmonized Commodity
   Classification System   22
Internationalizing   1–12
International law   98–100
International Monetary Fund (IMF)   18,
   79
International negotiations   232–237
International Trade Administration   138
International Trade Center   18
International Trade Commission   136
International transportation   202–215
Internet   224–225, 232
Internet marketing   46–48
ISO 9000   124–125, 134

J
JLG   141
Journals   221–223
Jurisdictional disputes   99–100

K
Knorr   127
Komatsu   167

L
Land Rover   150
Laws   95–100
Leasing   168–169
Legal environment   88–90, 93–95
Letters of credit   158–161
Levi   198
Licensing   48–50   *See also* Franchising
Logistics   202–205
Lowenbrau   50
Low-margin pricing policy   *See*
   Penetration pricing policy

M
Mack International   124
Madrid Agreement for International
   Registration of Trademarks   99
Maggi   127
Mano River Union   83
Marginal cost method   145–146
Market development   104–115
Market development financing   67
Market-differentiated pricing   145, 146
Market-driven pricing policy   *See*
   Competitive pricing policy
Market environment, product adjustments
   and   123–134
Market growth strategies   110–115
Market research   *See* Research
Marketing budget   244
Marketing communications process
   216–218
Marketing communications strategy
   218–221
Marketing opportunities, evaluating
   104–105
Market opportunity analysis   15–16
Marketing plan, developing   239–243
Market segmentation   113–115
Marlboro   129
Matsushita Electric   167
McDonald's   52, 140
Medtech International   187
Mercado Commun del Sur (Mercosur)
   82
Michelin   75
Microsoft   109
MicroTouch   133
Miller Brewing Company   50
Mixed aid credits   87
Mohammed   127
Most-Favored Nation (MFN)   78, 97
MTV   113
Multifiber accord   79
myExports.com   61, 222

N
NameLab   130
National Association of Credit
   Management   191

National Trade Data Bank (NTDB) 19
Negotiation, in other countries 234–237
Negotiation process 232–234
Nintendo 137
Nokia 107
Nontariff barriers 123–124, 125
Normal trade relations (NTR) 97
North American Free Trade Agreement (NAFTA) 8, 80–82, 138
NRL (no license required) 89

O
Official trade financing 69–73
Office of Export Trading Company Affairs 61
Omnibus Tariff and Trade Act 137
Organization for Economic Cooperation and Development (OECD) 18
Overseas Private Investment Corporation (OPIC) 72

P
P&D Creative, Inc. 187
Paris Convention for the Protection of Industrial Property 137
Parochialism 232
Patent and Trademark Office 138
Patent Cooperation Treaty 137
Payment barriers 162–164
Payment terms 155–162, 163–164
Penetration pricing policy 144
Philip Morris 129
Pillsbury 127
Political risk 66, 93–95
Politics, influencing 96–98
Price controls 95
Price dynamics 141–142
Price escalation 147–150
Price negotiation 167–168
Price setting 142–147
Pricing 141–169
Primary research 17, 24–25
Product adaptation 119–123
  company considerations 135–136
Product adjustments 116–140
Product appearance 132
Product categories 16
Product characteristics 128–129

Product counterfeiting 136–139
Product operation, in foreign markets 133
Product packaging 131–132
Product quality 133–134
Product service 134
Product standardization 119–121
Product usage, in foreign markets 133
Promotional strategy 216–237
Proxy variable 20
Psychological proximity 7–8

Q
QVC 47

R
Range Rover 150
Reach 67
Reebok 113
Regulatory activities 88, 91–93
Research 13–42
  primary 17, 24–25
  secondary 17, 22–25
Risk modifying 74
Risk shifting 74

S
Sales contract 101–102
Scenario building 28
Secondary data 22–25
Secondary research 17, 22–25
Semiconductor Chip Protection Act 138
Seminar missions 228
Shipping 203–205 *See also* Transportation infrastructure
Shipping documents *See* Transportation documents
Silicon Valley Bank 67
Silkience 130
Skimming pricing policy 144–145
Sogoshoshas 59, 87
South Africa Customs Union 83
South African Development Community (SADC) 83
South Asia Association for Regional Cooperation (SAARC) 83
Standard worldwide price 145
Starbucks 176

Statistical Yearbook 17
Stereotyping 232
Strategic planning process 105–110
Symbian 109

T
Target market selection 238–239
Target markets, evaluating 105
TeleGea 128
Terms of sale 150–154
Terrorism, export controls and 90–91
Tesco 198
Tetra Pak International 132
Total Credit Management Group 164
Trade Act 92
TradeCard 161
Trademark 129
Trademark Counterfeiting Act 138
Trademark licensing 50
Trade missions 225–228
Trade Opportunities Program 183
Trade Promotion Coordination Committee (TPCC) 87, 102–103
Trade-Related Aspects of Intellectual Property Rights (TRIPS) 79, 138
Trade-related investment measures (TRIMS) 79
Trade sanctions 88, 91
Trade shows 225–227
Transnational institutions 78–84
Transportation documents 210–214
Transportation infrastructure 202–207
Transportation management 207–209
Transportation services 209–214
Turbo Tek, Inc. 133

U
UN Center on Transnational Corporations 18
UN Conference on Trade and Development (UNCTAD) 18, 49
Unilever 75, 121
United Nations (UN) 17, 18, 73
Universal Copyright Convention 127
U.S.-Canada Free Trade Agreement 82
U.S. Census Bureau 27
U.S. Customs Service 150, 198
U.S. Department of Commerce 19, 60, 124
  Certified trade show program 227
  Commercial Service 86–87, 183–187
U.S. Exporters Yellow Pages 183
U.S. Munitions List (USML) 89
U.S. Treasury Department 91

V
Value-added tax (VAT) 147
Video exhibitions 228
Virtual trade show 228

W
Wachovia 68
War Weapons Control Law 88
War Weapons List 88
WatchGuard Technologies 80
WD-40 Co. 139
Webb-Pomerene Act 58
Webb-Pomerene Export Associations (WPEAs) 58–59
Whirlpool 114
World Atlas 18
World Bank 18, 79–80
World Bank Group 73
World Intellectual Property Organization (WIPO) 137
World Trade Organization (WTO) 5, 18, 78–79, 97
  intellectual property protection 49, 138